WOMEN AND POPULAR CULTURE IN CANADA

WOMEN AND POPULAR CULTURE IN CANADA

Edited by Laine Zisman Newman

WOMEN'S
PRESS

Toronto | Vancouver

Women and Popular Culture in Canada
Edited by Laine Zisman Newman

First published in 2020 by
Women's Press, an imprint of CSP Books Inc.
425 Adelaide Street West, Suite 200
Toronto, Ontario
M5V 3C1

www.womenspress.ca

Library and Archives Canada Cataloguing in Publication

Title: Women and popular culture in Canada / edited by Laine Zisman Newman.
Names: Zisman Newman, Laine, 1987- editor.
Description: Includes bibliographical references.
Identifiers: Canadiana (print) 20200188895 | Canadiana (ebook) 20200188933 |
    ISBN 9780889616158 (softcover) | ISBN 9780889616165 (PDF) |
    ISBN 9780889616172 (EPUB)
Subjects: LCSH: Women in popular culture—Canada.
Classification: LCC HQ1453 .W66 2020 | DDC 302.230820971—dc23

Cover art: Kelsy Vivash
Cover design: Rafael Chimicatti
Page layout: S4Carlisle Publishing Services

20 21 22 23 24   5 4 3 2 1

Printed and bound in Ontario, Canada

Canadä

To the Girls Club

Table of Contents

Mediated Nation: Genders and Geographies of Popular Culture

Laine Zisman Newman

And where the words of women are crying to be heard, we must each of us recognize our responsibility to seek those words out, to read them and share them and examine them in their pertinence to our lives. That we not hide behind the mockeries of separations that have been imposed upon us and which so often we accept as our own.
   —Audre Lorde

INTRODUCTION

This book is about women who make media, women represented in media, women who develop, resist, change, and influence media. It is about how representations of gender intersect with conceptions of nationhood, citizenship, and space. And it is about how media culture shapes our daily experience, how it frames and directs our everyday relations. We are constantly using our phones, inundated with ads, creating soundtracks for our daily commutes, learning through podcasts, and connecting on social media. Alongside our education, kinship circles, and upbringing, media and popular culture have a notable influence on our daily existence and what we perceive to be natural or normal. But media is not, as we well know, neutral or equitable. Thus, we must critically explore how the media of our popular culture operates in relation to nation, identity, and power in order to grapple with how it can simultaneously uphold and challenge systemic inequities in this country.

While there is a growing mainstream interest in gender inequities in media and popular culture—evident from the visibility of the #MeToo and #TimesUp movements—there is relatively little published on the historical and contemporary achievements and struggles of women in popular culture in Canada. Analyzing the intersections of popular culture and gender in Canada means considering both the significance of media development, production, and reception, and also how these categories relate to space, geography, and conceptions of nationhood and belonging. The aim of this collected volume is not simply to provide an opportunity to gain media literacy skills or understand the correlation between power and popular culture, but also to share and celebrate women's work in this country and to create an alternative archive of culture in Canada.

When I began theorizing and planning this collection, I felt an urgent need and drive to create something that was relevant to a spectrum of communities and experiences. These chapters demonstrate a commitment to resist simplistic interpretations of a "Canadian Canon." They reimagine and reconstitute an understanding of women's media production and representation. They ask us to ask more questions. And they elevate the voices and stories of feminists and women to create a radical new feminist archive of women and pop culture in Canada. Readers are encouraged to think carefully about the role women continue to play in the cultural landscape in Canada as active viewers, creators, and participants.

Other significant works have developed a foundation for this kind of critical theorization and analysis. Both *Gendering the Nation: Canadian Women's Cinema* (1999) and *The Gendered Screen: Canadian Women Filmmakers* (2010), for example, discuss creative works by women in Canada, focusing particularly on the big screen. Angelia Wagner and Joanna Everitt's (eds.) *Gendered Mediation: Identity and Image Making in Canadian Politics* (2019) and Cheryl Thompson's *Beauty in a Box: Detangling the Roots of Canada's Black Beauty Culture* (2019) expand the conversation on cultural and media studies in Canada to think critically about politics and aesthetics, beyond a normative white mainstream canon. *Women and Popular Culture in Canada* contributes to these timely conversations, challenging a simplistic understanding of women and media in Canada. While I will not provide a historical overview of women's contributions to or representation in media in Canada—a project that warrants a book-length survey of the multiple histories that have led to our current media culture in this country—in this introduction, I will endeavour to briefly explore the main themes of the book, namely what constitutes *women*, *popular culture*, and *Canada*.

WOMEN

Gender and the Category of "Woman"

Focusing on women throughout this collection implicitly means focusing on *gender*, a surprisingly complex and controversial term, despite the frequency with which we employ it. While gender is often thought of as synonymous with sex and in conjunction with normalized ideas of female/male and man/woman, queer and feminist theorists have argued that sex and gender are different from each other and that the conflation of the terms categorizes experiences into constructed false binaries. To say that these categories are constructed is not to say that our physical or experiential identities are *not real*, but rather that the normalized Western categories assume an "either/or" dynamic that does not account for the spectrum of experiences and bodies that exist in the world. Importantly, terms like *sex*, *gender*, *sexual orientation*, and *gender expression* are fluid and changing. We define them and react to them differently based on our historical time period, cultural background, and geography (among other factors). They are not universal or static categories.

In the context of Western feminist and queer frameworks, we can think of *sex* as a reference to constructed classifications of biological attributes and *gender* as a reference to socially constructed behaviours, roles, and identities. When I say that sex references "constructed classifications," I am asserting that the labels we put on some bodies and not others are based on human attempts to neatly categorize anatomy, hormones, and other biological attributes to set expectations of what it means to be male or female. But rigid definitions of the body do not account for the complexity of human biology or experience. With this in mind, it is not my job (or your job) to police or surveille anyone's anatomy. Womanhood and femaleness cannot be defined through a simplistic assumption of what people should look like, because all of us look different. Not only is everyone's body different, but who we are is also much more than our physical biology. Gender is the identity we live in the world: the way we perceive ourselves and experience our lives. Gender expression is how we choose to express that identity. In a heteronormative and heterosexist conception, gender is perceived as a binary (man/woman). However, if we think of gender as a spectrum, there are countless identities we may identify as and with.

There are multiple theorists who have discussed how gender is constructed and performed. Building on Simone de Beauvoir's assertion, "One is not born, but rather becomes, a woman," Judith Butler argues that gender is something that we do—not something that we are. In *Gender Trouble: Feminism and the Subversion of Identity*, Butler famously argues that gender is *performative*. This does not mean that gender is a performance. Rather, saying gender is *performative* means that gender is created through the repetition of normalized behaviour and acts and that such repetition works to reify gender categories, making them appear as though they were always there. Butler argues that "gender is a kind of imitation for which there is no original" (Butler 722), meaning that our understanding and enactment of gender has become so ingrained in Western culture that we are conditioned to behave in particular ways and do not notice that we are copying a copy of a copy of a copy, with no essential original. If there is no essential gender, there is no "right" or "wrong" way to be a woman.

Importantly, while Butler's work has been foundational in critiquing gender expectations and behaviour, her theorizations on gender have been critiqued by trans and non-binary scholars who argue that her work emerges from a cisgender perspective that does not reflect concrete social practices and experiences. Viviane Namaste, for example, argues that Butler's theorizations of gender as socially constructed fail to make space for those with lived experiences of transsexual and transgender identities (14). Namaste argues that Butler exploits trans subjects and violence against trans bodies in her case studies in order to assert a position that does not adequately represent the voices or experiences of those she discusses. Similarly, in *Second Skins: The Body Narratives of Transsexuality*, Jay Prosser argues that while discussing notions of embodiment and bodily practice and behaviour, Butler's abstract theories of gender performativity distance theory from lived experience. Butler has contributed enormously to queer and feminist theories, but it is important to problematize her work and position it within the layered and complex theorizations on gender performance and identities.

It is clear from these theories and critiques that definitions of gender and sex are messy and changing; they are not static concepts that can be defined simplistically or narrowly. While recognizing the distinct and different ways women experience inequity and oppression, *women* is conceived as an identity, experience, and subject position that can be adopted, performed, and complicated. Throughout this volume, when we talk about women in pop culture, we include all those who identify as women.

Feminist Intersectionality

This book takes an intersectional approach to studying women and popular culture in Canada. This means that we are starting from the understanding that it is impossible to analyze the relationship between gender and popular culture without considering experiences of class, ability, race, sexuality, and settler colonialism. Intersectionality provides a framework for considering how privilege and oppression are experienced simultaneously. For example, my own experiences are not marked separately as Jewish, as queer, as a woman, as able-bodied, as white, as a settler—rather, each of these positions informs the others. I experience privilege and oppression through how I live these experiences and social locations simultaneously.

Even before the terms *intersectionality* or *feminist* were coined, there were many women, particularly Black women and women of colour, who had already identified the ways in which white supremacy informs and shapes women's liberation and later the feminist movement. For example, Sojourner Truth's 1851 speech at an Ohio women's rights convention refused a universalized conception of femininity and womanhood—noting the ways in which the women's rights movement was only ever talking about white women. Later, the Combahee River Collective, a Black feminist lesbian organization in Boston between 1974 and 1980, set the groundwork for feminist intersectional thought through their considerations of *simultaneity*, or the ways in which experiences of oppression (race, class, gender, sexual orientation, and ability) are experienced at the same time. In 1977, the collective released a statement defining the politics of their movement:

> The most general statement of our politics at the present time would be that we are actively committed to struggling against racial, sexual, heterosexual, and class oppression, and see as our particular task the development of integrated analysis and practice based upon the fact that the major systems of oppression are interlocking.

More than a decade later, in 1989, law professor Kimberlé Crenshaw continued to develop this framework, and was the first woman to employ the term *intersectionality* in her essay "Demarginalizing the Intersection of Race and Sex: A Black Feminist Critique of Antidiscrimination Doctrine, Feminist Theory, and Antiracist Politics." She explains intersectionality using the analogy of traffic accidents:

> Discrimination, like traffic through an intersection, may flow in one direction, and it may flow in another. If an accident happens in an intersection, it can be caused by cars traveling from any number of directions and, sometimes, from all of them. Similarly, if a Black woman is harmed because she is in an intersection, her injury could result from sex discrimination or race discrimination.... But it is not always easy to reconstruct an accident: Sometimes the skid marks and the injuries simply indicate that they occurred simultaneously, frustrating efforts to determine which driver caused the harm. (149)

Crenshaw argues that Black women can not be understood simply in terms of gender or in terms of race, but at the intersections of these identities—identities are not experienced independently, but reinforce and inform each other. In the 1990s, sociologist Patricia Hill Collins applied Crenshaw's ideas to her framework on Black feminism and argued that intersectional systems of power, privilege, and oppression rely on each other, producing discrimination, segregation, and injustice. Today, the experiences and voices of Indigenous, disabled, trans, and queer women of colour continue to shape intersectional feminism.

Intersectionality is discussed in multiple ways throughout this collected volume. For example, Cheryl Thompson's chapter, "Representing *Misogynoir* in Canadian News Media," outlines the history and framework of intersectionality and explores the necessity of utilizing an intersectional approach; Jessica Watkin examines the ways in which otherwise progressive disability podcasts can fail to account for the experiences of women when they do not take an intersectional approach; and T. Nikki Cesare Schotzko uses an intersectional approach and critiques by Black feminist theorists to consider how white feminism animates Margaret Atwood's *The Handmaid's Tale*, erasing and rewriting histories of anti-Black racism and the transatlantic slave trade. Intersectionality is present in each chapter, as the authors refuse to theorize and analyze gendered experiences in silos. One of the underlying assertions throughout this text is that as we develop, produce, and consume media and popular culture, we must understand it through this complex intersectional feminist framework.

Identifying Privilege

It is not simply that media texts represent gendered identities in particular ways, but also that gender dynamics shape how media is developed and produced. This discussion is directly connected to experiences of privilege and power, because people with more privilege can more easily obtain and maintain access and resources. Privilege, as feminist queer theorist Sara Ahmed notes in her discussion of whiteness, allows particular objects to be situated within reach of some bodies and out of reach of others. Ahmed notes that some forms of privilege are inherited and in receiving that inheritance we also

> *inherit the reachability of some objects*, those that are "given" to us, or at least made available to us, within the "what" that is around.... By objects, we would include not just physical objects, but also styles, capacities, aspirations, techniques, habits. Race becomes, in this model, a question of what is within reach, what is available to perceive and to do "things" with. ("Phenomenology of Whiteness" 154)

Simply put, privilege increases the ease with which we can attain particular objectives and the plausibility of attaining them. Inheriting ease of access and reachability extends to shared attributes: we can imagine ourselves winning a Juno or a Tony or an Oscar more easily when we see like-bodies receive them. These awards might not quite be "within reach" (getting an Oscar is by no means an easy task), but privilege makes them more "available to perceive." Ahmed further argues that privilege is an "energy-saving device" that allows certain bodies to pass through space with less effort. Those who are not born into or do not acquire privilege, via settler colonialism, race, gender, sexual orientation, ability, or class, must work harder to assert their right to space, to belonging, and indeed to mere existence. Ahmed utilizes the analogy of a lock. She writes, "If less effort is required to unlock the door for the key that fits the lock, so too less effort is required to pass through an institution for bodies that fit. Social privilege is like an energy-saving device: less effort is required to pass through" (*Willful Subjects* 148).

Analyzing and understanding privilege in terms of race, gender, and class is by no means a new endeavour. Feminist and queer theorists have long discussed these dynamics. In 1989, Peggy McIntosh argued that privilege is not earned, it is something that is given. In McIntosh's "White Privilege: Unpacking the Invisible Knapsack," which first appeared in *Peace and Freedom* magazine, she argues that while many might acknowledge that women are disadvantaged, it is less common for men to explicitly acknowledge the other side of the equation: male privilege. Similarly, she argues, "whites are carefully taught not to recognize white privilege" (2). McIntosh argues that privileged positionalities are typically neutralized, but in order to be accountable, we must learn to see the unconscious privileges that animate our experiences in the world. Just as Ahmed and McIntosh unpack the ways that privilege manifests in daily life, so too can we unpack the ways these dynamics are normalized and perpetuated on screen. Identifying privilege and understanding how it functions is not only part of media literacy, but also part of fostering active and meaningful accountability.

POPULAR CULTURE

Mediating Realities

When I was 12 years old, I went to Los Angeles to visit my "honorary mother," Rhonda Hammer. I had recently hit puberty and I was excited to dress the way I wanted to dress; to be a woman with agency; to look like (what I perceived to be) a grown-up. I wore low-cut crop tops and short skirts. My honorary mother was inquisitive: I wasn't shamed for my clothing choices and she respected my style, but as a cultural studies professor, she did have a few questions for me: "Why do you dress the way you do? Who told you to wear that? What makes this 'cool'?" As a 12-year-old, I remember being *very* annoyed. I was sure I was making choices for myself and wasn't being persuaded by anyone anywhere. My clothing was about me and me alone. But her point was not that I was necessarily being negatively influenced, that I was objectifying myself, or even that I was a victim of the patriarchy. Her point was that all of our clothing choices have meaning and are always mediated by the socio-political and economic context. How we dress is one way we enact the norms we see in our cultures and embody what we perceive as "normal." Our clothing is not neutral. It is influenced by the media we consume and is itself a form of media—shaping our realities and how we are perceived. I share this anecdote because it has stuck with me and I believe it is a useful entry point in our efforts to define media and popular culture because it shows that the influence of popular culture is pervasive, that it is not detached from everyday choices or experiences.

The works in this collection speak to this reality and critically engage with media through a cultural studies approach, considering how media can both reproduce and challenge dominant norms and oppression and privilege. "Cultural studies," as Morag Shiach explains, "is an interdisciplinary space whose contours and energies express the complex and shifting relations between cultural analysis and political critique" (1). It is a complex and shifting field that evades a singular approach or narrative, focusing on the multiple factors shaping relations between culture and power. Here, Shiach explains:

> Culture has been understood in a number of different ways: as specific texts; as the practices which construct national, class, or gender identities; or as the interconnection of different modes and systems of communication. But each of these understandings has led to analyses which aim to capture the ways in which culture interacts with social inequalities. Thus the focus of analysis might be the ways in which particular subcultural groups use and modify cultural artefacts, or it might be the ways in which a particular film constructs its audience, or it might be the ways in which different cultural forms interact at a given historical moment. Overall, however, cultural studies is interested in the practices and texts through which individuals and groups come to understand or to imagine themselves as social beings. (3)

In this understanding, the *culture* engaged in popular culture is inextricable from the political. Studying media as a part of culture begins from an understanding of "culture" as the practices and activities that people participate in and through which communities and individual identities are formed. Beyond what appeals to individual people, or what they enjoy or believe, culture is deeply connected to how societies are organized, how power is distributed, and what is perceived and idealized as the norm. Our culture is highly mediatized, so much so that mass media is not an auxiliary or secondary consideration in our daily lives, but explicitly shapes them. A cultural studies approach to media and popular culture is not simply about mass media production and consumption, but also social practices and power distribution in everyday life. While there are many histories and theories that reside under the umbrella of cultural studies, the various subjects and theories within the field share a focus on how power operates through and with cultural practices.

If cultural studies is the study of practices that shape societies and individuals, and media are material objects that shape and mediate those realities, how might we conceive and engage *popular* culture? The word *popular* itself comes from the latin word *popularis*, meaning "of or belonging to the people." The first question that might come to mind when we read this definition is: *Who are these people?* While typically "popular culture" is uncritically assumed to refer to a range of commercial media that reaches wide audiences, labelling mass media "popular" (or "of the people") has the capacity to erase the top-down systems of power and domination that shape mainstream media—that distance it from "the people." For this reason, we cannot consider popular culture without thinking about larger institutions and systems of power that shape our realities: capitalism, patriarchy, settler colonialism, racism, and white supremacy. These all contribute in some way to processes of production and consumption of mass media. In the chapters included in this text, "popular culture" is conceived of widely, in order to both recognize and resist dominant ideological power dynamics embedded in a term that claims to be "of the people" and simultaneously to redefine who "the people" are.

Leading British cultural studies scholar Stuart Hall offers nuanced definitions of popular culture in "Notes on Deconstructing 'The Popular,'" wherein he emphasizes the dynamic and ongoing process through which popular culture is created and consumed. Hall maps the history and uses of the word *popular* and asserts that in defining the term we must consider its relationship to power, class, and political sites of struggle. While the mediums and roles of popular culture in political struggles consistently shift and change, the increasing presence and power of digital media and social media in our lives demonstrates how relevant Hall's foundational 1981 text remains. He explains, "In the study of popular culture, we should always start here: with the double-stake in popular culture, the double movement of containment and resistance, which is always inevitably inside it" ("Notes on Deconstructing" 228). Popular culture is therefore both a means of political resistance and empowerment and a means of circulating and upholding dominant norms and perceptions.

A Brief History of the Gaze

As many of the chapters in this book suggest, it is important not only to understand how women create media in Canada, but also to explore how we, as spectators, consume it. Cinema studies, alongside cultural studies, has provided essential theorizations on how we perceive the media, and in turn how the media affects us. In 1975, Laura Mulvey's foundational essay, "Visual Pleasure and Narrative Cinema," used Lacanian psychoanalysis as an entry point into a discussion of the male gaze (or the ways in which filmic representation assumes a male standpoint via the protagonist, the director, and the spectator). Mulvey argues that women on screen are defined by their "to be looked-at-ness," while the male gaze of the director, the protagonist, and the camera constitutes the "bearer of the look." Mulvey's work shaped the groundwork for feminist analysis in film studies and introduced tools and standpoints to consider the ways sexual inequities were reproduced on screen.

While Mulvey's work is undeniably influential, theorists critiqued her on multiple fronts, namely noting that her theories assume a lack of agency on the part of the spectator—conceiving of media consumption as a passive experience. This passivity has been challenged by theorists such as Stuart Hall, who notes the active ways in which audiences decode the messages and ideas encoded by media producers. Furthermore, Mulvey's work assumes a singular and universal woman's perspective and does not take into account the ways other positionalities and social locations shape viewing experiences. In her work "The Oppositional Gaze," Black feminist scholar bell hooks explains that Mulvey's theory speaks specifically to white women's experiences and also does not account for how the gaze itself can be a form of resistance for Black women. She argues that while Mulvey's gaze is always white and male, the gaze can also be a site of active resistance, particularly, as hooks notes, "for colonized black people globally.... In resistance struggle, the power of the dominated to assert agency by claiming and cultivating 'awareness' politicizes 'looking' relations—one learns to look a certain way in order to resist" (116). She continues:

> Feminist film theory rooted in an ahistorical psychoanalytic framework that privileges sexual difference actively suppresses recognition of race, reenacting and mirroring the erasure of black womanhood that occurs in films,

silencing any discussion of racial difference—of racialized sexual difference. Despite feminist critical interventions aimed at deconstructing the category "woman" which highlight the significance of race, many feminist film critics continue to structure their discourse as though it speaks about "women" when in actuality it speaks only about white women. (123)

We must expand our understanding of film analysis beyond a single-axis model of oppression and consider the multiple ways in which people experience and consume media—forms that are both resistant and conforming.

Commodifying Resistance: The Feminist Brand

Cultural studies scholar Douglas Kellner argues that media culture is a "contested terrain" (101), which has the capacity to perpetuate dominant ideologies and induce identification with them and also to produce opportunities for resistance. While mainstream media "is severely limited in the extent to which it will advance socially critical and radical positions" (102), it also provides audiences with the ability to resist, rewrite, and negotiate the messages encoded by the producers, making them, as Stuart Hall argues, active participants in meaning-making. Therefore, at the same time as it teaches compliance, it also, as Kellner explains, "provides resources which individuals can appropriate, or reject, in forming their own identities against dominant models. Media culture thus induces individuals to conform to the established organization of society, but it also provides resources that can empower individuals against that society" (3). To further complicate this understanding of popular culture, we must grapple with the reality that capitalist and consumerist institutions often subsume seemingly radical and progressive standpoints in order to attract audiences and shape their own image as one that aligns with women and minority rights. Therefore, we cannot assume that all images that appear to be feminist (or claim to be feminist) actually enact and embody the values and beliefs embedded in feminist frameworks. In 2009, Angela McRobbie argued that feminist images and ideas

have been absolutely incorporated into political and institutional life. Drawing on a vocabulary that includes words like "empowerment" and "choice," these elements are then converted into a much more individualistic discourse, and they are deployed in this new guise, particularly in media and popular culture, but also by agencies of the state, as a kind of substitute for feminism. (1)

Feminist ideologies are recreated and represented in popular culture and reshaped to fit a neoliberal capitalist discourse that prioritizes the individual over the collective and uses the "freedom to choose" as a catchy tagline for freedom to choose *what to buy*, *what to watch*, or *what to wear*, but not the freedom to opt out of the culture, to resist the culture, or to change the culture.

This is by no means a new endeavour. It is evident that popular culture and mainstream media have long recognized the value in targeting women as consumers. We may think back to Edward Bernays's campaign to sell cigarettes to women in 1929. Bernays, who was Sigmund Freud's nephew, was hired to increase women's cigarette purchases. To do so, he hired women to pose as suffragettes at the Easter Sunday parade and instructed them to stop in front of a group of reporters, pull a pack of cigarettes from their garter belts, and light them in front of the cameras. Bernays aimed to make cigarettes more appealing to women by bridging an association between women's rights, agency, and smoking. The press referred to them as "torches of freedom," effectively using women's liberation as a marketing ploy to increase sales. When women later remarked that the green Lucky Strike cartons clashed with their wardrobes, Bernays created a media campaign to make green more fashionable.

Our advertisements still do this work all the time. Even seemingly progressive or feminist depictions are nonetheless trying to "sell." Think about empowering makeup campaigns, deodorant commercials, or menstrual product ads. How do these advertisements portray women and what is their underlying objective? Working within a capitalist system means that the underlying goal of products, TV series, and movies is to sell. The objective of major corporations and production companies will *always* be to sell. As such, one (not so radical) claim that the texts in this book suggest is that not all women's media is feminist media, and not all media that claims to be feminist is feminist at all. In this regard, I want to think seriously about what it means to commodify feminism in popular culture. What does it mean to buy a shirt that says "This is what a feminist looks like!," to listen to music dubbed "feminist," to buy deodorant, menstrual products, organic food, or popular magazines called "feminist"? More urgently, what does it mean, in a Canadian context, when a Canadian prime minister, Justin Trudeau, labels himself a feminist but does little to address the missing and murdered Indigenous women in the country?

In *We Were Feminist Once*, Andi Zeisler clearly charts an evolution of what she calls "marketplace feminism." From Edward Bernays's "torches of freedom" to Beyoncé's feminist signage and nasty women T-shirts, Zeisler explicates the way in which feminism has been co-opted and transformed, from a movement of resistance to a static identity position devoid of activist *action*. Zeisler's work on marketplace feminism is not a sudden revelation, but adds to the collective call for action over empty performances of feminist standpoints and celebrity endorsements:

> The rise of feminist underpants is a weird twist on Karl Marx's theory of commodity fetishism, wherein consumer products once divorced from inherent use value are imbued with all sorts of meaning. To brand something as feminist doesn't involve ideology, or labor, or policy, or specific actions or processes. It's just a matter of saying, "This is feminist because we say it is." (62)

Capitalist and consumerist conditioning compels us to buy in order to substantiate—to associate what we wear with who we are. Dawn L. Rothe and Victoria E. Collins argue that rather than increasing visibility or popularity, "the commodification of resistance serves to perpetuate the system" (609). Citing Jean Baudrillard, they note that capitalist systems work to internalize critique and adopt it to the benefit of the system. "Commodity feminism," they explain, "embraces women as neo-liberal subjects as they purchase corporate approved ideals of gender equality" (Rothe and Collins 612). This is not to discount activists or their objectives, but instead to recognize our implicit perpetuation of a system that we attempt to discredit and dismantle. We can hold this contradiction, rather than trying to rectify, justify, or defend.

We can extend this discussion to consider digital media such as YouTube, Instagram, and other social media platforms, which can possess the appearance of user control and easy access to media development (I can shoot videos from my cellphone that reach millions of people) but nonetheless conform to and help to secure consumer capitalism and neoliberal individualism. An influencer becomes the ideal celebrity endorser for products. The feminist Instagram account is a way to propagate white beauty ideals, oppressive fitness regimes, and "healthy living" products made at the expense of marginalized communities, all under the guise of camaraderie, women's lib, and personal engagement. We feel closer to the celebrities and then feel closer to the products. This is where we might also see underlying contradictions of activism and resistance produced in mainstream media. They are always in connection to and complicit in a neoliberal patriarchal system. This sentiment echoes ideas espoused by Black feminist theorist and poet Audre Lorde, who explains, "For the master's tools will never dismantle the master's house. They may allow us temporarily to beat him at his own game, but they will never enable us to bring about genuine change. And this fact is only threatening to those women who still define the master's house as their only source of support" ("The Master's Tools" 112).

Thinking of media as a contested terrain means we can hold all of these realities at the same time. It is not to discount the incredible political efficacy and power of social media in feminist resistance, particularly in racialized and Indigenous communities. Black Twitter and other social media communities not only construct alternative and powerful opportunities for media dissemination and resistance, they also directly influence mainstream news content. Thus, while mass media may use the "master's tools," at the same time, narratives that effectively depict a resistance against patriarchal corporate entities, against systems of oppression, against naturalized norms, are not only empowering to the individual, but also help all of us to imagine a different world. And a utopian imaginary is powerful.

CANADA

The national is the political is the cultural. Canadian media and popular culture are tightly braided into the country's national identity. In "Marginal Notes on Cultural Studies in Canada," Jody Berland tracks "the history of discourses about culture, politics, and the nation in Canada" (514). Berland's work constructs an essential perspective on "Canadian identity" and nationhood, in relationship to media, technology, and broadcasting. She explains that Canada's cultural institutions have a long history and deep-rooted connection to the country's identity crisis and ongoing battle to assert itself amidst the anxiety of the imperial gaze and in the shadow of a bigger nation next door. Since the Canadian government initiated the Aird Royal Commission in 1928—which aimed to address the American and foreign monopoly of Canada's airwaves—Canada has had a vested interest in the "proactive development of an autonomous national culture" ("Marginal Notes" 515). This is further evident in the 1951 Massey Report, which directly linked autonomous media to national defence, by propagating the threat of Americanization and promoting the efficacy of film to solidify and disseminate a national presence through Canada's media landscape ("Marginal Notes" 517). Such a connection between defence, identity, and media should give us pause. We should ask who and what is "Canadian" in this context and what are we defending? We cannot understand Canadian cultural identities, media, or broadcasting without an understanding of how power operates to construct our understanding of nation and belonging. In order to critically engage the history and current state of women in popular culture in Canada, we must explore systemic power structures related to settler colonialism, race, gender, class, and ability. Berland explains:

> Art is not just about art, and Canadian cultural studies can never be singly about culture, because that is a misinterpretation of what culture is. "Culture" is where we make meaning in relation to power, geography, technology, race, language, sex, memory, time or space, weather or animals or food, et cetera. ("Politics of the Exasperated" 26)

With this in mind, popular culture in Canada is not simply about representation, style, or mediums, but also about how meaning and identities are shaped, embodied, and transformed through the national context. Rather than being lodged in the present, it is predicated on a history of colonialism and helps to form what we imagine as possibilities for the future. Understanding settler colonialism and how it frames and influences media production and reception in Canada is therefore essential to this text.

Settler Colonialism

The focus in the remainder of this section is not on the character or history of "Canadian" popular culture, but rather on the ways in which settler colonialism has shaped popular culture in the country, and how media might also offer a means of decolonization and resistance for Indigenous peoples. Aimee Carrillo Rowe and Eve Tuck define settler colonialism as

> the specific formation of colonialism in which people come to a land inhabited by (Indigenous) people and declare that land to be their new home. Settler colonialism is about the pursuit of land, not just labor or resources. Settler colonialism is a persistent societal structure, not just an historical event or origin story for a nation-state. Settler colonialism has meant genocide of Indigenous peoples, the reconfiguring of Indigenous land into settler property. In the United States and other slave estates, it has also meant the theft of people from their homelands (in Africa) to become property of settlers to labor on stolen land. (4)

Settler colonial ideologies work to normalize white settler supremacy by erasing Indigenous peoples and making settler presence appear inevitable, universal, and eternal. These naturalized standpoints influence our daily lives, as well as the narratives and stories we see in mainstream culture. In Canada, settlers are permitted to forget or excuse the histories of violence that enabled our presence here in order to justify the power we still maintain.

In popular culture, settler colonial ideologies are perpetuated through multiple mechanisms. Two major ways in which they are maintained through mainstream media representation are the continuing erasure of Indigenous presence and the neutralizing of settler identity. In addition to these tactics, when Indigenous people are seen on screen, they are frequently universalized as one type of group (rather than recognizing the diversity of nations that are lumped under this umbrella term), and they are typically situated within the past, rather than in the present, which works to erase the possibility of their ongoing futures. A settler colonial temporal logic influences characterization, as well as plot development on screen, because progress is associated with white settler nationhood and Indigeneity is situated as primitive and in the past.

While these representations have been contested by Indigenous peoples for quite some time, cultural studies scholars tend to position the study of settler colonialism as something relatively new. As Rowe and Tuck further argue,

> theorizations of settler colonialism as a new trend are missing the turn beneath the turn, or perhaps the "turn to where we already were" (Tuck, 2014). The turn beneath the turn is a fulsome apprehension of the implications of ongoing settlement of Indigenous land, the persistent presence of Indigenous life on that land, and the relationships between human and nonhuman lives on that land. (6)

They continue to note that while cultural studies and cultural production may work toward equitable practices, they nonetheless can perpetuate Indigenous erasures. "Popular cultural studies," they argue, "should be radically rethought through a critical examination of pervasive representations that disappear Indigenous peoples" (7). There are relatively few cultural studies scholars who incorporate theorization on settler colonialism, and when concepts related to the subject appear, they are often secondary (7). In this sense, we must not only consider what is said and written in cultural studies, but what is left unsaid.

By and large when a mainstream television series or film does mention Indigenous identities or acknowledge settler colonialism, it is typically a one-off plot. One- or two-episode story arcs assume that settler colonialism and anti-Indigenous oppression are situational and limited, rather than pervasive. Exceptionalism and short-lived plotlines do not simply trivialize the ways that settler colonialism functions in our society but further preclude settler accountability, supposing that the problem is circumstantial or short-term. They may focus on the victims but less frequently identify settlers as the continuing perpetrators.

As much as media can work to disseminate and perpetuate settler colonial ideologies, such a stance can also be combated within media culture. By revealing and challenging the dynamics at play in Canada, media and visual culture have the capacity to illuminate how settler colonialism shapes our understanding of nationhood and "Canadian" subjecthood. Here, media is not simply seen as a reflection of the world, but a mode of resistance (Rowe and Tuck 7). The role of narrative, media, and creativity in resistance should not be underestimated. Tarah Hogue discusses the importance of storytelling as a means of Indigenous healing and resistance in her article "Strategies of Aboriginal Performance Art and the Aesthetics of Diaspora," and argues that storytelling is a means of reconnecting with severed traditions and healing the wounds and loss that have resulted from colonization and continued oppression. In her article, she specifically considers performance artist Rebecca Belmore's work and emphasizes the importance of storytelling in Aboriginal performance art in relation to memory and diasporic representation. Similarly, Leanne Simpson explains that stories are not a simple form of recollection; they are a way to create, to reclaim, and to decolonize. They are active forces in creating alternative presents and new futures:

> Nishnaabeg and Indigenous artists like [Rebecca] Belmore interrogate the space of empire, envisioning and performing ways out of it. Even if the performance only lasts twenty minutes, it is one more stone thrown in the water. It is a glimpse of a decolonized contemporary reality; it is a mirroring of what we can become. (Simpson 98)

Thus, storytelling, and by extension narratives and media, need not primarily be about recalling a precolonial past but calling on it to reproduce an alternative future. Storytelling here is not a tool of remembrance or victimhood. On the contrary, it is about survivorship. Stories are not merely accessories, decorating daily life. They are essential to meaning-making, to culture, and to education.

CHAPTER BREAKDOWN

Women and Popular Culture in Canada is a collected volume intended for a broad audience of feminists, students, teachers, scholars, and artists. It brings together a range of researchers, scholars, and artists whose diverse voices and methodologies—and variation in styles and theoretical frameworks—refuse a singular defining approach and focus, pointing to how expansive and encompassing explorations of popular culture can be. They share personal experiences, subjective viewing perspectives, and stories that relate to their pedagogical approach and theoretical framing. This feminist practice resists singularity, jargon, or high theory, in favour of valuing dynamic difference in style, approach, and focus. In many cases, these chapters opt to introduce perspectives and case studies that are not part of mainstream culture, putting pressure on the term *popular* itself.

There are also mainstream television shows, musicians, and films that are not addressed in these chapters. For example, *Anne of Green Gables*, Celine Dion, and Canadian sports media are perhaps surprisingly absent from the topics discussed. There is no doubt an incredible number of critical interrogations on these performers and media, and their impact on women in Canadian culture should not be trivialized. With that said, one text can only do so much. The choice to focus on a diverse scope of projects and media texts is not an assertion of impact or influence. It is a choice to elevate the current and historical voices of diverse women in the country to construct a critical entry point into a much larger discussion on women in media and popular culture in Canada.

The chapters in this collection are organized into five distinct (but overlapping) parts. While these sections offer an approach to organizing the texts, it is clear that their themes, case studies, and approaches intersect across multiple axes. The volume begins by emphasizing the connection between politics and popular culture, providing a socio-political context and framework for analyzing the relationship between women and media through a discussion of representation, journalism, and news media. In chapter 1, Cheryl Thompson's work focuses on how Black women are represented in journalism, specifically looking at the experiences of Black Canadian journalist Marci Ien. In the second chapter of this section, Dilyana Mincheva complicates simplistic readings of Muslim women's voices on Western and non-Western media channels through an analysis of Irshad Manji. Finally, the role of South Asian women journalists in activism is examined in chapter 3, wherein Syeda Nayab Bukhari looks at ethnic media and journalism as a driving force in political and social change. Taken together, part I demonstrates how journalism and news media are not neutral reports of events, but part of a complex system of the politics of representation in Canada. The chapters move beyond mainstream representation to explore how communities represent themselves and voice their own standpoints and experiences through different mediums. The volume begins with these chapters in order to situate our critique of the media within an intersectional context of politics and resistance.

To continue to explore feminist and women's representation in media, part II begins with a rejection of one-dimensional analyses of a canonical Canadian figure. Analyzing Margaret Atwood's "bad feminism," T. Nikki Cesare Schotzko outlines how Atwood's *The Handmaid's Tale* appropriates the Black experience of chattel slavery. In so doing, the novel and the subsequent television series reproduces a "white feminist" pattern of erasing oppression of racialized and Indigenous women. In chapter 5, Christine Mazumdar traces the representations of pregnancy and motherhood over the course of various incarnations of the *Degrassi* series, noting both the show's groundbreaking representations and its shortfalls. With an undeniable impact on Canadian television history, the *Degrassi* franchise is an essential text for analysis of media in Canada. Finally, Claire Carter looks to the *Baroness von Sketch Show*, the first all-female feminist sketch comedy show in Canada, to consider the queering potential of the series, as it disrupts widespread heteronormative norms and tropes. Looking at specific case studies from the series, Carter demonstrates the potential for women's programming to queerly question and combat normalized gender expectations through humour. While noting the subversive ways in which the show highlights heteronormativity, Carter also problematizes how white privilege frames the series. Together, these chapters combat a simplistic understanding of gendered representations in the media, unpacking canonical images on screen. They focus on both empowerment and subordination, complicity and resistance.

Part III critically explores how gender norms and national ideologies are upheld through portrayals of crime, criminal justice, and (super)heroism. What might women's presence or absence from heroic narratives tell us about conceptions of strength and gender in Canada? How might the presence of an empowered woman conceal otherwise problematic representations of race, settler colonialism, and nationhood? This section begins with Andrea Braithwaite and Olga Marques's chapter, which questions why women have been absent from the role of detective in Canadian crime films and explores how their representations in these narratives mark some bodies as victims and others as accountable for their own destruction. They note that Canadian media has long been used as a means to construct and perpetuate a national (settler colonial) identity, and analyze how media representations shape our conceptions of crime, gender norms, and nationhood. The following chapter considers how Canadian sci-fi and fantasy series, particularly those with women leads, are shaped in part by Canada's multiculturalism and diversity policies. While noting that women protagonists are worthy of celebration, this chapter argues that the characters' differences are only celebrated insofar as they can align with and promote complicity with other national ideologies and practices.

And finally, Chris Klassen troubles a reading of a Canadian woman superhero, outlining the history and diverging interpretations of Canadian comic-book heroine Nelvana: a character sometimes read as white and other times as Inuk. Klassen argues that "Nelvana's role in maintaining Canada's interests in the North make her an agent of the colonial nation regardless of her racial categorization." This attempt to create a distinctly Canadian and patriotic hero is part of the history and present of Canadian media production.

The final two sections of the volume depart from mainstream television and film to consider other modes and mediums of representation. These chapters continue to reflect on the incredible ways women resist and subvert mainstreamed patriarchy, racism, and oppression by elevating marginalized voices and questioning white settler gender norms in pop culture in Canada. Writing about the efficacy of participatory media as refusal and resistance, part IV provides insights into how social media and the gaming industry reimagine and recast narratives in Canada to account for the voices and experiences of those who are underrepresented or erased. Questioning and troubling the very notion of "canon," the first chapter in this section, by Anuppiriya Sriskandarajah, challenges our preconceptions of dominant mainstream media in Canada by exploring how online platforms and social media provide opportunities to rewrite and reimagine what the canon might be, particularly for second generation immigrant women. Next, Roxanne Chartrand and Pascale Thériault analyze how "AltGames" are political acts of resistance in their chapter "The Videoludic Cyborg: Queer and Feminist Appropriations and Hybridity," which builds on the works of Donna Harraway and other feminist theorists. Here, Chartrand and Thériault outline the origins of prototypical masculinized and militarized video games, creating a timeline leading up to the #GamerGate crisis. They move to discuss how the Canadian AltGames community might work to dismantle toxic masculinity in virtual space, and recast and redefine identity through virtual spaces. In the final chapter of this section, Victoria Kannen and Aaron Langille continue to discuss the role of gaming as a subversive cultural text, utilizing a queer and feminist video game as a case study for queer and non-binary participatory presence. Here, Kannen and Langille explore feminist ethics of care in relationship to death positivity through participatory engagement and play. Games provide an opportunity not only to reimagine identity and gender in this context, but also to reposition mortality in the growing movement of death positivity.

"Necessary, Not Radical," the fifth and final part of the collection, explores off-screen media texts. Part V begins with Jill Carter's chapter, "Indigenous Rage Incarnate: Irreconcilable Spaces and Indigestible Bodies." Here, Carter addresses the ways in which settler representations of missing and murdered Indigenous women on stage can work to make Indigenous bodies and struggles hyper-visible, without enacting real change. Rather than fuelling settlers' objectified, tortured, or murdered Indigenous representations, Carter calls instead for the "'indigestible' Indigenous body." Performing the monstrous and rejecting settler expectations is a form of resistance from a voyeuristic settler gaze. The following chapter, by Valley WeeDick, discusses the works of trans women in music in Canada, specifically considering the works of Black soul singer Jackie Shane, and explores trans women's experiences in the music industry, and trans identity, spatiality, and inclusion more broadly. This chapter, rather than solely focusing on exclusion and disappearance, ultimately responds to erasures by refusing their normalization. WeeDick provides insight into how trans artists take space, make space, and reject cissexist social spaces in Canada. Finally, Jessica Watkin takes an intersectional approach to disability podcasts, discussing the ways in which seemingly progressive (and necessary) disability podcasts can fail to account for the experiences of women and marginalized communities. Advocating "care-full-ness" over curiosity, Watkin notes the necessity for intersectional engagement within disability podcasts. The texts demonstrate how women resist oppressive and inequitable media logics and contest mainstream norms using off-screen mediums including live performance, podcasts, and music. Rather than positioning such representation as a radical proposition, these chapters demonstrate why intersectional gender inclusivity is an irrefutable necessity.

The volume concludes with a list of suggested additional readings, meant to evoke questions and provide opportunities for further exploration. The list of recommended texts put this collection in conversation with the pasts, presents, and futures of feminist writing and media in and beyond Canada. These resources are an intentional act of citationality. The suggested reading list, alongside the works cited in each chapter, are maps we follow to find our feminist genealogies. Commit to reading these sources and to finding the histories and foundations that these chapters are built on; expand your knowledge of where these ideas come from, to understand where they might go. Allow these citations to act, as Sara Ahmed aptly describes them, as "feminist bricks: they are the materials through which, from which, we create our dwellings" (*Living a Feminist Life* 16).

We might think of this book too as a feminist dwelling—it houses the narratives, the voices, the histories, and the futures of women in arts and culture in Canada. But this house is not yet built. We must not think of it as static or complete. This is a house always in need of renovation, recreation, repairs, and renewal. I invite you to build this house with us, by asking questions about the media you see around you, what you observe, and the conversations you contribute to. This is an act of scholarly resistance, as we refuse erasure and elevate the voices of women in popular culture in Canada.

WORKS CITED

Ahmed, Sara. "A Phenomenology of Whiteness." *Feminist Theory*, vol. 8, no. 2, 2007, pp. 149–168.

———. *Living a Feminist Life*. Duke UP, 2017.

———. *Willful Subjects*. Duke UP, 2014.

Armatage, Kay, Kass Banting, and Brenda Longfellow, editors. *Gendering the Nation: Canadian Women's Cinema*. University of Toronto Press, 1999.

Austin-Smith, Brenda, and George Melnyk, editors. *The Gendered Screen: Canadian Women Filmmakers*. Wilfrid Laurier UP, 2010.

Berland, Jody. "Marginal Notes on Cultural Studies in Canada." *University of Toronto Quarterly*, vol. 64, no. 4, 1995, pp. 514–525.

———. "The Politics of the Exasperated: Arts and Culture in Canada." *ESC: English Studies in Canada*, vol. 33, no. 3, 2007, pp. 24–30.

Butler, Judith. *Gender Trouble: Feminism and the Subversion of Identity*. Routledge, 2011.

———. "Imitation and Gender Insubordination." *Literary Theory: An Anthology*, edited by Julie Rivkin and Michael Ryan, John Wiley & Sons, 2017, pp. 955–962.

Combahee River Collective. *A Black Feminist Statement*. 1977.

Crenshaw, Kimberlé. "Demarginalizing the Intersection of Race and Sex: A Black Feminist Critique of Antidiscrimination Doctrine, Feminist Theory, and Antiracist Politics." *Feminism and Politics*, edited by Anne Phillips, Oxford UP, 1998, pp. 314–343.

Greensmith, Cameron, and Sulaimon Giwa. "Challenging Settler Colonialism in Contemporary Queer Politics: Settler Homonationalism, Pride Toronto, and Two-spirit Subjectivities." *American Indian Culture and Research Journal*, vol. 3, no. 2, 2013, pp. 129–148.

Hall, Stuart. "Encoding, Decoding." *The Cultural Studies Reader*, edited by Simon During, Routledge, 1993, pp. 90–103.

———. "Notes on Deconstructing 'The Popular.'" *People's History and Socialist Theory*, Routledge & Kegan Paul, 1981, pp. 227–249.

Hogue, Tarah. "Strategies of Aboriginal Performance Art and the Aesthetics of Diaspora," *Vancity Art*, 4 Feb. 2009.

hooks, bell. "The Oppositional Gaze." *Black Looks: Race and Representation*, South End Press, 1992, pp. 115–131.

Kellner, Douglas. *Media culture: Cultural studies, Identity and Politics Between the Modern and the Post-Modern*. Routledge, 2003.

Lorde, Audre. "The Transformation of Silence into Language and Action." *Identity Politics in the Women's Movement*, 1977, pp. 81–84.

———. "The Master's Tools will Never Dismantle the Master's House." *Feminist Postcolonial Theory: A Reader*, 2003, pp. 25–27.

McIntosh, Peggy. "White Privilege: Unpacking the Invisible Knapsack." *Peace and Freedom*, 1988, pp. 10–12.

McRobbie, Angela. *The Aftermath of Feminism: Gender, Culture and Social Change*. Sage, 2009.

Mulvey, Laura. "Visual Pleasure and Narrative Cinema." *Visual and Other Pleasures*, Palgrave Macmillan, 1989, pp. 14–26.

Namaste, Viviane. *Invisible Lives: The Erasure of Transsexual and Transgendered People*. University of Chicago Press, 2000.

Prosser, Jay. *Second Skins: The Body Narratives of Transsexuality*. Columbia University Press, 1998.

Rothe, Dawn L., and Victoria E. Collins. "The Illusion of Resistance: Commodification and Reification of Neoliberalism and the State." *Critical Criminology*, vol. 25, no. 4, 2017, pp. 609–618.

Rowe, Aimee Carrillo, and Eve Tuck. "Settler Colonialism and Cultural Studies: Ongoing Settlement, Cultural Production, and Resistance." *Cultural Studies, Critical Methodologies*, vol. 17, no. 1, 2017, pp. 3–13.

Shiach, Morag. *Feminism and Cultural Studies*. Oxford UP, 1999.

Simpson, Leanne. *Dancing on Our Turtle's Back: Stories of Nishnaabeg Re-creation, Resurgence and a New Emergence*. Arbeiter Ring, 2011.

Thompson, Cheryl. *Beauty in a Box: Detangling the Roots of Canada's Black Beauty Culture*. Wilfrid Laurier UP, 2019.

Wagner, Angelia, and Joanna Everitt, editors. *Gendered Mediation: Identity and Image Making in Canadian Politics*. UBC Press, 2019.

Zeisler, Andi. *We Were Feminists Once*. Public Affairs, 2016.

PART I

NOTEWORTHY AND NEWSWORTHY:
THE POLITICAL AND THE POPULAR

CHAPTER 1

Representing *Misogynoir* in Canadian News Media: From BLMTO to Marci Ien

Cheryl Thompson

INTRODUCTION

On December 10, 2018, International Human Rights Day, the Ontario Human Rights Commission (OHRC) released an interim report on racial profiling and racial discrimination against Black persons by the Toronto Police Service (TPS). The OHRC found that between 2013 and 2017, a Black person in Toronto was nearly 20 times more likely than a white person to be involved in a fatal shooting by the TPS; despite making up only 8.8 percent of Toronto's population, Black people were overrepresented in use of force cases (28.8 percent), shootings (36 percent), deadly encounters (61.5 percent), and fatal shootings (70 percent) (3). These findings affirm what Toronto's Black community has been saying for decades—there is a policing crisis in Canada. In an article penned for the *Washington Post*, Robyn Maynard concluded, "The refusal to acknowledge [this crisis] is not only a negation of present-day realities but also an erasure of history" ("Over-policing").

The issue of Black women and policing became headline news on February 26, 2018, when Black Canadian journalist Marci Ien penned an opinion-editorial for the *Globe and Mail*, titled "The Double Standard of Driving While Black—Canada." The article begins with Ien recounting the events that took place between her and Toronto police:

> Another sleepless night. I keep thinking about what happened. I keep thinking about what could have happened. What was meant to be a quiet Sunday evening last week turned into something else. That I am an award-winning journalist didn't matter. That I co-host a national television show

didn't matter. That I live in the neighbourhood for 13 years didn't matter. But being black mattered.... I was being stopped by a police officer in my driveway outside of my house in Toronto.

Almost one year before, a six-year-old Black girl was thrust into the media when her mother (both names were never released) launched a formal complaint against Peel Regional Police officers who had handcuffed the little girl at her elementary school in Mississauga in September 2016 because the unarmed child was supposedly acting in a "violent" manner. Toronto media outlets reported the story in February 2017 after the mother's formal complaint.

This chapter will probe Ien's case while drawing parallels between it and incidents involving Black children in our schools. I use *intersectionality* as a framework to describe the ways different forms of discrimination overlap and relate to Black women's/girl's lives, and how racism and sexism play out on our bodies. The aim is to also explore how *misogynoir* appears in Canadian media and, through media coverage, is reified onto Black women/girls. According to *Vice*, public awareness about the Mississauga school incident came one week after Ontario's then–education minister Mitzie Hunter ordered a probe into systemic racism at the York Region District School Board following reports of a trustee using hate speech (Krishnan, "Why Was"). School board trustee Nancy Elgie, 82, an elected official for Georgina, found herself at the centre of the controversy after she was overheard referring to a Black parent as a "nigger" after a public meeting in November 2016 (Krishnan, "Look at All"). Both incidents became a lightning rod for Black Lives Matter Toronto (BLMTO), which launched a campaign to eliminate the School Resource Officer (SRO) program. The SRO program started in 2008—one year after 15-year-old Jordan Manners, a Black grade nine student at C. W. Jefferys Collegiate in Toronto's Jane and Finch area, was shot and killed on school grounds. The SRO program stationed uniformed officers in Toronto District School Board (TDSB) schools. Because of pressure from BLMTO and members of Toronto's Black community, as well as the fact that 2,000 out of the 15,000 students surveyed, from 45 schools, said that they felt intimidated, watched, and targeted by SROs in November 2018, TDSB trustees voted 18–3 to cancel the SRO program (Freeman and Goodfield). Since 2017, BLMTO has also run a Freedom School, a three-week program for children aged 4 to 10. This school has received little media attention, except for a short 2018 CBC documentary, discussed later in this chapter.

This chapter will engage with Maynard's *Policing Black Lives: State Violence in Canada from Slavery to Present*, one of the first book-length critiques of policing in

Canada. In order to contextualize Ien's case, I first explain my theoretical frameworks and methodological approach.

THEORETICAL FRAMEWORKS: INTERSECTIONALITY AND *MISOGYNOIR*

In 2016 Kimberlé Crenshaw, along with legal scholar Andrea Ritchie and others,
published *Say Her Name: Resisting Police Brutality against Black Women*. This book
was in response to multiple policing shootings of unarmed Black men and women
that have taken place since 2012, when 17-year-old African American teenager
Trayvon Martin was fatally shot in Sanford, Florida, by George Zimmerman.
The book was also a response to Sandra Bland, a 28-year-old African American
woman who was found hanged in a jail cell in Waller County, Texas, in 2015,
three days after she was arrested during a traffic stop. While her death was ruled
a suicide, it sparked allegations of racially motivated police murder and, within a
few months, Bland's death, under the hashtag #SayHerNameSandraBland, was
used to mobilize against police violence. HBO also produced a documentary, *Say
Her Name: The Life and Death of Sandra Bland*, that followed the two-year case,
questioning what really happened to her.

In 1991 Crenshaw used the term *intersectionality* as a framework to "illustrate that many of the experiences Black women face are not subsumed within
the traditional boundaries of race or gender discrimination as these boundaries
are currently understood, and that the intersection of racism and sexism factors
into Black women's lives in ways that cannot be captured wholly by looking at
the race or gender dimensions of those experiences separately" (1244). Since then,
one of the core tenets of *intersectionality* includes the notion that critical inquiry
must emanate within and from multiple theoretical frameworks. In their book
Intersectionality, Patricia Hill Collins and Sirma Bilge argue that understanding
intersectionality as a *heuristic*, a problem-solving or analytical tool, means that it
can assume different forms (4). Specifically, it can be used to understand and analyze the social world and human experience; it can help to make sense of social
inequalities; it can unpack power relations through a lens of mutual construction;
and it fosters relational thinking that rejects *either/or* binary thinking in favour of
a relationality that embraces a *both/and* frame (25–27). The aim, then, is to contextualize issues like social inequality, relationality, and power (29).

There is now a robust literature on *intersectionality* but not a lot in the broad-
est scope of Internet studies, specifically concerns about how race, gender, and
sexuality often preclude intersectional interrogations of the structure, activities,

representations, and materiality of the Internet (Noble and Tynes 4). Hill Collins has also observed that there are "definitional dilemmas" to the term where there is a risk of it being defined so narrowly or too broadly that it loses its meaning altogether; but if we conceptualize *intersectionality* as a framework, not as a theory, "the critical insight that race, class, gender, sexuality, ethnicity, nation, ability, and age operate not as unitary, mutually exclusive entities, but as reciprocally constructing phenomena that in turn shape complex social inequalities" (32) can be understood and articulated. By using *intersectionality* as a framework for this chapter, my aim is to explore the ways in which race and gender shaped how the media reported on Ien and how this intersection ultimately played a role in shaping public discourse on Black women/girls and criminality.

The term *misogynoir* was coined by Moya Bailey in 2010. "I wanted to develop a term that addressed the specific violence of representational imagery depicting Black women," (341) Bailey explains, adding, "I coined *misogynoir* to name this particular kind of racist sexist tropes. As a result of its utility, *misogynoir* has been used frequently within the Black feminist blogosphere" (341–342). Where *intersectionality* allows for a complexity of understanding of the experiences of Black women/girls across multiple axes, *misogynoir* gives us the tools to deconstruct how sexism and racism depict Black women/girls on digital platforms, such as web news and social media. The goal of Black feminist scholars is to add to the toolbox on Black feminist thought. My aim is to engage in a dialogue with these Black women, but to also locate the topic in Canada, which is often left out of similar discussions.

METHODOLOGY

As the cases discussed in this chapter are relatively recent, I rely heavily on news reports and social media discussions. Specifically, the news articles include both TV and print media—traditional news sources (i.e., CTV, CBC, Citytv, *Toronto Star*, and *Globe and Mail*) and non-traditional online sources (i.e., *Vice*, *Now Magazine*, and Rabble.ca)—and Twitter. The articles were culled based on three criteria: (1) discussion and/or debate about Ien; (2) police response to Black children in schools; and (3) racial profiling and the Black community. In this regard, the chapter aims to explore the relationship between discourses and ideology. Discourses are ideological insofar as their "meanings serve the interests of that section of society within which the discourse originates and which works ideologically to naturalize those meanings into common sense," but they are not "produced by individual authors or speakers" (Fiske 14). Rather, discourses are socially produced and often institutionalized ways of making sense of a certain topic that constructs a "sense of social identity" (14–15). Critical discourse analysis (CDA) is a useful method of analysis for media because it allows for the identification and probing of social practices, including economic, class, political, cultural, and others while positioning discourse not singularly as language but as visual images as well as social practices and social actors. Using CDA to examine news media coverage of Black women/girls allows for a deeper understanding of how Black feminism, media studies, and critical theory overlap and intersect. This chapter ultimately explores two questions. First, who are the Black women/girls under discussion, what embroiled them into the media, and how did the media subsequently report on their encounters with police? Second, given the interactivity of online media sources, what can a discourse analysis of the commentary section reveal in terms of *misogynoir*?

THE MEDIA AND POLICING BLACK LIVES

Maynard asserts that *misogynoir* "extends across society, including and well beyond the state," and "while all Black women experience misogynoir and are vulnerable to state violence, all Black women do not experience identical forms of oppression. Black women outside of the realm of 'respectability' are more vulnerable to victimization by state-sanctioned processes" (*Policing Black Lives* 125–126). These comments are especially important to consider given the different ways in which Ien, an accomplished journalist, versus a young Black girl in public school versus queer-identified Black women members of BLMTO were framed within the media and, most importantly, how they have (and have not) been given the agency to speak on and about being Black *and* a woman in Canada. The issue of police and the Black community is decades long.

Most notably, there were six high-profile shootings of Black men and women in Canada between 1978 and 1990. On August 9, 1978, 24-year-old Buddy Evans was killed by a white police officer at a nightclub on King Street West in Toronto; on November 11, 1987, unarmed 19-year-old Anthony Griffins was shot and killed by a white police officer in a Montreal police station parking lot; on August 9, 1988, 44-year-old Lester Donaldson was shot to death in his rooming house apartment by a white police officer; on December 8, 1988, Michael Wade Lawson, a 17-year-old Mississauga teenager, was shot in the back of his head and killed by a white police officer while he was joyriding in a stolen car; on October 27, 1989, 23-year-old Brampton resident Sophia Cook was shot by a white police officer in the back (and left paralyzed) while strapped down in the passenger seat of a car;

and on May 14, 1990, unarmed 16-year-old Marlon Neal was shot after fleeing a police radar trap in Scarborough (Nangwaya).

In 1988, activist Dudley Laws co-founded the Black Action Defence Committee (BADC) along with Charles Roach, Sherona Hall, and Lennox Farrell (Winsa). Laws, who was born in Jamaica, passed away in 2011. In 1990, he called on then-premier Bob Rae to establish an independent body to investigate the police shootings. The Special Investigations Unit (SIU), which looks at all police shootings, was formed in the wake of the Donaldson killing, but also because of the BADC's advocacy work (Winsa). Similarly, Roach, who immigrated to Canada from Trinidad, also worked alongside Laws and others in the 1980s and 1990s to seek justice for Black men and women who were killed at the hands of white police officers.[1]

The above cases predate BLMTO and the 24-hour news cycle and, in some ways, are forgotten by mainstream media. Recent police shooting cases such as that of Jermaine Carby, who was shot and killed by Peel Regional Police in Brampton on September 24, 2014; Andrew Loku, a refugee from South Sudan who was shot and killed by Toronto Police on July 5, 2015; and Bony Jean-Pierre, who was shot and killed by police while trying to flee a drug raid in a Montreal North apartment on March 31, 2016, have been framed as "new" phenomena rather than the continuation of long-standing issues with police and the Black community in the GTA and beyond. Desmond Cole's April 2015 article in *Toronto Life*, "The Skin I'm In," in which the journalist-activist talked about his experiences with carding,[2] an intelligence-gathering practice used by police across the country, also made the police's targeting of the Black community seem new.

BLMTO launched in late 2014 as a coalition to speak out against police brutality. It followed the creation of a hashtag on Twitter, #BlackLivesMatter (BLM), created by three African American women—Alicia Garza, Patrisse Cullors, and Opal Tometi—in 2013, following the death of Trayvon Martin (Tynes et al. 22). BLMTO, co-founded by Yusra Khogali, Sandy Hudson, and others, first caught the Canadian media's attention the night Carby was fatally shot. In an interview with the *Toronto Star*, Hudson explained, "I got a call from my brother, who said something needs to be done," and so the next day Hudson and approximately 3,000 others held a candlelight vigil at the Superior Court across from the US consulate in Toronto (Reynolds). "Where did this movement [BLMTO] come from? Who's behind it, how did it snowball? And what are its goals?" asked the *Star* (Reynolds). Given the decade-long history of police violence against unarmed Black people, the media's reporting on BLMTO has de-historicized and de-contextualized a long-standing issue. As evidenced by BLM's use of social media, the Internet has served as a site of expanding coverage of Black violence at the hands of police, often produced in the interest of creating a media spectacle through discourses of Black criminality (Tynes et al. 22). Ien's case speaks to the entanglements of social media, race, and discourses of Black criminality.

MARCI IEN AND THE INTERSECTIONALITY OF RACE AND GENDER

Since 2016, Ien has been a co-host on the Canadian Television Network's (CTV) daytime panel talk show *The Social*. Before this, she was a co-host of CTV's *Canada AM*, an English-language morning news show that aired from 1972 to 2016, and a reporter for CTV News and anchor for CTV News Channel. Ien is also a graduate of Ryerson University's RTA School of Media. In 2014, she was granted the Planet Africa Award for excellence in media, and in 2015, Ien garnered a Canadian Screen Award nomination in the Best Host category for her work on *Canada AM*. In 2016, she also received an African Canadian Achievement Award for her journalism. By all accounts, Ien is an accomplished journalist with a national profile.

On December 6, 2018, she appeared on the front page of *Share* magazine, a Caribbean community publication founded in 1978. "A powerful woman," declared the frontpage headline. In a two-page feature titled "Broadcaster Marcia [sic] Ien one of Canada's 'most powerful women,'" staff writer Ron Fanfair introduced Ien as someone "to be celebrated among Canada's highest achieving women in diverse fields" (3). Ien, the magazine reported, was to be listed among the Women's Executive Network's Top 100 Most Powerful Women in Canada. "It means that when I call, people might just pick up the phone," she said, adding, "It means when I say something, people listen.… It means that I can make decisions and I am in spaces where my word counts. That means I can pull others up if my word counts. That's what power is. It means I can continue to make change" (3). These statements are a far cry from her *Globe and Mail* op-ed.

Between February 26 and March 4, 2018, Marci Ien appeared in five op-eds in the national news media, including the one she penned herself for the *Globe and Mail*. In addition to pointing out that she was an award-winning journalist and a Black woman, she stated, "Maybe the hooded parka I was wearing mattered, too. I was being stopped by a police officer in my driveway outside of my house in Toronto. I was at home. My safe place. And I was scared." The "hooded parka" reference is a clear signal to Trayvon's hoodie, which became a symbol for how Black men/boys are viewed as "suspects," especially in encoded white places.

Media discourse following Trayvon's death has revealed a deeply entrenched racial bias against Black people and hoodies. In 2012, for instance, journalist Geraldo Rivera said on the *Fox & Friends* TV show that "the hoodie is as much responsible for Trayvon Martin's death as George Zimmerman was" and that, in his opinion, parents should not let their children wear hoodies—unless it is raining or they are at a track-and-field event; he also said it sends a sinister signal (Weeks). Ien's reference, then, was a signal that in Canada, like in the US, the clothing on Black bodies can also be a contributing factor in encounters with police.

There were four takeaways from Ien's op-ed. First, contrary to the popular Canadian ethos of "multiculturalism," racism exists in Canada. Second, the history of the Black community's negative relationship with the police cannot be ignored. A 2017 study of 1,500 Black-identified people conducted by Toronto's Black Experience Project, for instance, found that nearly 80 percent of Black men between the ages of 25 and 44 said they had been stopped by police in public in the GTA (Breen). Overall, 55 per cent of Black GTA residents surveyed reported being stopped by police at some point, the Black Experience Project report found (Breen).[3]

Third, Black women also experience carding. Profiling, which many believe carding to be, "is a self-fulfilling prophecy. The more that a group is targeted, the greater the likelihood that criminality will be discovered—particularly for those offenses that are prevalent in society" (Tanovich 916). Repeatedly, Toronto Police claimed that Ien was stopped on her driveway for her "driving behaviour" for failing to stop at a stop sign, and that on video footage, her race was "not visible," so therefore race was not the reason she was stopped (Hayes, "Toronto Police"). In response, however, Ien defended herself by stating that it was not about whether she incorrectly came to a complete stop at a stop sign that mattered, it was "how I felt [in my driveway] … it was his tone. It scared me" (Hayes). Fourth, even though she is an accomplished professional, Ien said she has often noticed how Black bodies are frequently presumed, by police, to be "out of place" and/or "dangerous" in majority white spaces.

For example, in the case of the six-year-old Black girl handcuffed (at the ankles and wrists) at school, police said they were called to Nahani Way Public School by school officials three times to deal with this particular little girl (Krishnan, "Why Was"). According to Peel Sergeant Josh Colley, "the officers arrived on scene and found a young girl who was acting extremely violent, punching, kicking, biting, spitting. And their first priority is her safety"; Colley, speaking to CityNews, said further that the officers used de-escalation techniques to try to calm the child down (Mulligan). "When that didn't work the officers, with the resources that they had, used what they could to restrain her in a safe manner and ultimately ensure her safety and the safety of the others," he added (Mulligan). Peel Sergeant Colley, who is also Black, believed that "it's an insult to think that someone would say that race played a part in the way that we dealt with the situation" (Mulligan). Historically, as Robin Bernstein writes, "white children have been constructed as tender angels while black children have been libeled as unfeeling, noninnocent, nonchildren" (33). Ien opined that Black Canadians are subject to different standards and laws, and that racial biases are real; they are formed in our childhood. Given this young Black girl's treatment, it is extremely difficult to not agree with her.

Danardo Jones, legal director of the African Canadian Legal Clinic, told *Vice* that there is no justification for handcuffing a little girl. "Is there anything else that two 200-pound men could have done to restrain a 48-pound child? Did they try giving her a lollipop or maybe a colouring book with some crayons? The kind of stuff any compassionate adult would do," he said (Krishnan, "Why Was"). The polarization between Black and white children has existed in Western visual culture since the nineteenth century, and it is because of this polarization of racial innocence or lack thereof that white childhood always appears innocuous, natural, and therefore justified, but Black children are somehow comparatively inherently "violent" and more "adult" than childlike (Bernstein 33). This case is a clear example of racial bias—there has yet to be reports of six-year-old white children being handcuffed by police in GTA schools.

While it is true that the Internet can serve as an alternative space for conceiving of and sharing empowering images of Black people, it happens in a highly commercially mediated environment. As Safiya Umoja Noble writes, "it is simply not enough to be 'present' on the web; we must consider the implications of what it means to be on the web in the 'long tail' or mediated out of discovery and meaningful participation, which can have a transformative impact on the enduring and brutal economic and social disenfranchisement of African Americans, especially among Black women" (165). The way that the police responded to Ien's op-ed revealed how "intersectional identities reproduce oppression found within dominant discourse and how intersectional identities present counter-narratives to stereotypical mass media depiction involving [Black women]" (Korn 120). It also sheds light on how grossly underrepresented racialized groups and women are in Canadian media.

A 2010 study conducted by Ryerson University found that only 4.8 percent, or 14 of the 289 leaders in Canadian media examined, were racialized ("Toronto, DiverseCity"). In 2014, J-Source, a news website geared toward journalism professionals, surveyed 76 English-language daily newspapers in Canada and found that 73 percent of all columnists were men (Robertson). Many of Canada's media elites have chosen to continue publishing homogenous news, often defending their right to freedom of speech (Anderson). Shree Paradkar, race and gender columnist for the *Toronto Star*, one of the few racialized reporters in Canadian news, wrote a response to Ien's op-ed that echoed the sentiment of others. "How Black people (and Indigenous people and other marginalized people) experience police is different from how people with specific status of race and age and wealth experience police," she wrote. In response to Ien's piece, a senior Toronto police officer went on Twitter to dispute her account that race played a factor in her being pulled over for what was the third time in eight months. "You failed to stop at a stop sign," a tweet by then–Staff Superintendent Mario Di Tomasso read. "It was dark. Your race was not visible on the video and only became apparent when you stepped out of the vehicle in your driveway" (@DM_COMM_SAFETY).[4] Inasmuch as social media is an empowering force for Black women to speak for ourselves, some of the tweets in reply to Di Tomasso speak to the ways in which social media has, through the circulation of "cybertypes," propagated, disseminated, and commodified "images of race and racism" (Nakamura 3). As a function of the *new racism*, which as Hill Collins describes purports to be colour-blind, "multiculturalism … and other ideologies that justify inequalities not just of race, but also of class, gender, religion, sexuality, age, and ethnicity, are increasingly reproduced by an influential … popular culture industry" (*From Black Power* 8). "Since she is a Reporter (Marci Ien) who works for @BellMediaPR, her honesty and judgement need to be questioned moving forward if from what has been said here about what happened is true" said one white man on Di Tommaso's Twitter (@News_Drunk). "Please stop screaming racism as a defence for committing a crime! Obviously your driving is a danger to the public & your neighbours!" (@bconnolly00) added another. The tweets affirm what Maynard describes as a "societal erasure" and "tacit acceptance" of the racialized and gendered surveillance and punishment "levelled at Black women in their everyday lives[, which] belies an ongoing and institutionalized disregard for experiences of racism that do not fit within more classical views of racial profiling or gendered violence" (150).

"When you look at the world and all the things that are happening in it, to be in a place where you have an opinion and you can state what you want, what you stand by and your feelings about certain things is special," Ien told *Share* (Fanfair 14). "You can't do that as a news reporter. The show that I am on now is about us. Our personalities and how you feel are what drive the show. What a privilege it is to have a voice and to be able to speak to certain things I believe in on a daily basis," she added. Ien's voice is her cultural capital. That is what afforded her the opportunity to share her experiences with police. It was, paradoxically, that same voice and visibility that made her a target for what Nancy Leong calls *racial capitalism*, or "the process of deriving social or economic value from the racial identity of another person" (2153). Stated otherwise, racial capitalism occurs when a white individual or a predominantly white institution derives social or economic value from associating with people with non-white racial identities. In a society preoccupied with diversity, "nonwhiteness is a valued commodity," Leong asserts, adding, "And where that society is founded on capitalism, it is unsurprising that the commodity of nonwhiteness is exploited for its market value" (2154).

Why was Ien, an employee of Bell Media, left to fend for herself in the Twitter battle with police? Instead of using the platform of her show to talk about anti-Black racism in Canada, Ien had to *become* the story. In that sense, part of her value became tied to *being* Black—not just a journalist—which she then performed in a way that met with the expectations of the dominant culture, that is, a (Black) adversarial relationship with (white) police. Ien's case illustrates how *misogynoir* works; "being Black encompasses *both* experiencing white domination *and* individual and group valuation of an independent, long-standing Afrocentric consciousness" (Hill Collins, *Black Feminist Thought* 27). Prior to February 2018, Marci Ien was a Black journalist who did not embroil herself in public discussions about anti-Black racism. Today, she stands as a Black feminist example of the ways in which domination is experienced and resisted in social institutions controlled by the dominant group, like the media. When young Black girls have encounters with police, unfortunately, they are not afforded the opportunity to defend themselves. BLMTO's Freedom School, then, is a vital step toward shifting the focus away from Black violence to encouraging Black children to be proud of who they are, even if they live in a society that does not always affirm who they are. "[The Freedom School] is another beautiful model of teaching Black youth not only about Black contribution to history, and also of the realities of Black queer and Black trans people, but also the contributions of different Black liberation movements," Maynard told me (Thompson 23).

In the 2018 film *Freedom Summer*, we learn that BLMTO's Freedom School, a three-week summer program for Black youth in Toronto, aims to tackle the issue of Black erasure in public education curriculum head-on. The film uses statistics such as one finding that only 65 percent of Black youth in Toronto graduate high school, due to factors like disengagement, discipline, and suspension, also known as "push out," to illustrate why Black children urgently need to learn about our history and Black identity. As one Freedom School parent, D'bi Young (who is also a renowned dub poet, playwright, and performer) says, "It is so important to have a space where he [her son, Moon] can lead while learning because developing your autonomy, developing your sense of self, those things are important" (Asfaha). "To be in a space that will nurture that, but also challenge irresponsibility, and also challenge a lack of empathy, and challenge a lack of compassion … in a gentle and supportive way," she explains further, "I think that's healthy, that's how we grow." The question that programs like the Freedom School and critical analyses, like this one, aim to probe is ultimately *What can we do today to change what we learn about Black history and culture, and by extension, how can we shift the interactions the Black community too often has with police?*

CONCLUSION

In January 2019, after an 11-month review, Ontario Court of Appeal Justice Michael Tulloch called for the end of carding. According to CBC News's reporting, in a 310-page review on the police practice, Tulloch said, "there is no evidence that random street checks lead to fewer crimes, and that the roll back of carding practices has, in some cases, resulted in lower crime rates" ("An Ontario Judge"). Mike McCormack, Toronto Police Association president—who has been a long-standing critic of any complaints against Toronto Police, especially those made by BLMTO—said in response to the report, "There's going to have to be a training curriculum involved in this, retraining of police officers. Where are we going to find the time and people to do this when we can't even put people out on the street" (Gibson). His comments are another example of tone-deaf policing. Despite documented evidence of the ineffectiveness of carding and anecdotal accounts like that of Marci Ien's, many police officers continue to make excuses about a decades-long problem of over-policing the Black community. Rather than use conjecture to defend police tactics, the real change will happen when honest conversations about anti-Black racism and police services are had.

CRITICAL REFLECTION QUESTIONS

1. How does media reporting shape public opinion on policing and perceptions of anti-Black racism?
2. Would Marci Ien have been given the same media attention if she was not a TV personality?
3. Is social media a useful tool to bring the issue of policing into the public's awareness or does it create more of a combative relationship between the public and police?

NOTES

1. Roach, who died in 2012, received an honorary street, Charley Roach Lane, in 2018; it can be found in Toronto's St. Clair Avenue West area, where Roach's law firm, Roach, Schwartz & Associates, operated for decades (Rankin).

2. Carding involves stopping, questioning, and documenting individuals, even when no particular offence is being investigated; their information is then collected and kept on record for unspecified periods.

3. There were no clear statistics on the policing experiences of Black women in the GTA.

4. Mario Di Tommaso was appointed Deputy Minister of Community Safety in October 2018.

WORKS CITED

@bconnolly00. "@MarciIen Please stop screaming racism as a defence for committing a crime! Obviously your driving is a danger to the public & your neighbours! Re: Toronto Police response to allegation of racism. #TOpoli #Toronto #onpoli #cdnpoli #Racism #StopSpreadingHate #FakeNews." Twitter, 28 Feb. 2018, 7:37 p.m., https://twitter.com/bconnolly00/status/969053945141350400.

@DM_COMM_SAFETY. "I have viewed the video footage of your vehicle stop. You were stopped because of your driving behaviour. You failed to stop at a stop sign. It was dark. Your race was not visible on the video and only became apparent when you stepped out of the vehicle in your drive way." Twitter, 27 Feb. 2018, 7:03 p.m., https://twitter.com/DM_COMM_SAFETY/status/968682944024989696.

@News_Drunk. "Since she is a Reporter (Marci Ien) who works for @BellMediaPR, her honesty and judgement need to be questioned moving forward if from what has been said here about what happened is true." Twitter, 1 Mar. 2018, 9:10 a.m., https://twitter.com/News_Drunk/status/969258616543948800.

Anderson, Septembre. "Diversify or Die: Canadian Media Choosing the Latter." *Torontoist*, 17 May 2017, https://torontoist.com/2017/05/diversify-die-canadian-media-choosing-latter/. Accessed 24 Jan. 2019.

"An Ontario Judge Says Carding Doesn't Work. But Will Politicians Listen?" *CBC News*, 4 Jan. 2019, https://www.cbc.ca/news/canada/toronto/ontario-carding-review-michael-tulloch-1.4964768. Accessed 5 Jan. 2019.

Asfaha, Lu. "Freedom Summer." *YouTube*, commentary by D'bi Young, 3 Jan. 2018, https://www.youtube.com/watch?v=f9hUB9edi8I.

Bailey, Moya. "New Terms of Resistance: A Response to Zenzele Isoke." *Souls*, vol. 15, no. 4, 2013, pp. 341–343.

Bernstein, Robin. *Racial Innocence: Performing American Childhood from Slavery to Civil Rights*. NYU Press, 2011.

Breen, Kerri. "55% of Black Toronto-area Residents Report Being Stopped by Police: Survey." *Global News Radio*, 19 July 2017, https://globalnews.ca/news/3609874/55-of-black-toronto-area-residents-report-being-stopped-by-police-survey/. Accessed 20 Jan. 2019.

Cole, Desmond. "The Skin I'm In: I've Been Interrogated by Police More than 50 Times—All Because I'm Black." *Toronto Life*, 21 April 2015, https://torontolife.com/city/life/skin-im-ive-interrogated-police-50-times-im-black/. Accessed 25 May 2015.

Crenshaw, Kimberlé. "Mapping the Margins: Intersectionality, Identity Politics, and Violence against Women of Color." *Stanford Law Review*, vol. 43, no. 6, 1991, pp. 1241–1299.

Crenshaw, Kimberlé, et al. *Say Her Name: Resisting Police Brutality Against Black Women*. African American Policy Forum, 2016.

Fanfair, Ron. "Broadcaster Marcia Ien One of Canada's 'Most Powerful Women.'" *Share*, vol. 41, no. 19, 6 Dec. 2018, 3, 14.

Fiske, John. *Television Culture*. Methuen, 1987.

Freeman, Joshua, and Kayla Goodfield. "TDSB Votes to Scrap School Resource Officer Program." *CP24*, 22 Nov. 2018, https://www.cp24.com/news/tdsb-votes-to-scrap-school-resource-officer-program-1.3689573. Accessed 21 Jan. 2019.

Gibson, Victoria. "Ontario Police Call for More Funding in Wake of Justice Tulloch Carding Report." *Globe and Mail*, 2 Jan. 2019, https://www.theglobeandmail.com/canada/toronto/article-ontario-police-call-for-more-funding-in-wake-of-justice-tulloch/. Accessed 5 Jan. 2019.

Hayes, Molly. "Toronto Police Reject The Social Co-Host Marci Ien's Claims of Racism." *Globe and Mail*, 1 Mar. 2018, https://www.theglobeandmail.com/news/toronto/toronto-police-reject-the-social-co-hosts-claims-of-racism/article38178365/. Accessed 7 Mar. 2018.

Hill Collins, Patricia. *Black Feminist Thought: Knowledge, Consciousness and the Politics of Empowerment*. Routledge, 1990.

———. *From Black Power to Hip Hop: Racism, Nationalism, and Feminism*. Temple UP, 2006.

———. "Intersectionality's Definitional Dilemmas." *Annual Review of Sociology*, vol. 41, no. 1, 2015, pp. 1–20.

Hill Collins, Patricia, and Sirma Bilge. *Intersectionality*. Polity Press, 2017.

Ien, Marci. "The Double Standard of Driving While Black—in Canada." *Globe and Mail*, 26 Feb. 2018, https://www.theglobeandmail.com/opinion/driving-while-black-in-canada/article38107157/. Accessed 3 Mar. 2018.

Korn, Jenny Ungbha. "Black Women Exercisers, Asian Women Artists, White Women Daters, and Latina Lesbians: Cultural Constructions of Race and Gender Within

Intersectionality-Based Facebook Groups." *The Intersectional Internet: Race, Sex, Class, and Culture Online*, edited by Safiya Umoja Noble and Brendesha M. Tynes, Peter Lang, 2016, pp. 115–128.

Krishnan, Manisha. "Look at All the Ridiculous Excuses This School Trustee Used After Calling a Parent the N-word." *Vice*, 27 Jan. 2017, https://www.vice.com/en_ca/article/3dpbmj/look-at-all-the-ridiculous-excuses-this-school-trustee-used-after-calling-a-parent-the-n-word. Accessed 20 Jan. 2019.

———. "Toronto Cops Ganged Up on a Black Journalist Who Accused Them of Racial Profiling." *Vice*, 2 Mar. 2018, https://www.vice.com/en_ca/article/neqmgb/toronto-cops-ganged-up-on-a-black-journalist-who-accused-them-of-racial-profiling. Accessed 7 Jan. 2019.

———. "Why Was a Six-Year-Old Black Girl Handcuffed by Police at School?" *Vice*, 3 Feb. 2017, https://www.vice.com/en_ca/article/4x4qvn/why-was-a-six-year-old-black-girl-handcuffed-by-police-at-school. Accessed 3 Mar. 2018.

Leong, Nancy. "Racial Capitalism." *Harvard Law Review*, vol. 126, no. 8, 2013, pp. 2151–2226.

Maynard, Robyn. "Over-policing in Black Communities is a Canadian Crisis, Too." *Washington Post*, 24 April 2018, https://www.washingtonpost.com/news/global-opinions/wp/2018/04/24/over-policing-in-black-communities-is-a-canadian-crisis-too/?noredirect=on&utm_term=.dc41a56fa64b. Accessed 25 April 2018.

———. *Policing Black Lives: State Violence in Canada From Slavery to the Present.* Fernwood Publishing, 2017.

Mulligan, Cynthia. "Exclusive: Mom Outraged After Six-Year Old Daughter Handcuffed by Police in School." *CityNews*, 2 Feb. 2017, https://toronto.citynews.ca/2017/02/02/exclusive-mom-outraged-six-year-old-daughter-handcuffed-police-school/. Accessed 22 Jan. 2019.

Nakamura, Lisa. *Cybertypes: Race, Ethnicity, and Identity on the Internet.* Routledge, 2002.

Nangwaya, Ajamu. "Factsheet on Police Containment of and Violence in the African Community." *Toronto Media Co-op*, http://toronto.mediacoop.ca/blog/ajamu-nangwaya/6183. Accessed 20 Jan. 2019.

Noble, Safiya Umoja. *Algorithms of Oppression: How Search Engines Reinforce Racism.* NYU Press, 2018.

Noble, Safiya Umoja, and Brendesha M. Tynes. "Introduction." *The Intersectional Internet: Race, Sex, Class, and Culture Online*, edited by Safiya Umoja Noble and Brendesha M. Tynes, Peter Lang, 2016, pp. 1–20.

Ontario Human Rights Commission. *A Collective Impact: Interim Report on the Inquiry into Racial Profiling and Racial Discrimination of Black Persons by the Toronto Police Service.* Government of Ontario, Nov. 2018.

Paradkar, Shree. "Toronto Police Reaction to Marci Ien Shows Woeful Ignorance of Racism Basics." *Toronto Star*, 4 Mar. 2018, https://www.thestar.com/opinion/star-columnists/2018/03/04/toronto-police-reaction-to-marci-ien-shows-woeful-ignorance-of-racism-basics.html. Accessed 11 Mar. 2018.

Rankin, Jim. "City of Toronto to Honour Legendary Black Activist and Civil Rights Lawyer Charles Roach." *Toronto Star*, 15 July 2018, https://www.thestar.com/news/gta/2018/07/15/city-of-toronto-to-honour-legendary-black-activist-and-civil-rights-lawyer-charles-roach.html. Accessed 21 Jan. 2019.

Reynolds, Christopher. "Deaths Ignite Grassroots Black Lives Matter Toronto Movement." *Toronto Star*, 28 July 2015, https://www.thestar.com/news/gta/2015/07/28/deaths-ignite-grassroots-black-lives-matter-toronto-movement.html. Accessed 21 Jan. 2019.

Robertson, Dylan C. "Surprised? Canadian Newspaper Columnists are Mostly Male, Middle-Aged." *JSource*, 2015, http://j-source.ca/article/surprised-canadian-newspaper-columnists-are-mostly-male-middle-aged/#. Accessed 24 Jan. 2019.

Say Her Name: The Life and Death Of Sandra Bland. Directed by Kate Davis and David Heilbroner, appearances by Sandra Bland, Robert E. Brzezinski, and Brian Encinia, HBO, 2018.

Tanovich, David M. "E-Racing Racial Profiling." *Alberta Law Review*, vol. 41, no. 4, 2004, pp. 905–933.

Thompson, Cheryl. "Interview with Robyn Maynard." *Herizons*, vol. 32, no. 1, Spring 2018, pp. 21–23.

Toronto, DiverseCity: The Greater Toronto Leadership Project. *A Snapshot of Diverse Leadership in the GTA*. Ted Rogers School of Management, Ryerson University, 2010.

Tynes, Brendesha, et al. "Digital Intersectionality Theory and the #Blacklivesmatter Movement." *The Intersectional Internet: Race, Sex, Class, and Culture Online*, edited by Safiya Umoja Noble and Brendesha M. Tynes, Peter Lang, 2016, pp. 21–40.

Weeks, Linton. "Tragedy Gives The Hoodie A Whole New Meaning." *NPR*, 24 Mar. 2012, https://www.npr.org/2012/03/24/149245834/tragedy-gives-the-hoodie-a-whole-new-meaning. Accessed 22 Jan. 2019.

Winsa, Patty. "'Fearless' Black Activist Dudley Laws Dies at Age 76." *Toronto Star*, 24 Mar. 2011, https://www.thestar.com/news/gta/2011/03/24/fearless_black_activist_dudley_laws_dies_at_age_76.html. Accessed 21 Jan. 2019.

CHAPTER 2

Reform and Utopia in Canadian Islamic Feminism: The Contradictory Project of Irshad Manji

Dilyana Mincheva

WHO IS IRSHAD MANJI?

Irshad Manji is perhaps the most controversial and unsettling Muslim woman in Canada, and possibly the world. She is many things: queer woman and feminist; dedicated Canadian and Muslim; radical intellectual whose anarchic thinking equally disturbs conservative, liberal, and postcolonial scholars of the left and right; human rights activist; successful writer; victim of misogynistic Islamic orthodoxy; and tabloid-like media persona. These multiple identities, somehow combined within the all-encompassing image of a Canadian Muslim reformer and dissident, make engaging her ideas an intellectually challenging and politically risky task. Yet this engagement is necessary since it expands the limits of public communication by pushing us to seek, and sometimes create, communicative avenues, incorporating identities whose existence we all recognize but over whose content and centrality we may significantly disagree. To engage Irshad Manji is not to endorse her positions. Instead, it is an attempt to see Manji, in her spectacular divisiveness, as part of a conceptually contested, pragmatically impossible, and infinitely utopian yet politically important project of communication: pursuit of a public sphere that is shared, normatively groundless, inter-subjective, internally poetic, self-critical, and, therefore, potentially subversive to the status quo. At its limits, this public sphere should not be understood as purely propositional and speculative. Rather, its essence lies in its praxis: bringing together people with clashing convictions and values—bigots, cosmopolitans, public authority figures, journalists, experts, marginals, radicals, and everyone in between—whose multiplicity and irreducible heterogeneity secure the anarchic, skeptical, poetical, experimental, and ever transformative process of democratic communication. Regardless of whether one assesses Manji as a false expert, self-hating Muslim, and instigator, or sympathizes with her ideas of reform, her projects, activism, and public persona are indispensable to any theoretical or pragmatic speculation on the boundaries and opportunities presented by the Western-Islamic, and particularly the Canadian-Muslim, public sphere, as well as to discourses of Muslim feminism.

Irshad Manji is a Canadian public figure with international presence in global media. In Canada specifically, she has appeared on CBC, Vision TV, Citytv, and TVOntario, and has hosted and produced TV shows on topics ranging from queer identities to religious devotion. In 2006, Manji wrote the script of *Faith Without Fear*, a Grammy-nominated documentary for PBS in which she explores issues of religious orthodoxy and orthopraxy, freedom, and religious ethics. Her articles and opinion pieces have been published in *Maclean's*, the *Globe and Mail*, the *Ottawa Citizen*, the *New York Times*, and the *Wall Street Journal*. She has received human rights awards from various public institutions, including the Mansoor Hallaj Award for Free Expression (2013), granted by the Muslim Canadian Congress in Canada.

In writing and media discourse, Manji positions herself as an intellectual historian, queer feminist, loyal Canadian, Muslim reformer, and true believer, whose conscience responds only to God, not to institutionalized forms of Islam. Her prose brims with affect and rebellion,[1] despite her glorification of reason and rational dissent. While her call for reform appeals to a wide majority of Muslims inside and outside of the Western world, intellectuals, journalists, and common people,[2] she also often manages to alienate her readers. In particular, Manji's gay identity has been seen as performative camouflage—an empty signifier—meant to advance a politically conservative agenda against Islam.

Given that extensive and legitimate critique against Manji exists (Ahmad 113; El-Ariss 94; Mahmood 197; Vanzan 3–14), what can further engagement with Manji provide? I argue that the risks of deeply exploring Manji, while maintaining critical distance, are worth taking for two distinct reasons, which neither the media nor academia have ever articulated.

First, Irshad Manji presents a complex dilemma for Muslim feminism, particularly that informed by postcolonial critique, which cannot be sufficiently addressed by outright dismissal of her as orientalist, racist, and Islamophobic. Central to this dilemma are the responses to Manji's work from ordinary, non-theologically trained Muslim women who have similar concerns, also based on their lived experiences. Such women and young girls are not necessarily driven by any ideological agenda, hold no political power, and do not hate Islam but recognize in Manji and other critical Muslim voices (Raheel Raza, another Canadian example) someone who articulates in simple, everyday language some of the issues experienced inside religious-cultural communities: patriarchy, homophobia, glorification of tradition, religiously sanctioned misogyny, communal violence, and female subjugation. In its historical trajectory, postcolonial feminist thought has developed an important anti-racist, feminist agenda, celebrating "authenticity" as a counter-narrative to paternalistic forms of white Western feminism. However, in this significant endeavour, the Muslim women who are followers of Manji, Reza, and Hirsi Ali have seemingly been overlooked.[3] In a pluralist approach to celebrating the diversity of Muslim female voices, are not the religiously justified, traumatic lived experiences of Manji and other women worthy of addressing? Does the potential instrumentalization of Manji's critique for conservative political purposes make her suffering (or that of her followers) less authentic and less worthy of engagement? Manji's generalized interpretation of Islamic theology, her partial knowledge of Arabic scripture and culture, her clichéd prose, and the politics channelled through it are issues that can be vehemently raised against her; but can we remain unresponsive to her testimony of suffering, or oblivious to the fact that some women choose to support her because of similar lived experiences? Bluntly, as a feminist deeply partial to the stories of misogyny and abuse described during the #MeToo campaign, why might I, as a Muslim feminist, remain silent in the face of the #MosqueMeToo[4] campaign? By engaging with Manji's message, though politically disturbing for scholars who self-identify as committed opponents of racism, hegemony, and oppression, we also demonstrate a readiness to confront the issues on which past silence has been interpreted as excessive political correctness or moral blindness to injustice and suffering. This space is currently occupied by Manji and similar voices; they market themselves as speaking "unpleasant truths" in a world overwhelmed by fake talk, which further reinforces the "authenticity" of their testimonies among the general public.

Second, the questions raised above cannot be easily answered only from the perspective of postcolonial feminist theory. Historically, postcolonial feminism has argued that culture and tradition, in all their complexity, should be embraced as sources of authentication and empowerment that can combat widespread racism and whitewashing. Communal solidarity against the racist oppressor has been prioritized over conversations about gender equality.[5] Indeed, a sustained accusation against Manji is that she is too Western and largely detached from any *authentic* form of Muslim religious life.[6] I suggest that, in addition to the postcolonial feminist reading of Irshad Manji, her activism and public persona may be tentatively analyzed within the communication framework of the emergent Western-Islamic public sphere. Inasmuch as the Western-Islamic public sphere is a communication space of infinite (self-)critique and (self-)interrogation—a space without rigid hierarchies in which, through the anarchist praxis of *parrhesia* (i.e., free speech), forms of truth are discovered, contested, modified, and denounced; a space that is poetic, inherently immanent, grounded in the world of human action, inclusive, utopian, and radically dedicated to autonomy—then Irshad Manji merits engagement within its parameters. Manji's constant presence in the media at all possible levels—as a producer, decorated journalist, social media guru, interlocutor, and critical consumer—also makes her a particularly challenging case study for reflection on the risks, opportunities, and pragmatics of the Western-Islamic public sphere.

MANJI AND THE DILEMMAS OF ISLAMIC FEMINISM

In *Allah, Liberty and Love*, Manji's 2012 response to accusations of simplicity, Islamophobia, and conservatism, she collects and showcases a variety of Muslim voices (predominantly female) responsive to her message. Rather than acting as a Muslim exegete, Manji's main point is to draw attention to Muslim women whose voices have been muted by the forces of dogmatic religious authority or left-leaning political discourses of "excessive political correctness."[7] To this end, she presents a cacophony of repetitive electronic correspondence with her followers: emails, text messages, and Facebook and Twitter exchanges, consistent with her pop culture style. Manji understands her mission as a public figure whose occupation is beyond a specific expert role. She occupies a media space and exhibits "moral courage" in the face of authorities that ignore the multiplicity of Muslim experiences "from below." Such authority includes not only dogmatic Islamic thinking but also discursive power that, in other contexts and under different historical circumstances, engages eloquently in battling racism, sexism, and neocolonialism. Manji maintains that her project of reform reflects the spiritual and pragmatic needs of a specific type of invisible and global Muslim demographic, neglected by both conservative and liberal institutions. In 2016, Manji participated in a memorable hour-long discussion on Islamophobia on Mehdi Hasan's Al-Jazeera talk show, *Head to Head*. She was quick to mention that many Muslims around the world support her ideas, but powerful Islamic authorities always silence her arguments and prevent young people from engaging with her. During this discussion, Sheik Ibrahim Mogra, an imam from Leicester and assistant secretary general of the Muslim Council of Britain, accused Manji of not talking to Muslim scholars. She responded:

> Sir, with all due respect, you guys, as you put it, have not actually engaged
> with people like me. In fact I've received a number of invitations from

ordinary Muslims who are part of congregations all over the world, who are excited about these arguments. But in every single case, no exaggeration, in every single case, they have written back to me to say, "Actually I'm sorry Irshad, the board has decided that they're not ready and the congregation is not ready to hear these arguments." (Al Jazeera)[8]

Strong support for Manji was provided by Dr. Halla Diyab, a Libyan-born Syrian-Egyptian-British journalist for Al Arabiya and Al Jazeera and a feminist activist. While based on opposite sides of the Atlantic, both Diyab and Manji claim to speak on behalf of invisible Muslim women who position themselves between competing discourses of belonging, living each day with divided identities: Islamic, queer, feminist, Middle Eastern, South Asian, African, Western, liberal and conservative, secular and pious. Muslim women who exhibit a wide range of anxieties over possible conflicts between their bodies, desires, everyday loyalties, and faith should be encouraged to critically re-examine scripture and question the traditions for themselves. They must do this because their faith contains complex and unexamined spaces that could be opened for feminist (self-)discovery in environments (mostly in Western societies) where Muslim clerics cannot dominate political discourse.

The testimonies of Irshad Manji's female followers, eloquently reprinted or summarized in *Allah, Liberty and Love* and referenced whenever she appears in the media, have indeed received some confirmation in anthropological work "from below" in Western Muslim communities. In Toronto, for example, Islamic conservatism triggered heated debates in the early 2000s over Toronto District School Board policies for gender equality, particularly the stipulation that "no accommodation made by a school to protect freedom of expression of religious beliefs of its students should interfere with the equality of female students in the school system."[9] At the time, conservative Muslims explained that the religiously mandated gender roles in Islam are fairly distinct and not compatible with commitment to equity and homophily in Canadian public education. In fact, between 1980 and 1999, in only the Greater Toronto Area, 19 conservative Islamic educational institutions were established in which gender segregation was actively practised, as the parents were "most concerned about their children's socialisation into a Muslim environment … in agreement with" their own (Marcotte 361). In 2006, the former director of the Islamic Society of North America's Canadian chapter, Mr. Khalid, publicly announced that "very attractive women" should cover their face—a statement over which he was sued by the Muslim Canadian Congress.[10] It should be noted that the rise of ultra-conservatism in Canada's Muslim diaspora is a recent phenomenon and represents an extremely small proportion of the diverse, kaleidoscopic Muslim populations in the country.

Manji's claims to speak for the underrepresented seem further legitimized by the many women across the Middle East, Africa, Asia, Europe, and North America who describe their first-person experiences in the tropes of Manji's prose. Their discourses are available online and on social media,[11] in interdisciplinary scholarship,[12] through NGO accounts,[13] and through email correspondence with Manji and others like her. These women are underrepresented inasmuch as we know they exist to the extent that we know violence and misogyny exist in the world. However, these women are invisible to us, the Western and postcolonial feminists, even if we encounter their stories, faces, and tragedies, and we need to acknowledge that their plight results from complex intersections of cultural, educational, socio-economic, and (indeed) *religious* factors. Here, of course, religion is understood as a complex habitat grounded materially in cultural praxis and belief, rather than just a set of theological texts. It is important to clearly note that the theological corpora of Islam—the Qur'an and the authentic hadith traditions—do not sanction honour crimes against women in any way; nonetheless, the fact that they are practised in some Muslim majority societies and among some immigrant families should be open for public, plurivocal, and gender-specific discussion in the same way that gender violence is currently discussed in the West. The fact that sexism, racism, and xenophobia are widespread Western malaises (as the #MeToo campaign tried to disclose) does not mean that these practices do not exist in non-Western societies or inside families of Muslim origin in the West. Raheel Raza, a Canadian Pakistani Muslim, journalist, and human rights activist, and the first woman to perform a controversial mixed gender Friday prayer in Cabbagetown, Toronto, is particularly critical of Western feminists and their silence on crimes committed against women in the name of religion and culture. In the context described by Raza, women who have been victims of Muslim male sexism and racism are often left disempowered and resentful, either because their voices are reduced to "false consciousness" and "self-hate" by left-wing academics and Western feminists,[14] or because the concerns they raise are weaponized by Islamophobic right-wing parties.

We can hardly deny that in a divisive communicative climate these women's voices are often instrumentalized by conservative politicians to attack Islam, minorities, and immigrants. However, if we fail to take seriously these women's stories, rebellion, and resentment, and fail to discuss these openly and within the frameworks that they establish, then Irshad Manji will remain the only point of reference for these abandoned voices. I argue here that Manji's global popularity among disenfranchised Muslim youth, as well as her absolute stardom on social media but marginality in academia, can be interpreted as marking the fundamental absence of communicative spaces and practices that allow these initially apolitical voices to be heard, on their own terms, without direct political instrumentalization.

At the same time, this is precisely the domain of the unimaginable double bind of feminism, thought of simultaneously as Western and secular, Islamic and pious, and imagined as one universal network of solidarity among women. Feminism, of course, has complex historical trajectories; various waves, faces, and agendas; and its own complicated relationship with power and other solidarity movements. Racialized women and middle-class white women do not share, either historically or presently, the same struggles. Muslim women in Canada and Saudi Arabia do not enjoy the same rights and do not face the same struggles. By contrast, Muslim women in Iran and those in Yemen have their own divisions and localized fights for recognition. Meanwhile, transgender, bisexual, homosexual, and non-binary women face their own struggles, which may or may not intersect with those of other feminist movements.[15] The female identity is always infinitely complicated by intersections of class, race, education, socio-economic status, politics, culture, religion, geography, and the unexpected contingencies of personal biographies.

In short, the enormous diversity of feminist struggles and the variety of epistemological frameworks within which these struggles are justified might explain why Western feminism, when conceived as one formation, is not massively engaged with intra-communal and familial abuses against Muslim women. In addition, the involvement of Western, secular, liberal feminists in the struggles of their Muslim "sisters" involves several theoretical and pragmatic risks that activists and scholars may prefer to avoid. Most important among these dangers is that the terminology genealogically related to female emancipation in the West—and, by extension, the notions of gender, sexuality, human rights, and freedom—is burdened by Western forms of rationality, indispensably tainted by histories of imperialism and colonialism, and, in some cases, even related to Christian understandings of the world.[16] Therefore, solidarity from Western feminist organizations, NGOs, or simply scholars of Western feminism, even when premised on good intentions, may be criticized for perpetuating imperialist thinking. We can perhaps distinguish, here, between Western feminist discourses, classifying them as "good" feminism, full of epistemic humility, or "bad" missionary feminism, which is hegemonic and culturally insensitive. However, even feminist scholars of Middle East studies, such as Lila Abu-Lughod, who are completely aware and critical of the missionary position of Western liberal feminism, are not spared critique when advocating radical international solidarity among Western women and Muslim women (Provitola and Steinmetz-Jenkins). Such scholars and activists appear to run the risk of being considered politically committed to anti-imperialism but epistemologically committed to imperialism.

At the same time, feminisms based in non-Western countries, if not constructed in complete opposition to all values espoused by whatever are perceived to be Western colonial and imperialist feminisms, also face being criticized as too "Westernized," inauthentic, and ultimately subjugating. Uma Narayan, for example, reveals the impossibility of overcoming the negative association of the term *feminism* with the imperialist West, regardless of how localized and historically deviant from Western debates the feminist struggle is in multiple "Third World" contexts (Narayan 3; Parashar). Moreover, in a post-9/11 world where stereotyping of Islam as the ultimate Other to the civilized West dominates media and security discourses, many Muslim women choose to rediscover and reaffirm their Muslim identity by adopting more conservative versions of Islam, acting as if Islamic and Western understandings of female agency indeed have nothing in common.

It should not be surprising, then, that Irshad Manji appears to her followers as someone prepared to take risks on their behalf that no one else will. She is not theoretically sophisticated and does not use the abstract anti-imperialist apparatuses of critical discourse. Her messages are simple and unifying: everyone deserves dignity; abuse against women and gender minorities does not need epistemological, cultural, or religious yardsticks for measurement and punishment; all women and minorities who are victims of abuse deserve equal attention, regardless of race, religion, class, education, or geographical location; even if some crimes against Muslim women or gender minorities are viewed as legitimate by clerics and religious authorities, this does not mean that Islam—understood as civilizational and spiritual praxis and, fundamentally, as the testimony of one's individual consciousness before the One and Only God—should be tarnished.[17] Most importantly, Manji's message asserts that Islam is plural and plurivocal, and while it houses extremes (like every universal religion), it also contains multiple voices who position themselves, at the risk of facing vitriolic attacks by conservatives and liberals alike, in vehement resistance to these extremes. She claims that these dispersed people are not "community representatives" and do not stand for some kind of manufactured diversity with political stakes; instead, they represent the extraordinary amalgamation of Muslim identities, a true plurality, made visible by digital communication (to those prepared to break the boundaries of their "filter bubbles"), which cannot be reduced to the binary spectra of liberal versus conservative, Western versus Islamic, or free versus subjugated. For Manji, Muslim agency is much more complicated than is expected by what she regards as the ready-made theoretical frameworks of feminism and multiculturalism. Even on the most heated and divisive topics, Manji tells us that Muslim responses are multiple, variegated, and unexpected. Some radically veiled Muslim women can be crusaders for the legalization of female toplessness: she has met them, and they supported her (Manji, *Allah* 170).

Manji's writing and activism pose yet another theoretical and pragmatic challenge to postcolonial feminism: they are always presented as personal testimony, a genre historically related to the anticolonial struggles of Latin American activists. In her books, articles, op-eds, social media contributions, and multiple television appearances, Manji discusses her personal experiences in an Islamic household and the Islamic madrasa in Vancouver; she refers to her own correspondence with Muslim youth; she reveals her own clashes and, at times, collaboration with Islamic clerics; and she recounts her personal journey from submission to rebellion, then activism and resistance. In these respects, Manji is, indeed, quite similar to other divisive and controversial Muslim women (Ayaan Hirsi Ali, Halla Diyab, Rana Husseini, Raheel Raza, Gina Khan, Mona Eltahawy, and Asra Nomani). Yet she is also similar to such iconic anticolonial activists as the Mayan Rigoberta Menchú, who used the genre of personal testimony to resist colonial power: "What has happened to me has happened to many other people too: my story is the story of all poor Guatemalans. My personal experience is the reality of a whole people" (qtd. in Grewal 571). From a theoretical perspective, it is difficult to distinguish personal testimony of suffering—which we recognize as an authentic and subversive tool and celebrate as a sincere challenge to power (Rigoberta Menchú)—from personal testimony of injustice, regarded as instrumental to hegemony (the critique raised against Manji).[18] After all, none of us (scholars or activists) has personally witnessed Manji's life, whether inside her family home or her local madrasa, and so we cannot know if she speaks the truth. We have not lived what these women—Menchú, Manji, and the Muslim women whose personal testimonies populate Manji's books—have lived, so how can we decide who among them is the truth teller and the authentic fighter? To put it simply: if we are prepared to embrace Rigoberta Menchú's personal testimony of suffering as authentic, we do not have any grounds on which we could dismiss Manji's testimony of suffering as inauthentic.

MANJI AND THE CANADIAN-ISLAMIC PUBLIC SPHERE: REFORM AND UTOPIA

Along these lines, Manji's case raises other important theoretical and pragmatic concerns: even if we know that her story is not representative of a whole class of women, does this mean we should dismiss it? Marginal voices are celebrated more in postcolonial studies, critical race studies, and feminism (in all their historical forms and debates) than in any other field of the humanities, championing the right of the subaltern to speak. This is also essentially a public sphere issue, concerning who has the right to speak "truth to power," when, and under what circumstances. Manji presents an incredibly complex dilemma: her critique of Islam and descriptions of Islamic-driven misogyny from an "insider's" perspective do benefit conservative political discourses, yet we must simultaneously acknowledge the right of this voice to communicative spaces of expression, since doing otherwise would seemingly betray the fundamental tenets of our fields. Moreover, both theoretically and pragmatically, the public sphere is the precise space where we can test what seems at odds with our own expectations or biases as feminists, scholars, and activists. Manji presents us with a challenge because she is a woman of colour and an immigrant who belongs to a sexual minority and exhibits conservative views, if we assume that her voice is, indeed, conservative.[19] From the perspective of the communicative ideal of the public sphere, should Manji's voice be considered legitimate?

Both Irshad Manji and her critics tend to see her writing and activism as a type of central political discourse. Manji frames herself as emerging from the margins as the disobedient voice of young Muslim women that no one is willing to notice. Her project is to give media and political visibility to the voices of the disenfranchised. To her opponents, Manji's activism is already too loud, politically destructive, and damaging to the Muslim identity. None of these propositions, however, seem to be entirely grounded. For instance, Alia Hogben (executive director of the Canadian Council of Muslim Women) informed the *Star* that Manji's name is rarely mentioned in Muslim circles in Canada (Scrivener). This is despite Manji holding similar positions on gender equality and justice to those publicized by the Canadian Council of Muslim Women, the first Muslim feminist organization to hold regional meetings across Canada in 2005 and 2006, addressing questions of gender injustice in Canadian society and specifically inside Muslim households and Canadian mosques (Marcotte 359). Furthermore, when the introduction of religious arbitration in family matters was debated in Ontario in the mid-2000s, members of the Canadian Council of Muslim Women shared personal stories and testimonies in the media—similar to Manji's biographical narrative—as a vociferous form of protest against establishing sharia-based family courts (360). It is possible that Muslim feminist organizations do not officially ally with Manji principally because controversy often follows her public appearance, causing many activists to prefer to maintain distance from her.

I argue that a healthy and democratic public sphere, open to infinite reinventions and grounded in human praxis, should be able to accommodate polemical figures such as Manji and to use the hyper-mediatized controversy surrounding them for widely inclusive debate and (possibly) profound reflection on female solidarity. What I term the "Western-Islamic public sphere" remains a politically utopian project, currently sustained by the discourses of diasporic intellectuals whose ideas on Islam clash, coalesce, and perpetuate the internal production of Muslim debate within the limited world of academia. The Western-Islamic public sphere, as described in my previous work (Mincheva 13–25), depends heavily on the ability of smart and intellectually curious people to exchange arguments publicly with other intellectually curious people who disagree with them. Among these people, the discussion—a life-power in itself, which alters the world by creating radically new forms of thinking, expression, and connection—does not have an end point and is not impeded by oppressive orthodoxies, even if the curious minds involved belong to ideologically driven camps in scholarship or theology. Therefore, the Western-Islamic public sphere thrives in an atmosphere of heterodox discussion, largely facilitated by open and unbiased media, where diverse perspectives encounter one another and inspire radically new forms of thinking or connection: Otherness in its pure form. Manji and similar activists are important contributors to expanding the boundaries of the Western-Islamic public sphere beyond purely intellectual discussion; they do so by translating its stakes into popular language that the digitally overwhelmed generation of Muslim millennials, living with divided loyalties, can easily understand.

Particularly in Canada, where multiple versions of Islam simultaneously reside, figures like Irshad Manji may be instrumental in bringing Islamic diversity to both internal conversations and those with the larger Canadian society. Recent debates around Canadian Islam have clearly shown the increasing difficulty of identifying who speaks authoritatively for Muslims in Canada (Syed); yet the expression of Muslim women is even more complicated. They are often subject to othering and silenced on multiple fronts: as visibly Muslim, as predominantly women of colour, and (simply) as women (Marcotte 369). As someone who has somewhat transcended these limitations, Manji can be productively included in debates around the pragmatic stakes of the Western-Islamic public sphere and its feminist dimensions. It usually goes unnoticed that, despite her polemical edge, Manji knows that she occupies the margins of Islam. Through her multiple references to a traumatic childhood, specific verses from the Qur'an, and a pool of correspondence with young Muslims shines a deeply nourished insecurity. Perhaps this derives from knowing that whatever message she tries to promote is already judged by identity markers—female, Muslim, queer, public figure—that are constantly in flux and endless negotiation for the one who lives with them.

Manji's attempt to reform Islam through the effort of individual consciousness—beyond religious authorities and outside the boundaries of established interpretations—also fits within the model of the Western-Islamic sphere due to its poetic and distinctly idealistic dimension. This aspirational sphere is based on the infinite urge of critical minds to resist embodiments of heteronomous thinking by historicizing and relativizing them. In Manji's case, this involves relentlessly attacking the institutions that execute canonical Islam: mosques, imams, and local communities, defined exclusively in the closed and self-sufficient universes of ethnic and religious reasoning. Manji's project calls, therefore, for radical openness, freedom, and solidarity with other human beings, regardless of whether they identify as Muslims, based on a moral *Islamic* imperative rooted in individual agency and reason (Manji and Dajani).

While it is true that authority in Islam comes from numerous canonical texts, transmitted and negotiated in the *longue durée* tradition of Islamic authoritative exegeses, we should not forget that Islamic texts and practices are always a product of human and historical interpretations through the centuries. For Manji, the whole concept of Allah becomes meaningful only if human things and actions can be imbricated in life-affirming and infinitely inclusive conversation about what submission to Him entails. Otherwise, Allah is a meaningless absolute that requires blind and repetitive following, devoid of moral agency; the mute and distant authority of Allah and anyone who claims to be His ambassador on Earth becomes a breeding ground for fundamentalism. Precisely the concept of reconciliation between reason and faith is what informs the reformist project of Manji that she terms "the project ijtihad." When Manji is accused of not showing solidarity with Muslim women who choose the Islamic veil, she responds that many of her followers choose to wear the hijab but are, nonetheless, fervent supporters of Manji's and any other woman's right to choose, including their clothing, partners, words, and the way they practise and understand Islam. Manji maintains it is wrong to assume that a derogatory description of the hijab offends the women who choose to wear it. If we respect their choice, we need not protect them from another perspective on the hijab.[20] One who is an authentic, autonomous agent—and who truly makes a choice—is not threatened by the plurality of perspectives laid before them.

Manji's radical utopian individualism contains the important intuition that in an individual encounter—with scripture or with the Other (understood broadly as all kinds of uncomfortable difference existing in the world)—something with extraordinarily transformative potential occurs. This encounter is a foundational event, which should not be understood in theological or dogmatic terms. Rather, it pertains precisely to human communication and history, being deeply rooted in praxis rather than abstract thinking, and alterity is immanent to it. If one admits that the eventful encounter with difference is possible—and, indeed, as any human practice it is precarious and open to both tremendous success and abysmal failure—then the discourses and practices that contain this encounter are essentially an issue for the public sphere. The immanent differentiality of human existence and experience is the foundation of the Western-Islamic public sphere as a communicative universe, which has the potential to turn the impossible—*self-alteration*—into a pragmatic possibility. Most important here is the proposition that the communicative world of the Western-Islamic public sphere is completely free from teleology or prior calculation and is, therefore, in a sense, utopian. This essentially means that in desiring this seemingly impossible world to be realized—a world of open, meaningful, and always precarious communicative encounters, in which all recognition is possible—one must inevitably commit to this project as if it is completely possible in the future.

CONCLUSION

Manji's project obviously involves radical communicative openness and global connections with a multitude of digitally present young people, rather than the membership of traditionally structured organizations such as the Muslim Canadian Congress. She claims to talk directly to everyone concerned about issues around Islam, but primarily identifies her interlocutors as the young, lost, and often neglected Muslim voices of the Canadian and global Muslim Ummah. To these young people, Manji offers the perspective of "a life beyond categories" and, therefore, a project of reform beyond the traditional restraints of political and social identities. Her personal and political choices attempt to embody this life in and with contradictions. In a sense, her media presence— which is global and traverses the left, right, and radical spectra—also speaks to this.

There is clear scholarly consensus in media studies that encountering people with whom we disagree, particularly online, tends to make us more convinced and committed to our own perceptions.[21] We either retreat into closed communicative spaces, such as filter bubbles or echo chambers, or, when exposed to uncomfortable opinions, become angrier and radicalized: the "backfire effect" (Nyhan 1). Perhaps people like Irshad Manji do exacerbate pre-existing biases rather than helping to eradicate them. Is there a solution to this, other than shutting her down? One option is to take her seriously, as someone who genuinely points to problems and, paradoxically, embodies a problem. This also means committing to interpret her actions, writing, and activism as a playful intermingling of multiple discursive registers, both real and fictional, political and anarchist, Canadian, Muslim, queer, and cosmopolitan: all of them, when taken together, being infinitely unsettling, alternative and solitary, controversial, divisive, oppositional, and non-canonical. An indispensable voice, therefore, to any public sphere committed to disagreement and utopia.

CRITICAL REFLECTION QUESTIONS

1. Are such controversial women as Irshad Manji instrumental to a critical project of Islamic feminist reformation? Do you know other women whose public activity is similar to Manji's?
2. Is it possible for Muslim women of public standing in Canada to address, publicly and honestly, religiously driven Islamic misogyny without falling into the trap of legitimizing the nefarious—and quite real in Western societies—political game of Islamophobia? Is Irshad Manji one of these women "entrapped in binary thinking"?
3. How is Islamic feminism related to global expressions and movements of feminism? Is a project of universal female solidarity possible in a world divided along cultural, economic, and geographic lines?

NOTES

1. See Ahmad (117); El-Ariss (97); Lallami; Podur; Rasheed; Whitaker.
2. I have previously described the multifarious ways in which Islamic thinking on reform takes shape and informs citizenship projects within Western-Islamic intellectual circles (Mincheva). For complex theological discussion of Islamic reformation, see Kamali.
3. In an illuminating article about Hirsi Ali, informed by fieldwork in France, Kiran Grewal reports that many Muslim members of the French feminist organization for prevention of domestic violence *Ni Putes Ni Soumises* are surprisingly sympathetic to Hirsi Ali's message. They support Hirsi Ali because they recognize the female misery and suffering described in her books as their own. See Grewal (570–571).
4. The #MosqueMeToo movement was started on Twitter by the Egyptian-American Mona Eltahawy. No less scandalous than Manji, she is a feminist and media persona based in Cairo and New York (Tong). Manji and Eltahawy could be regarded as part of the same activist

campaigns to replace fundamentalist Islam with an Islam of reform and liberation (Nuzhat 181–208).

5. In a series of important studies—*Yearning: Race, Gender and Cultural Politics* (1990), *Black Looks: Race and Representation* (1992), *Outlaw Culture: Resisting Representation* (1994)—bell hooks describes how, during the US civil rights movement, Black women were not supposed to rebel against their own intra-communal oppression, as this may have harmed the racial struggle. Uma Narayan also describes being muted in classroom conversations or in discussions with peers when she seeks to raise concerns about troubling aspects of Indian culture. The reason is clear: critique of Indian culture fuels Western stereotypes and so needs to be restrained (32). This text is comprehensively discussed in Grewal (578).

6. See Manji's exchange with As'ad AbuKhalil regarding the Danish cartoons (Hearn).

7. This is the ground on which Manji criticizes Canadian multiculturalism, which she aspires to substitute with "honest diversity."

8. The interview is available on Manji's website, YouTube, and in Al-Jazeera's archives (with a full transcript as well).

9. For a comprehensive discussion, see Azmi (262).

10. This example is discussed in Marcotte (367).

11. The success of the #MosqueMeToo movement on Twitter, for example, is a sign that Muslim women are prepared to pressure their communities to discuss the interplay between culture and Islamic law, and to address previously taboo issues concerning the female body (Hanifie).

12. A vast literature in the fields of social work, human rights, and international law acknowledges that honour crimes thrive in a cultural-religious-educational-economic habitat specific to tribal societies and inherited by some Muslim majority societies (Al Gharabeh 133).

13. The most famous feminist organizations in the lands of Islam are the Egyptian Centre for Women's Rights, KAFA (Lebanon), the Dubai Foundation for Women and Children, the Arab Women Organization of Jordan, and the Association for the Development and Enhancement of Women (Egypt). Their work is often criticized in Western academic circles as ideologically driven by Western liberalism, which aims to replace Islamic authenticity with the false universal of liberal values (Massad, *Islam* 110–213).

14. See Grewal 575–576.

15. See controversies around the term *TERF* (*trans-exclusionary radical feminist*) in a philosophy paper (Allen et al.).

16. For detailed examples of Islamic radicalization and case studies, see Davis (279–291).

17. This particular point is made in the viral "Manifesto of 12," written in the wake of the Danish cartoon controversy in Europe. The full text is reproduced in *Allah, Liberty and Love* (Manji 166–168).

18. Whereas postcolonial theory has widely agreed to view Menchú's personal story as the ultimate representation of suffering, the scarce postcolonial scholarship that engages with

Manji has labelled her representation partial, misguided, and Islamophobic, though she denies each aspect of this critique.

19. Manji is not affiliated with any political party, refusing to identify herself with any currently existing political definitions. If we consider her conservative, she is the first publicly conservative Canadian Muslim woman. See Marcotte (363–364).

20. See Mehdi Hasan's *Head to Head* (Al Jazeera).

21. For a recent study regarding the 2016 US presidential election, see Groshek (1389–1407).

WORKS CITED

Ahmad, Irfan. "Immanent Critique and Islam: Anthropological Reflections." *Anthropological Theory*, vol. 11, no. 1, 2011, pp. 107–132.

Al-Alawi, Irfan. "FGM Debate Continues in Muslim Lands." *Gatestone Institute International Policy Council*, 18 July 2013, www.gatestoneinstitute.org/3859/fgm-islam.

Al Gharabeh, Fakir. "Debating the Role of Custom, Religion and Law in 'Honour' Crimes: Implications for Social Work." *Ethics and Social Welfare*, vol. 10, no. 2, 2016, pp. 122–139.

Al Jazeera. "Irshad Manji on Islamophobia." *Head to Head*, 8 Feb. 2016, www.aljazeera.com/programmes/headtohead/2016/01/transcript-irshad-manji-islamophobia-160123075229052.html.

Allen, Sophie, et al. "Derogatory Language in Philosophy Journal Risks Increased Hostility and Diminished Discussion." *Daily Nous*, 27 Aug. 2018, dailynous.com/2018/08/27/derogatory-language-philosophy-journal-hostility-discussion/.

Azmi, Shaheen. "Muslim Educational Institutions in Toronto, Canada." *Journal of Muslim Minority Affairs*, vol. 21, no. 2, 2001, p. 262.

Cuomo, Kerry Kennedy. "Rana Husseini: Honor Killings." *Speak Truth To Power*, www.pbs.org/speaktruthtopower/rana.html.

Davis, Jessica. "Evolution of the Global Jihad: Female Suicide Bombers in Iraq." *Studies in Conflict & Terrorism*, vol. 36, no. 4, 2013, pp. 279–291.

Donegan, Moira. "How #MeToo Revealed the Central Rift Within Feminism Today." *The Guardian*, 11 May 2018, www.theguardian.com/news/2018/may/11/how-metoo-revealed-the-central-rift-within-feminism-social-individualist.

El-Ariss, Tarek. "The Making of an Expert: The Case of Irshad Manji." *The Muslim World*, vol. 97, no. 1, 2007, pp. 93–110.

Farah, Tareq. "Don't Paint Muslim People as Nazis." *Globe and Mail*, 27 Nov. 2003, www.theglobeandmail.com/opinion/dont-paint-muslim-people-as-nazis/article774078/.

Gewen, Barry. "Muslim Rebel Sisters: At Odds with Islam and Each Other." *New York Times*, 27 April 2008, www.nytimes.com/2008/04/27/weekinreview/27gewen.html.

Goodman, Lenn. *Islamic Humanism*. Oxford UP, 2003.

Grewal, Kiran. "Reclaiming the Voice of the Third-World Woman. But What Do We Do When We Don't Like What She Has to Say? The Tricky Case of Ayaan Hirsi Ali." *Interventions*, vol. 14, no. 4, 2012, pp. 570–571.

Groshek, Jacob. "Helping Populism Win? Social Media Use, Filter Bubbles, and Support for Populist Presidential Candidates in the 2016 US Election Campaign." *Information, Communication & Society*, vol. 20, 2017, pp. 1389–1407.

Hanifie, Sowaibah. "#MosqueMeToo campaign empowering Muslim women to break sexual harassment taboo." ABC.Net.Au, 12 April 2018, http://www .abc.net.au/news/2018-04-12/hashtag-empowering-muslim-women-challenge-cultural-taboos/9640364.

Hearn, Kelly. "Freedom of Speech or Incitement to Violence?" *Democracy Now!* 7 Feb. 2006, www.democracynow.org/2006/2/7/freedom_of_speech_or_incitement_to.

Holland, Jessica. "Highlighting Arab Women via Television." *The National*, 3 Sept. 2013, www.thenational.ae/arts-culture/highlighting-arab-women-via-television-1 .649735.

Ibish, Hussein. "Ijtihad, Rethinking and Islam." *NewAgeIslam*, 3 Oct. 2009, www .newageislam.com/articledetails.aspx?ID=1840.

"Irshad Manji Best Selling Author, Speaker, and Advocate." Macmillan Speakers, https://www.macmillanspeakers.com/irshadmanji.

Kamali, Muhammad Hashim. "Issues in the Understanding of Jihād and Ijtihād." *Islamic Studies*, vol. 41, no. 4, 2002, pp. 617–634.

Lallami, Laila. "The Missionary Position." *The Nation*, 19 June 2006, www.thenation .com/article/missionary-position/.

Mahmood, Saba. "Feminism, Democracy and Empire." *Gendering Religion and Politics: Untangling Modernities*, edited by Hanna Herzog and Ann Braude, Palgrave Macmillan, 2009, pp. 193–215.

Manji, Irshad. *Allah, Liberty and Love*. Vintage Canada, 2012.

Manji, Irshad. *The Trouble with Islam Today: A Muslim's Call for Reform in Her Faith*. St. Martin's Griffin, 2005.

Manji, Irshad, and Mohammed S. Dajani. "Is There Moderate Islam?" Discussion hosted by the Washington Institute for Near East Policy, 16 Dec. 2015, www .washingtoninstitute.org/policy-analysis/view/is-there-a-moderate-islam.

Marcotte, Roxanne. "Muslim Women in Canada: Autonomy and Empowerment." *Journal of Muslim Minority Affairs*, vol. 30, no. 3, 2010, pp. 357–373.

Massad, Joseph. *Desiring Arabs*. University of Chicago Press, 2007.

Massad, Joseph. *Islam in Liberalism*. University of Chicago Press, 2015.

Mernissi, Fatema. *The Veil and the Male Elite: A Feminist Interpretation of Women's Rights in Islam*. Translated by Mary Jo Lakeland, Basic Books, 1992.

Mincheva, Dilyana. *Muslim Intellectual Discourse in the West: The Emergence of a Western-Islamic Public Sphere*. Sussex Academic Press, 2016.

Narayan, Uma. *Dislocating Cultures: Identity, Traditions and Third-World Feminism*. Routledge, 1997.

Nuzhat, Sara Amin. "Dissent and New Diversities in Muslim Identity Discourses in the Wake of 9/11." *Muslim Identity Formation in Diverse Societies*, edited by Derya Iner and Salih Yucel, Cambridge Scholars, 2015, pp. 181–208.

Nyhan, Brendan. "When Corrections Fail: The Persistence of Political Misperceptions." *Political Behavior*, vol. 32, no. 2, June 2010, pp. 303–330.

Parashar, Swati. "The #MeToo Movement and Postcolonial Feminist Dilemmas: Reflections From India." *Duck of Minerva*, 22 June 2018, duckofminerva .com/2018/06/the-metoo-movement-and-postcolonial-feminist-dilemmas-reflections-from-india.html.

Pennington, Rosemary, and Hilary E. Kahn, editors. *On Islam: Muslims and the Media*. Indiana UP, 2018.

Podur, Justin. "A Multifaceted Fraud: Reviewing Irshad Manji's *The Trouble with Islam*." *podur.org* (politics and solidarity), 5 Dec. 2003, podur.org/node/881.

Provitola, Anna, and Daniel Steinmetz-Jenkins. "Why Liberalism Needs Islam." *Los Angeles Review of Books*, 11 Sept. 2015, lareviewofbooks.org/article/ why-liberalism-needs-islam/.

Rasheed, Sahireen. "The Politics of Neo-Liberalism, Sexuality and Islam." *Journal of South-Asia Women Studies*, vol. 14, no. 1, 2012, asiatica.org/jsaws/13-1/ politics-neo-liberalism-sexuality-and-islam/.

Scrivener, Leslie. "The Prime of Ms. Irshad Manji." *The Star*, 10 June 2011, www.thestar .com/news/insight/2011/06/10/the_prime_of_ms_irshad_manji.html.

Sharify-Funk, Meena. "Marketing Islamic Reform." *Islam in the Hinterlands: Muslim Cultural Politics in Canada*, edited by Jasmine Zine, UBC Press, pp. 150–155.

Syed, Naseer Irfan. "Who Speaks For Muslims In Canada?" *Globe and Mail*, 27 Oct. 2004, www.theglobeandmail.com/opinion/who-speaks-for-muslims-in-canada/article746643/.

Tamimi, Iqbal. "Bullying and Hijacking Muslim Women's Voices in the UK Live on Air." *London Progressive Journal*, 20 Dec. 2010, londonprogressivejournal.com/ article/view/792/bullying-and-hijacking-muslim-womens-voices-in-the-uk-live-on-air.

Tong, Tracy. "Muslim Women Are Speaking Against Abuse with #MosqueMeToo." *PRI,* 14 March 2018, www.pri.org/stories/2018-03-14/ muslim-women-are-speaking-out-against-abuse-mosquemetoo.

Vanzan, Anna. "Veiled Politics: Muslim Women's Visibility and Their Use in European Countries' Political Life." *Social Sciences*, vol. 5, no. 2, 2016, www.mdpi .com/2076-0760/5/2/21/htm.

Wente, Margaret. "Don't Ignore Women's Struggle in the Muslim World." *Globe and Mail*, 5 April 2014, www.theglobeandmail.com/opinion/ dont-ignore-womens-struggles-in-the-muslim-world/article17816899/.

Whitaker, Brian. "False Prophets." *Guardian*, 5 June 2006, www.theguardian.com/ commentisfree/2006/jun/05/nativemisinformants.

CHAPTER 3

Tales of Resistance and Activism: South Asian Women Journalists in Metro Vancouver

Syeda Nayab Bukhari

> Still there is a lot of bias against women [journalists], still there is gossip about women in media … it's also present in the white [media] community, but out here, it's just too much. That kind of bias, they can't see a successful woman, that's the problem.
> —*Elvis Lal, Male media practitioner, interview excerpt*

SOUTH ASIAN WOMEN: DANGEROUS OR DESIRABLE

Historically, South Asian women were "seen as either dangerous or desirable" in Canadian society and media alike, and very little has changed (Dua 110). Though South Asian women represent different and distinct cultures, religions, and backgrounds, they are often considered a homogenized group and are generally stereotyped as wearing saris, bindis, or hijabs. Each of these cultural identity markers is read differently by different audiences: a woman wearing a sari or bindi in Canada could be seen as an immigrant, struggling to keep her cultural identity alive, while another South Asian woman wearing a hijab might be forced to remove her hijab to keep the country's secularism intact. In either case, these women are hyper-visible—essentialized based on their "cultural and religious practices." Such narrow stereotyping significantly influences mainstream (white) discourse about South Asian women living in Canada and shifts focus away from the real issues South Asian and other immigrant women face in this country. Immigrant women's experiences are complicated further by the need to confront and negotiate experiences of patriarchy and racism not only from mainstream white media, but also from within their own communities. Yu Shi argues that because many immigrants are pressured to adopt and conform to Canadian norms:

> Dominant cultural values are communicated through the ethnic newspapers
> that the women read every day. These values penetrate their private lives and
> regulate their daily matters as minute as the color of their socks. Whether
> or not to conform is a decision that they have to make through painful ne-
> gotiations. (Shi 148)

Women must therefore address and combat negative representations and gendered
norms in mainstream media and in ethnic media.

People of disadvantaged groups, especially women and older adults in visible minority communities, face multi-layered racism and discrimination in their
day-to-day lives, within their workplaces and on the streets. Due to systemic racism, a lack of English language skills, and unreceptive mainstream media, these
disadvantaged groups do not find spaces of safety and inclusion (Cunningham
and Sinclair 31; Fleras 250). In part, their erasure is a result of a lack of positive
visibility in mainstream media in Canada, which fails to address their erasure or to
present their experiences from their perspectives. People of colour in general and
South Asian ethnic minorities more specifically are either ignored or negatively
stereotyped in mainstream media (Fleras 75; Ojo 347).

Women journalists in Canada have been playing a significant role in voicing
their communities' right to social inclusion through their work, contributing to
the historical trajectory of the development and growth of South Asian ethnic
media in Canada. Locally produced ethnic media outlets do not simply provide
significant space for underrepresented racialized and immigrant communities, but
also make space for issues related to women of colour (Matsaganis et al. 150–151).
However, as in many other industries, women are underrepresented in ethnic
media-making, facing far more challenges than their male counterparts.

This chapter highlights South Asian women's experiences, past struggles, and
contributions to social activism through ethnic media, especially highlighting how
they resist the gender- and race-related injustices they experience, alongside their
community members. The first part of this chapter examines the mainstream media's and ethnic media's portrayal of South Asian communities—focusing on gender, violence, and racism—with the goal of contextualizing and situating women's
work in ethnic media in Canada. These narratives and readings of the mainstream
media's portrayal of South Asian women help to outline the relationship between
their communities and white settler society. The second part of this chapter focuses on the historical and contemporary roles, contributions, and challenges of
South Asian women journalists working in ethnic media. Here, I outline gendered
experiences, struggles, and challenges that women journalists encounter inside

and outside of their communities, and consider the specific experiences of three prominent and popular women journalists in the South Asian communities, as well as focus groups with South Asian ethnic media audiences, including older adults, young adults, and community representatives.

This analysis is based on empirical data[1] including semi-structured interviews with ethnic media practitioners—including media owners, TV and radio show hosts and reporters, print media journalists, and filmmakers—and skilled women and men of Indian, Pakistani, and Bangladeshi origin. I highlight first-hand experiences and perceptions of producers and audiences to make visible their strategies and efforts to obtain gender equity, as well as socio-economic and political justice.

GROWTH OF SOUTH ASIANS AND THEIR ETHNIC MEDIA IN CANADA

South Asian ethnicities, though often presented as a homogenized group in Canadian political and public discourse, refer to a wide spectrum of identities, including people from Bangladesh, Bhutan, India, the Maldives, Nepal, Pakistan, and Sri Lanka, who practise major religions such as Hinduism, Sikhism, Islam, Christianity, and Buddhism, speak diverse languages, and participate in diverse cultures (Zaman and Bukhari 5, 20). In 2006, approximately 1.3 million self-identified South Asians made up 4 percent of the total Canadian population, surpassing Chinese Canadians as the country's largest visible minority (Jin and Kim 555). Many large urban cities in Canada have significant populations of South Asians thriving politically and economically. For example, in Toronto, South Asians represent 15 percent and in Vancouver they make up 11 percent of the total population (Statistics Canada). Increased economic performance and political participation in the Canadian system has changed the outlook of these communities, and with larger populations and ethnic concentration in big cities, their locally produced media is also growing. Murray and colleagues report that Vancouver is "a major hub for ethnic media" with about 144 listed outlets, among which South Asian media ranks number one with 33 outlets in Metro Vancouver (100). There are several newspapers and magazines such as the *Asian Journal*, the *Indo-Canadian Voice*, the *Link*, *Chardikala*, the *Miracle*, the *South Asian Post*, the *Urdu Journal*, and *Darpan Magazine* being published in Metro Vancouver. Most of these are published in Hindi, Punjabi, or Urdu, with some newspapers publishing English or multilingual content. Radio RedFM, Spice Radio, Radio India, Radio Punjab, and Sher-e-Punjab, as well as other online, locally produced radio stations, offer 24/7 transmissions that include news coverage, current-affair shows with a live call facility, entertainment, religious programs, and advertisements for businesses.

The Punjabi- and Hindi-speaking Indian populations make up the largest ethnic groups within South Asian communities in Metro Vancouver, and these numbers are reflected in the predominance of Punjabi and Hindi media. However, smaller communities face challenges in operating their often one-person media organizations. While there is a significant lack of income parity with mainstream media, many trained journalists are working in ethnic media outlets. Those working in the ethnic media sector note that their positions have afforded them increased space, opportunity, and respect in their communities. My own interaction and research in the field of ethnic media reveals that while a considerable number of women are working at ethnic media organizations, it is still a male-dominated industry, with very few women in leadership roles.

PERCEPTIONS OF GENDER, CLASH OF CULTURES, AND RACISM

Gender has a unique intersectional position in the project of nation-building in Canada. Historically, Anglo-Saxon women have signified the "mothers of race" (Dua 109) and, thus, all "other" women—specifically women of colour—have been racialized under the sign of racial inferiority. Little has changed. There seems to be a profound connection between the negative and racialized portrayal of South Asian communities in the mainstream media and perceptions of issues related to violence against women, honour killings, and cultural practices (Jiwani, *Discourses of Denial* 114; Thomas 188). During my doctoral research, as soon as a question about women's issues in South Asian communities was asked, participants would start or end their discussion with the topic of violence and honour killing,[2] as depicted in media. This consistent return to the topic demonstrates the pervasive ways that honour killings have been solidified as a fixed presence in South Asian communities for both media practitioners[3] and their audiences.

Like gender-based stereotypes, religious stereotypes also create an ongoing discourse against certain immigrant groups, framing them as objects to be spoken about rather than agentive human beings. A recent example are the mainstream representations of oppressive policies pertaining to the hijab and/or niqab, worn by select groups of Muslim women. News stories about these policies often position women in hijabs as victims who, as Yasmin Jiwani explains, are acted upon by others rather than [seeing these women] as active agents who are capable of determining their own course of safety or resistance to the perceived threat from the outside. Such a framing accords with one of the main features of news reporting, namely, the tendency to create binaries between the victims and perpetrators. ("Gendering Terror" 277)

News stories like those referenced in Jiwani's article classify Muslim women as a homogenous group that is vulnerable to attack because they are visibly identifiable, not aware of their rights, and, consequently, unable to fight for them (Jiwani, "Gendering Terror" 277; Thomas 191). Challenging the legitimacy of the hijab and niqab or focusing on how they put women at risk in North America reinforces the notion of Western supremacy and, by extension, the right of Western states to intervene in and take control of the cultural practices of the *Other*.

Mainstream media has played a central role in portraying Muslim women living in Canada as homogenous, victimized, and "unproductive," and, therefore, in need of reform to rescue them (Abu-Lughod 70). Sunera Thobani argues that the characteristics stereotypically seen as defining South Asian women (i.e., "passive and highly subservient") constitute an "insulting" attempt to disguise the racialized immigration policies that are actually perpetuating inequality for these women in their host country (132). This represents a bid by the state to shift blame to South Asian cultures instead of taking on responsibility to ensure gender and racial equality. There is a perception among South Asian communities that mainstream media not only fails to gratify the needs of their communities, but also misrepresents their communities' cultural practices and events. One of the focus group discussion (FGD) participants, Hartej Singh, a talk show presenter at a South Asian ethnic radio station, blames mainstream media for not only ignoring ethnic minorities but also siding with the government when framing news reports:

Mainstream media only picks up the bigger stories [related to immigrants], things at higher [levels. In terms of] their own focus and perspective.... They will present the news from the government's point of view; they will never add how it will affect immigrant communities. Ethnic media, however, will look after the interests of ... immigrants by presenting their side and how they can be affected.

Mainstream media's portrayal of gender in South Asian communities was regarded as especially biased and inappropriate by research participants. The case of Romana Monzur, a Bangladeshi student at the University of British Columbia who was ruthlessly tortured by her husband, is one such example. Fahmida, an FGD participant, provided a well-rounded analysis of the news coverage: "There was news about a Bangladeshi student, Romana; it was covered pretty widely and it's interesting how they [i.e., the Canadian mainstream media] pick up issues. Sometimes I see bias. On the other hand, there are a lot of happenings in Bangladesh politically; I don't see anything [about that] in the news." Mainstream media thus opts to disseminate stories that support particular ideas of belonging and Otherness in their country, but are silent on other issues impacting the communities represented.

Women journalists who work as reporters, talk show hosts, and editors often work to address the dearth of information on issues related to women by highlighting experiences and stories absent from mainstream reporting. These women journalists have close links with community, social, and women activist organizations and often engage with them on their radio and TV programs. When asked why only women journalists had women-related programs as their priority, Mukhtar Singh, an FGD participant, responded that it was culturally more suitable for women journalists to connect with women audiences, as women would feel safer and more comfortable sharing with women journalists as compared to men journalists. Criticizing the dubious role of mainstream media, women journalists, especially women in disadvantaged groups, are also taking on the task of social activism for their communities, addressing issues pertaining to settlement, integration, discrimination, and patriarchal and familial experiences of their audiences in Canada.

WOMEN JOURNALISTS PURSUING SOCIAL ACTIVISM

The vast majority of ethnic media organizations are owned and managed by men, with only a few women owning ethnic media organizations in the country. It appears that, in the case of small media organizations, such as local newspapers, the women of the family help the male owner run the business. For example, an owner of a Pakistani newspaper confirmed that his wife and daughter were working as editors and designers for his paper; he also added that his daughter had significant influence on his topic selection for editorials. Conversely, in the case of another newspaper published in Urdu, a woman is the owner but is not involved in the editing or newspaper compilation directly.

Many women journalists working in ethnic media came to Canada as immigrants at various times over the last four decades. Their experiences as immigrant women shaped their perceptions and reactions to issues related to settlement, integration, and discrimination, and later influenced the development and production of their media content. Experiencing and recognizing systemic barriers in achieving social inclusion and equality in mainstream society, some of them pursued journalism because of a commitment to creating social change with an informed intention. Pursuing social activism through ethnic media, however, is as challenging as it is demanding. Inherited patriarchal practices in South Asian immigrant communities, both from their own cultures and from adopted Canadian cultural values, also affect the media organizations and overall media-making environment for these women. Nonetheless, amid organizational policies and media restrictions, they are building their social activist agenda.

THREE WOMEN, THREE STORIES

In addition to gaining insight from ethnic media audiences through targeted focus groups, this research relies on the insights from three women journalists who shared their perspectives and first-hand experiences working in the ethnic media industry. Leela,[4] a seasoned journalist, started her career in the 1970s with the British Broadcasting Corporation (BBC), where she was trained to work as a broadcaster. Her migration history spans many years and many continents before arriving and settling in Canada. After her immigration to Canada, she started her career in broadcasting with a community TV and radio station in Metro Vancouver, where she did an entertainment show for many years. Her journalistic training at BBC and her experiences as a racialized woman immigrant in Canada inspired her to start her own radio station to entertain, educate, and advocate for her communities. However, the journey was not smooth for her. Male colleagues in the ethnic media industry used her gender, religion, ethnicity, and language against her. Despite these challenges, she was successful in establishing her own media organization, hosting a popular radio show about social issues, and also hosting her own TV shows featuring South Asian women and other significant community members. Her media organization is considered one of the most popular media outlets in Metro Vancouver today.

Anterpreet Kaur earned a PhD in political science from an Indian university with a study focused on women's participation in grassroots politics in India. Before immigration, she did not have any journalistic experience, but her research experience with women, specifically her interviewing skills, helped her find a job in Canadian mainstream media with a company that wanted to hire a Punjabi-speaking woman in order to cater to their Punjabi audiences. She is successfully working as a reporter, covering different stories related to South Asian communities in Metro Vancouver.

Finally, Preetam Kaur earned her master's degree in journalism and mass communication in India. Before immigrating to Canada, she worked with All India Radio and Dordarshan TV, both publicly owned media outlets. She also worked as a freelancer for Radio Hamsafar (Montreal) and Punjab Radio (London, UK), and with the *Hindustan Times* as a correspondent. She is currently working on a popular radio station as a news editor, as well as hosting a live show on social topics. Although all three of these women have Indian backgrounds, their work aims to serve all South Asian women. These women are creating a significant impact on the ethnic media industry through their presence, innovation in programming, and entrepreneurship.

The narratives of women journalists illuminate the gender dynamics in the ethnic media landscape. Anterpreet, for example, who only entered ethnic media recently, asserts that it is a requirement to work "like a man" in order to gain success in ethnic media. She says, "If you work in the media industry, you have to be as strong, intelligent, responsive, proactive, and brave as men; otherwise, as a woman, you cannot work in the field of journalism. Women who are not smart and strong, they cannot survive in the industry."

Similarly, Leela explains that being a woman in a male-dominated profession has posed serious challenges for her ever since the beginning of her career in the 1970s, especially as a media owner. These challenges include the constant pressure to demonstrate competency at a hyper-competitive level due to gendered double standards. She explains, "Because you are a woman, you have to work double or triple as [hard] compared to a man, to raise your voice, to convince people to listen to your point of view." Citing an example from her past, Leela shares how her interviewing of Indira Gandhi during the politically tense 1980s[5] had a particularly negative impact on her career, and she watched her community support evaporate. Her gender posed a threat as she occupied space in the knowledge sharing and producing forum (i.e., ethnic media), which is primarily considered a male domain:

> [The community] were scared of the [conservative] Sikh community, that they would also have to face the same backlash that I had to face. I will share an event with you: back then, I was told, one day, that I shouldn't go to Main Street [in Vancouver] that day because I would be beaten up, but I had to go shopping with my mother for my brother's wedding. It was 1984, '85, or '86; it was a very difficult time for us, for all of our community. For me to be in a position of power and not take sides … a handful of people would really dislike that I wouldn't take their side, but I couldn't; I was a broadcaster. I was supposed to be impartial.

Other media owners also indicated that Operation Blue Star and its aftermath among Punjabi- and Hindi-speaking Indo-Canadians created conflicted relations between Sikh and Hindu media owners in Metro Vancouver. Media owners on both sides of the issue claimed that, during the 1980s, a period of conflict and escalating tension in India, they had been objectively serving their communities in Metro Vancouver. While she confronted notable obstacles, such experiences did not discourage Leela from playing an impartial role in the news media, as well as advancing her agenda of social activism on two fronts: within her community and with the mainstream community. She produces radio and TV shows that promote awareness about socio-economic, cultural, and political issues in her community. She notes the important role her work plays in shaping their community and maintaining their culture:

> I think the biggest impact of my radio station is the retention of our culture, our civilization, our language. Secondly, our programming for seniors: keeping in mind their requirements, having special programs for them, the ways we can help them grow here [in Canada]. Women had a specific issue, especially in the 1980s, where husbands would take their wives forcefully to Blain [United States]. There was a doctor there; he would abort their female child within 12 weeks of their pregnancy, after sex determination through sonograms. God knows how many female fetuses and maybe some boys, too, have been killed like this.... We [also] talk about our history; for example, we talk about *Komagata Maru*[6] and when the ship came to Vancouver, what happened with that; we share those stories through TV.

Along with creating awareness and advocating for underrepresented people within her community, she is also addressing the representation of South Asians within dominant mainstream media. As a professional journalist, Leela is advocating for the rights and better understanding of her community to prevent their negative portrayal in mainstream media:

> We also inform outside communities about our community's living. For example, we informed other communities that family is the most important thing for our community; [similarly], buying a house is the most important thing for us. If you see any Indian or Pakistani [immigrants], the first thing they do is to buy a house; property is important. So, we informed them of our values, our way of thinking, our priorities, and our income to show that we are an important part of the entire cultural mosaic, and that we should be treated like that.

Preetam Kaur's journey illustrates how her transformation from an immigrant to a professional journalist shaped the ways she prioritizes addressing the concerns and needs of her community. As an editor and an anchor on a radio show, she remade herself by articulating her public presence, proposing new ideas, and relying on the feedback of her audience for setting the agenda for her programs. She explains:

> I think we have a major role in community service. When you are doing a music program, your focus is on music, but when you are doing news or a talk show, it is a bigger responsibility. For a talk show, choosing a topic, the level of involvement of the listeners, you come to know these things through their feedback, and it feels that we have a responsibility.... I mostly do shows on immigrant issues; I am also an immigrant, so often I compare new immigrants' situations with my own. You feel what others are going through because you have been there mentally.

Media owners claim to have a considerable number of women involved in their respective media organizations as employees, and media practitioners also confirm putting gender-related issues at the top of their agenda. However, while working for a popular radio station, Preetam Kaur explains that she faced resistance from within her community for advocating for gender-related issues. She explained that some audiences within South Asian communities criticized her for organizing frequent radio talk shows focusing on issues related to women; this resulted in her facing pressure from her superiors. She explains:

> My bosses would receive phone calls [criticizing me] and they would tell me, "Preetam, don't do too many shows on women's issues." Or, sometimes, my bosses would be told in their social circles ... gossip about my shows, that "Preetam was again doing a show on women today." So, they would tell me, "Don't do too many shows on women's issues." I couldn't understand it ... [I would think], "Then what type of shows should I do?" I do not do shows on fashion or clothing or makeup. I realized that people might be taking it the wrong way, so I changed my approach. I still talk about the same issues, but from a different [family] angle.

Women journalists seem to adopt subtle activism that diverts "valuable energies from less comfortable but more productive activities necessary to generate real change" (Nicol 11). Gender and disadvantaged groups remain the central focus of their content, but they bring them up under the cover of family- and community-related topics. Women journalists, while dealing with their communities, use their cultural lens to filter their messages in order to make them acceptable and appreciated to their target audiences. Rather than removing "women's issues" from her programming, then, Preetam finds ways to engage audiences in the issues.

Stereotypes within mainstream media are also addressed by women journalists and women-led programming. In our discussions, Anterpreet raised the issue of different cultural interpretations of "honour" and criticized mainstream media for linking honour in South Asian communities with gendered violence, especially while the media lacks the contextual and cultural knowledge of what honour means to these communities:

> I think the issue of honour killing in our community is complicated … like, we feel very bad when our children do not obey us [while disciplining them]; our prestige and ego gets hurt. But they [mainstream media] don't even know what "honour" is. That's the difference. When it comes to honour killings in our communities, it is a big blow, because there is this perception that our communities kill our women.

Anterpreet mentions that issues pertaining to women and gender are closer to her heart and she always focuses on them, but she complains about the lack of female participation in media. Entering the field of ethnic journalism in Canada, Anterpreet also encountered resistance and negative feedback from her community in regards to her career choice. She explains that many people condemned her decision to pursue a profession in media and warned her that she might lose respect in the community. Persevering in spite of this negative feedback, she has been able to establish herself as a professional journalist and seems content with her career choice. She urges more women to be active in ethnic media: "I would say this: our women have low levels of participation in ethic media. More women should participate in media; until they raise their voice, no one will be able to advocate for them. Still, there is a dearth of professional and educated men and women in our community. We can't find experts when we need them to talk about [social] issues." In general, women journalists face issues of a different and distinct nature compared to their male counterparts. Anterpreet received criticism for joining ethnic media as a woman, while Leela and Preetam Kaur had to fight for survival against their South Asian (male) ethnic media competitors and supervisors. Despite the efforts at creating social change made by women and other journalists, ethnic media is criticized for unprofessional and patriarchal practices.

Even whilst it is clear that violence against women in *all* communities is an issue that should receive more attention, given the stereotypes associated with honour killings, and the way these communities are overly identified through such violence, there is a mixed opinion among South Asian audiences of what ethnic media's role is in addressing the issue. While some feel that this issue is not specifically associated with their communities and should therefore not receive too much airtime, the majority of audiences seem to agree that ethnic media should highlight and prioritize violence against women as a major part of their content. Saman, an FGD participant, shares an experience of having her phone call cut off while she was taking a pro-woman stance during a live call-in talk show. She emphasizes the need for increased gender sensitivity for ethnic media practitioners in Canada:

> I had this experience twice; the hosts were talking about domestic violence, and I called with research data to show that there was a domestic violence issue in our community. Both of them cut off my calls because they didn't agree with me. Only one radio station with a female journalist invited me to talk about this issue.... I see a lot of bias against women, especially South Asian women [among ethnic male journalists]. I find there is a lack of education among [radio] talk show hosts, and an unawareness of how to correct their callers' information. Professionalism is a huge issue.

While news related to women remains a central point of discussion, the community is silent in general about the ethnic media's representation of LGBTQ people and issues. One ethnic media producer, Naseem, was vocal about the lack of representation of LGBTQ issues in ethnic media, saying, "There is a big void there. I think there isn't much representation of LGBTQ [issues] in ethnic media. But it is changing slowly. There are people like [Mr. Singh], who often call me and raise LGBTQ issues in ethnic media."

Naseem asserts that, in general, LGBTQ identities and issues are stigmatized in South Asian communities and many do not feel comfortable talking about and accepting the existence of LGBTQ people in their communities. It is worth mentioning that while media practitioners with a modern outlook mention women, youth, seniors, and even refugees as marginalized groups in their communities, none of them (aside from Naseem) mention the LGBTQ population or their issues. Naseem identifies the reasons for this lack of representation of LGBTQ people as stemming from religious groups, mainly Hindu, Sikh, and Muslim conservative groups. He mentions subtle resistance from religious institutions when it comes to bringing up LGBTQ issues in South Asian communities. It is significant to note that LGBTQ people of colour are reported to face racism when reaching out for support outside of their communities (Burtch et al. 158), thus making situations even tougher for them as a marginalized group. Though criticizing the failure of ethnic media to incorporate LGBTQ voices, Naseem seems hopeful for slow and gradual change in the communities' attitudes. He considers the youth—along with LGBTQ activists—as catalysts for social change, and believes in the possibility of increased non-judgmental and neutral treatment and representation of LGBTQ populations by ethnic media in the future. Leela also mentions that her new project—a new FM radio station—is targeting youth and producing youth-specific programming, and she seems hopeful about the participation and inclusion of LGBTQ youth in the project.

Despite negative experiences in their industry and underrepresentation in mainstream Canadian media, the women journalists' experiences captured in this chapter show resistance and resilience. They might not claim the title of social activists, but their journeys reveal a clear connection between their struggles against racism, sexism, and discrimination—both personally and more widely in their communities—and the media that they choose to produce. All three women journalists are committed to continuing their social activism by producing programming on issues pertaining to women, seniors, and other disadvantaged groups for social, political, and economic inclusion within their communities.

CRITICAL REFLECTION QUESTIONS

1. What is the role of media when it comes to representing immigrant communities and immigrant voices in Canada?
2. Do you think news media can effectively create space for public dialogue around the intersections of gender, cultural belonging, and immigration? What are the potential challenges for circulating news media within and outside of immigrant communities?
3. Research significant critiques of the portrayal of minority immigrant communities in the mainstream news media. Discuss potential ways to address these challenges.

NOTES

1. This chapter is based on my PhD thesis, defended in 2017.
2. This refers to killing women who have "dishonoured" the family by, usually, losing "sexual and moral purity." The killing is done by relatives, usually by the father, brother, husband, or son, and it is known as honour killing in certain patriarchal cultures.

3. *Media practitioner* is a broad term used for this research; it includes journalists, TV and radio anchors, producers, media managers, reporters, media owners, etc.

4. All names used in this chapter are fictitious to protect the identity of the research participants.

5. In 1984, Indira Gandhi, the prime minister of India at the time, ordered Operation Blue Star in the province of Punjab, India. The operation targeted armed separatist Sikhs inside the Golden Temple at Amritsar and killed hundreds; among those, most were pilgrims.

6. *Komagata Maru* was a steamship through which people from India tried to immigrate to Canada by way of Vancouver ports in 1914, but due to the racist and restrictive policies of the Canadian government, the people on board were not allowed to enter Canada. These passengers faced great challenges, some of which resulted in their deaths.

WORKS CITED

Abu-Lughod, Lila. *Do Muslim Women Need Saving?* Harvard UP, 2013.

Burtch, Brian, et al. "LGBTQ Movements in Western Canada: British Columbia." *Queer Mobilizations: Social Movement Activism and Canadian Public Policy*, edited by Haskell Tremblay, University of British Columbia Press, 2015, pp. 142–162.

Cunningham, Stuart, and John Sinclair, editors. *Floating Lives: The Media and Asian Diasporas*. Rowman & Littlefield, 2001.

Dua, Enakshi. "The Hindu Woman's Question." *Canadian Woman Studies*, vol. 20, no. 2, 2000, pp. 108–116.

Fleras, Augie. *Media Gaze: Representations of Diversities in Canada*. University of British Columbia Press, 2011.

Jin, Dal Yong, and Soochul Kim. "Sociocultural Analysis of the Commodification of Ethnic Media and Asian Consumers in Canada." *International Journal of Communication*, vol. 5, 2000, pp. 552–569.

Jiwani, Yasmin. *Discourses of Denial: Mediations of Race, Gender, and Violence*. University of British Columbia Press, 2006.

———. "Gendering Terror: Representations of the Orientalized Body in Quebec's Post-September 11 English-Language Press." *Critique: Critical Middle Eastern Studies*, vol. 3, no. 13, 2004, pp. 265–291.

Matsaganis, Matthew D., et al. *Understanding Ethnic Media: Producers, Consumers, and Societies*. Sage, 2011.

Murray, Catherine, et al. *Cultural Diversity and Ethnic Media in BC*. Centre for Policy Studies on Culture and Communities, School of Communication, Simon Fraser University, 2007.

Nicol, David. Su*btle Activism: The Inner Dimension of Social and Planetary Transformation*. State University of New York Press, 2015.

Ojo, Tokunbo. "Ethnic Print Media in the Multicultural Nation of Canada: A Case Study of the Black Newspaper in Montreal." *Journalism: Theory, Practice & Criticism*, vol. 7, no. 3, 2006, pp. 343–361.

Shi, Yu. "Chinese Immigrant Women Workers' Mediated Negotiations with Constraints on Their Cultural Identities." *Feminist Media Studies*, vol. 8, no. 2, 2008, pp. 143–161.

Statistics Canada. *2011 National Household Survey*. 11 Sept. 2013, https://www12 .statcan.gc.ca/nhs-enm/2011/dp-pd/prof/details/page.cfm?Lang=E&Geo1= CMA&Code1=535&Data=Count&SearchText=Toronto&SearchType= Begins&SearchPR=01&A1=All&B1=All&Custom=&TABID=1. Accessed 18 Jan. 2019.

Thobani, Sunera. *Exalted Subjects: Studies in the Making of Race and Nation in Canada*. University of Toronto Press, 2007.

Thomas, Jasmine. "Only If She Shows Her Face: Canadian Media Portrayals of the Niqab Ban during Citizenship Ceremonies." *Canadian Ethnic Studies*, vol. 47, no. 2, 2015, pp. 187–201.

Zaman, Habiba, and Syeda Nayab Bukhari. *South Asian Skilled Immigrants in Greater Vancouver: Formal and Informal Sources of Support for Settlement*. Metropolis British Columbia: Centre of Excellence for Research on Immigration and Diversity, 2013, http://mbc.metropolis.net/assets/uploads/files/wp/2013/WP13-09.pdf.

PART II

FEMINIST, EH? RE-READING CANADIAN
TEXTS AND TV

CHAPTER 4

"How Were We to Know We Were Happy?": Fairy Tale (Fr)antics and Margaret Atwood's Fickle Feminism

T. Nikki Cesare Schotzko

WITH ALL DUE RESPECT

When white author and literary celebrity Margaret Atwood began her January 13, 2018, *Globe and Mail* op-ed with the observation "It seems that I am a 'Bad Feminist,'" Twitter took note (Atwood, "Bad Feminist"). What became particularly contentious in the piece, directed to critics of Atwood's participation in UBC Accountable (a collective of North American scholars and literati protesting the University of British Columbia's allegedly unfair handling of sexual assault allegations against Steven Galloway), was Atwood's unacknowledged citation of Black feminist scholar Roxane Gay's hyper-successful 2014 book *Bad Feminist*. Gay took note as well, tweeting, "Actually, Margaret … with all due respect, this isn't what I meant by Bad Feminist" (Gay, "Actually, Margaret …").

Atwood's appropriation (wittingly or not—though given the caliber of Atwood's writing and the pop-cultural celebrity she maintains, it would be insulting to imagine that it was unwitting) of a phrase so popularly linked to Gay is emblematic of, as *Root* blogger Clarkisha Kent writes, "a long and ugly history of white feminists co-opting (if not outright stealing) black feminist theory and terminology" (Kent). And while Atwood may whimsically ruminate on what type of feminist she is, Kent has no trouble identifying it for her, specifically through Atwood's wildly renowned and beloved 1985 novel, *The Handmaid's Tale*:

> *The Handmaid's Tale* is not a feminist text. It is a white feminist text. And this is specifically the case because it imagines a white-woman dystopia by stealing and reappropriating the historical injustices done to black women in America by way of slavery. (Kent)

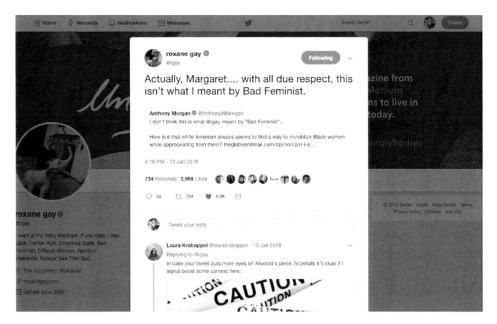

Figure 4.1: Roxane Gay's Tweet to Margaret Atwood, "Actually, Margaret ..." on January 13, 2018

Source: Twitter screen capture

Though an easy dismissal of the growing antagonism between various self-identified feminists has been to attribute it to generational differences, Kent's response, among several others' across mainstream and social media, makes clear that factors other than or in addition to age contribute to the dynamics of power and access afforded celebrity mentors like Atwood, including, in particular here, race.[1]

I adopt Gay's "bad feminism" as a critical methodology to approach Atwood's op-ed and to examine the racial overtones admitted to Hulu's television adaptation of *The Handmaid's Tale*, but determinedly not present in Atwood's novel. (While also remaining fully self-conscious, as an economically privileged, cisgender white woman with tenure, of the methodological hazards of appropriation hovering just under the pedagogical guise of such an adoption.) I borrow, too, the quotation in my title from *The Handmaid's Tale*. The protagonist (whom we now know as "June" from the television series) is remembering illicit afternoons spent in hotel rooms with Luke, before he left his wife to marry June. "The knock would come at the door; I'd open, with relief, desire. He was so momentary, so condensed. And yet there seemed no end to him," Atwood writes. "We would lie in those afternoon beds, afterwards, hands on each other, talking it over. Possible, impossible. What could be done? We thought we had such problems. How were we to know we were happy?" (Atwood,

Handmaid's Tale 79). And later, as June and Luke are planning their escape across the border into Canada, Atwood writes, "Luke was in the living room. He put his arms around me. We were both feeling miserable. How were we to know we were happy, even then? Because we at least had that: arms, around" (245).

Sara Ahmed, in the introduction "Why Happiness, Why Now?" to *The Promise of Happiness*, writes, "Happiness shapes what coheres as a world" (Ahmed 2). Happiness also, however, becomes a means "to justify oppression" (2). This is particularly so in expectations of happiness wrought on those subjugated within dominant power structures—especially those within the domestic sphere. Reading the power structures implicit within hierarchies of domestic and reproductive labour becomes tantamount to reading *The Handmaid's Tale*. Just as Aunt Lydia denotes the privilege of living a life with "freedom from" in the Republic of Gilead, as opposed to the "freedom to" of life before, Atwood too makes a world in which happiness is derived from, rather than opposed to, subjugation (Atwood, *Handmaid's Tale* 49).

To offer a very brief summary, in *The Handmaid's Tale*, Atwood writes the story of an unnamed white woman who, upon trying to escape the dystopian Republic of Gilead (a re-envisioning of the current United States via an ultra-Christian, alt-right agenda) with her white husband, Luke, and their daughter, is taken into custody as a "handmaid" and is expected to breed (white) children for the barren (white) political elite. In the novel, Luke is killed as they try to cross the Canadian border, while their daughter is relocated to a (white) privileged family. During their internment, the woman (henceforth referred to as "June," as suggested in the novel and realized in the television adaptation) becomes reacquainted with her more activist-minded friend from "before," Moira, as they are both indoctrinated into the new world by teachers/enforcers known as "Aunts": Lydia et al. Once placed in a high-ranking family, that of the "Commander," June carries out an affair with a low-ranking officer of Gilead, enabled by the Commander's wife, Serena Joy, who schemes of June bearing a child that would be recognized as the Commander and Joy's own. The novel ends (spoiler alert) as June becomes pregnant and stages yet another escape, this time from her reproductive servitude, during which she murders the Commander—all of which is provoked by the officer, who is part of the quietly active resistance to Gilead. This narrative, while predominantly first person, is framed as a retelling via tapes June made while in rural exile that have been discovered and are theorized by an imagined futuristic academic community.

The Handmaid's Tale does not provide the happy ending of fairy tales, but it does not *not* provide it either. It withholds this from the reader, perhaps to force the reader to take a position of either cynicism or hope, perhaps to leave room for the sequel—*The Testaments*, released in September 2019 (after this writing but before its publication, so as yet unknown in its culmination of June's story).

But *The Handmaid's Tale* is also involved as much in a remaking as a making of this world, wherein, as Kent demonstrates, Atwood is rewriting the story of systemic abuses within the transatlantic slave trade—a story that continues to shape daily Black and Brown life beyond Gilead's fictional borders and within very real and increasingly precarious ones—transposed upon a whitewashed narrative: a (could-be) happily ever after retold without reference to what came before. Atwood's own lack of narrative comment on Canada's history of slavery plays into the same process of nation-formation her own craft—and the celebrity it has afforded her—participates within, one that quickly and quietly dismisses its own complicity within this history. This should be incongruent with the very feminist ideology Atwood represents; that it is not incongruent with, or that it works against, such feminist theoretical positions and literary structures is what remains truly fantastical.

My reference, then, to "fairy tale (fr)antics" is neither to belittle the debates currently around Margaret Atwood's feminism nor to undercut the serious critical debate around the relevance of *The Handmaid's Tale* to contemporary political realities. Rather, my intention here is to note the retelling of historical atrocity within *The Handmaid's Tale* that is reinterpreted to speak to present and future injustices rather than to those it inherently references, and to highlight the fairy tale–informed dichotomy Atwood creates, present throughout the *Globe and Mail* op-ed, between those "Good Feminists" who criticize her and her own actions as a "Bad Feminist" (Atwood, "Bad Feminist"). That is, to read with and through each other both the untold story Atwood tells within *The Handmaid's Tale* and that which she tells of herself. While Roxane Gay does not uphold such a dichotomy—instead positioning her own "bad feminist" as a counter to "Essential Feminism" (Gay, *Bad Feminist* loc. 109)—Gay, not dissimilarly to Atwood, structurally and thematically alludes to fairy tales at various points throughout *Bad Feminist*.[2] Further, by prioritizing pop-cultural discourse as scholarly citation, I reflect not only on the impact mainstream and social media has had on these recent debates concerning contemporary feminisms, but also on how the more inclusive and diverse dialogue these forums generate might also broadly influence pedagogical approaches to the feminist Canadian Literature canon.

ONLY ONE OF THESE WOMEN IS THE QUEEN OF ENGLAND

On November 14, 2016, UBC Accountable published "An Open Letter to UBC: Steven Galloway's Right to Due Process," contesting the University of British Columbia's handling of its investigations into "serious allegations" made against Canadian author Galloway, who was then chair of the creative writing program.

The letter attests that UBC withheld information from Galloway about the allegations, "cast[ing] a cloud of suspicion over" Galloway and suggesting that "he was in some way a danger to the university community." BC Supreme Court Judge Mary Ellen Boyd conducted an investigation of the allegations in December, at the request of the university, finding that "all but one of the allegations investigated, *including the most serious one*, were unsubstantiated" (UBC Accountable; emphasis in original). UBC consequently "terminated Professor Galloway's employment without severance and without reference to the original allegations," citing "other allegations" as significant factors in their decision. The letter emphasizes the effects UBC's actions have had on Galloway—"severely damaging Professor Galloway's reputation and affecting his health"—and, while acknowledging the rights of complainants, asks UBC for a "public clarification" of the allegations and its internal process of investigation:

> The University's conduct in this matter is of great concern. We, the undersigned, respect the principle of protection for individuals who wish to bring complaints. We also respect the right of an accused to fair treatment. There is growing evidence that the University acted irresponsibly in Professor Galloway's case. Because the case has received a great deal of public attention, the situation requires public clarification. (UBC Accountable)

There were over 80 signatories on the letter, as of March 22, 2018, comprised of prominent and influential figures in the Canadian and US academic and literary community, including Margaret Atwood.

Following widespread controversy over the letter—what white feminist activist Julie S. Lalonde berated for having "prioritized a broken system over broken people" in an Open Letter to Margaret Atwood (Lalonde)—a number of the signatories provided statements on the UBC Accountable site explaining why they signed; several others removed their names from the letter (see Dean). White author Camilla Gibb apologized on Facebook for signing, writing (and reaffirming the so-called generational divide in early twenty-first-century feminisms), "I am guilty of showing my age and being a product of my generation where, in the late 80s when I was an undergrad, the sexual impropriety of professors was so commonplace we thought it was normal. I am listening to younger women, really listening now, and learning" (Gibb).

Margaret Atwood and Susan Swan, both of whom maintained their signatory status on UBC Accountable, posted a response on March 22, 2018, to a new site, Where We Are Now, in an effort to "shift this conversation to a more constructive place." Reiterating their lack of a personal relationship with Steven Galloway and acknowledging their regret over any harm UBC Accountable's Open Letter may have brought to complainants, Atwood and Swan reassert their motivation to support UBC Accountable in terms of UBC's (ethical) responsibility to its funders and the damage to Galloway's reputation the university's actions caused:

> We trust that in due course the University will see fit to do the right thing and issue an apology to the many writers, teachers, students and other individuals involved in the case. As a result of the University's prolonged lack of the transparency owed to its funders—both donors and the taxpaying public—and its opaque, divisive, and misleading communications, many of these have suffered silencing, loss of employment or the threat of it, and damaging attempts at character assassination and career destruction. (Atwood and Swan)

Atwood and Swan's letter ends with a link to a *Globe and Mail* article regarding Atwood's promise to donate in total $50,000 to the new fund organized by the group AFTERMETOO to provide assistance to survivors of sexual assault and harassment (Lederman). (Swan is noted in the article as also promising a donation, though it is Atwood who is featured in the headline.)

Atwood herself published a response in the *Walrus* on November 17, 2016, reciting her position that UBC mishandled the case and rallying the cry for due process, as

> to take the position that the members of a group called "women" are always right and never lie … and that members of a group called "accused men" are always guilty … would do a great disservice to accusing women and abuse survivors, since it discredits any accusations immediately. (Atwood, "Galloway Affair")

While I find Atwood's prose, and her logic, weirdly uneven in this piece, it is her January 13, 2018, op-ed in the *Globe and Mail*, "Am I a Bad Feminist?" that is the most jarring. This piece may or may not have been in at least some way a belated response to Lalonde's 2016 open letter, wherein Lalonde dismantles Atwood's argument in the *Walrus* that women are just as unscrupulous (Lalonde uses the term *shitty*) as men. To doubt that fact, which would mean *not* doubting women who accuse men of sexual assault, would contrarily risk, as Lalonde writes, "intellectual failure or *worse*, being a bad feminist" (emphasis in original).[3]

Acknowledging Atwood's intention toward a fairer system whereby institutions handle sexual assault claims, Toronto-based writer and editor Stacy Lee Kong, similarly to Lalonde, argues in *Flare* that Atwood, rather than dialoguing with the critiques levelled against her, instead "doubled down. She used her very powerful platform (she has 1.85 million Twitter followers) to troll those who disagreed with her" (Kong). Atwood's response in "Am I a Bad Feminist?" is not only, as Hannah McGregor identifies it on her peer-reviewed podcast, *Secret Feminist Agenda*, "an example of the kinds of damage that you can do when you are wielding power thoughtlessly" (McGregor), but, in its conjuring of Gay's book without reference to Gay herself, indicative of a perpetual erasure throughout social and cultural history of marginalized and underrepresented voices and bodies.

For Gay, feminism as a philosophy or movement or value system f(l)ails when it is attached to one figure: "feminism is not whatever philosophy is being spouted by the popular media feminist flavor of the week, at least not entirely" (Gay, *Bad Feminist* loc. 74). It particularly f(l)ails when that figure ascends the "Feminist Pedestal": "People who are placed on pedestals are expected to pose, perfectly. Then they get knocked off" (loc. 87). To be a bad feminist for Gay, then, is to be "human," "messy," and "not trying to be an example" (loc. 80). It is to advocate for equal access, equal rights, and equal pay, and, sure, to like shows made by Shonda Rhimes (loc. 164). It is also—and, for me, this is the most resonant point—to advocate for other women, whether or not they identify as feminists themselves. "Feminism is a choice, and if a woman does not want to be a feminist, that is her right, *but it is still my responsibility to fight for her rights*" (loc. 106; emphasis added).

Atwood has long occupied a pedestal, feminist or otherwise, within CanLit, even as, at least initially, she repeatedly had to reassert her own authorial plausibility as a woman within it. Atwood concluded a presentation at the University of Ottawa in 2004, as Lorraine York notes in "Biography/autobiography," with a photograph of Atwood shaking hands with the Queen of England. "Only one of these women is the Queen of England," Atwood remarked (qtd. in York 34). Having discussed Atwood's strategic handling of her literary celebrity, York observes, "Again we have the same self-deprecation, meant to poke a hole in the image of her as an all-powerful icon. Of course, in typically Atwoodian fashion, it also reinforced it" (34). Atwood employed a similar tone on Twitter, after feminist critics asked her to account for "Am I a Bad Feminist?" On January 14, 2018, just a day after the op-ed appeared, Atwood tweeted, "Taking a break from being Supreme Being Goddess, omniscient, omnipotent, and responsible for all ills. Sorry I have failed the world so far on gender equality. Maybe stop trying? Will be back later. (Next incarnation maybe)" (Atwood, "Supreme Being Goddess").

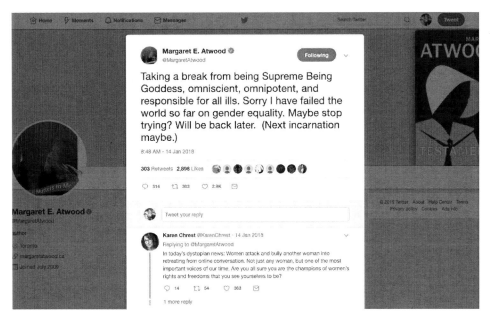

Figure 4.2: Margaret Atwood Renounces Her Claim to "Supreme Being Goddess," Temporarily, after Fallout from Her "Bad Feminist" Piece
Source: Twitter screen capture

Atwood's response here and in "Am I a Bad Feminist?" makes evident how the issue with UBC Accountable has become only nominally about the institution's handling of the Galloway controversy, and only more tenuously so about Galloway himself, or his actions. Rather, Atwood's chastisement of her detractors—"Are these Good Feminists fair-minded people?" she asks (Atwood, "Bad Feminist")—is about the growing antagonism between feminists, especially feminist writers and scholars, that, in this case, concerns the pervasiveness of sexual assault on campuses (and the pervasiveness of allegations of sexual assault in general) but is not exclusive to it. It is further about Atwood's own status—her "Supreme Being Goddess"-ness that she manages to claim not despite her disavowal but through it—and the audacity of questioning such righteous divinity.

Again, to call millennial feminists' critique of Atwood, or of Catherine Deneuve, say, ageist is to ignore factors of privilege and access these celebrity mentors hold that result from other identificatory and economic factors as well. Further, Atwood's unattributed use of Gay's terminology not only misconstrues Gay's argument, but, more importantly, reenacts an ongoing misappropriation by white women, and particularly by white feminists, of labour—intellectual, emotional, physical, and otherwise—performed by women of colour.

A HISTORY THAT GOES UNACKNOWLEDGED

When Dominican American writer Junot Díaz (a complicated figure given the multiple accusations of assault that followed his revelation in the *New Yorker* of having been sexually assaulted as a child [see Díaz, "The Silence"; Silman]) asked Margaret Atwood in a 2017 interview about how contemporary readers' experience of *The Handmaid's Tale* relates to those of its 1985 release, Atwood responded as follows:

> It is quite different now. There were national differences at the time of publication. In England it was viewed as a jolly good yarn, but they didn't think of Gilead as something that was going to happen to them, because they did their religious warfare in the seventeenth century and had lived through a lot of other bad stuff that they thought they had gotten over—although, in recent days, apparently not. In Canada it was the usual worried Canadian question—"Could it happen here?"—*though I didn't have to explain to Canadians why my characters were escaping to Canada, because we have been escaped to quite a lot in history.* But in the United States, particularly on the West Coast, they said—somebody spray-painted on the Venice Beach seawall—"The Handmaid's Tale is already here." That was in 1985. (qtd. in Díaz, "Fiction Again"; emphasis added)

Not only is *The Handmaid's Tale* set in a dystopian rendering of Cambridge, Massachusetts—"Would some people be affronted by the use of the Harvard wall as a display area for the bodies of the executed? (They were.)," she writes in the introduction to the 2017 Emblem edition of the novel (with its TV tie-in cover; 14)—but it is also directly predicated on recent US history.

> Would I be able to persuade readers that the United States of America had suffered a coup that had transformed an erstwhile liberal democracy into a literal-minded theocratic dictatorship? In the book, the Constitution and Congress are no longer: the Republic of Gilead is built on a foundation of the seventeenth-century Puritan roots that have always lain beneath the modern-day America we thought we knew. (Atwood, *Handmaid's Tale* 14)

That Gilead is predicated on white supremacy makes race, as Karen Crawley writes in "Reproducing Whiteness: Feminist Genres, Legal Subjectivity and the Post-racial Dystopia of *The Handmaid's Tale* (2017–)," "central to the novel's dystopian plausibility," even as Atwood rarely cites racial and ethnic difference within it (Crawley 335).[4] The television series, in contrast, elides any specificity of race or ethnicity, despite casting several characters who are white in the novel, and in Volker Schlöndorff's 1990 film adaptation, with people of colour. However, as in the vast majority of other "colour-blind casting," diversification is not equivalent to decolonization, and such superficial manipulation of race, without more profound discourse incorporated into the story itself, at best neutralizes but more often erases race (see Bastién; Jones; Sears).

Much is, of course, made of the reproductive violence women endure in Gilead, in both the novel and series, and, particularly in the series, of sexuality-based discrimination and violence. In the novel there is even a brief interlude on the Nazi Holocaust (though Atwood never actually uses the terms *Nazi* or *holocaust*; Atwood, *Handmaid's Tale* 187–190). Yet, even as it structurally borrows from the Black enslaved woman's narrative and "allegorizes the slave experience" (Crawley 341), *The Handmaid's Tale* never identifies the Black history it refers to—instead assimilating it into white women's experience. Or, as Crawley (whose article should be compulsory reading alongside any Atwood novel or adaptation thereof) writes,

> The spectre of historical slavery, in its classed and racialized aspects, hovers in the background of the show to provide a fantastic space of engagement for its target audience of white liberal feminists, because it allows an affect of detachment—the only loyalties the audience is being positioned to question are to themselves and other white women. (Crawley 344)

This is even more substantially evidenced in Atwood's setting of white women against each other in the novel—a preface of sorts to her arguments concerning UBC Accountable. "By trying to show white women's complicity in patriarchy but ignoring race, however, the show is performing that which it critiques," Crawley indicates. "It is complicit in upholding whiteness and white women's complicity in reproductive violence and other forms of state violence against women" (341). Crawley continues—her critique, again, making blatantly evident the friction in Atwood's own argument both in her piece for the *Walrus* and in "Am I a bad feminist?"—"The show's thematic insistence on female complicity tends to function regressively ('women can be monsters too!') in ways that are individualizing and moralizing" (Crawley 341).

The overt appropriation of the Black experience of chattel slavery, repurposed toward white women's subjugation at the hands of the theocracy the United States, however, is only part of the story that Atwood leaves untold. That is, even as she situates Canada as the harbour of enlightenment to the north—"I didn't have to explain to Canadians why my characters were escaping to Canada, because we have been escaped to quite a lot in history"—Atwood makes no effort to indicate Canada's own colonial project of slavery of both Indigenous and Black people. "A history that goes unacknowledged," writes Robyn Maynard in *Policing Black Lives: State Violence in Canada from Slavery to the Present*, "is too often a history that is doomed to be repeated" (Maynard loc. 300)—in art, apparently, as in life.

THE FUTURE IS A F*CKING NIGHTMARE

Robyn Maynard states early on in *Policing Black Lives* that "anti-Blackness often goes unspoken. When acknowledged, it is assumed to exist, perhaps, but in another time (centuries ago), or in another place (the United States)" (Maynard loc. 268). Citing several prominent Canadian scholars whose work discloses Canada's own participation in two hundred years of chattel slavery, including Afua Cooper, Ken Donovan, Délice Mugabo, Harvey Amani Whitfield, and Sylvia Hamilton, among scores of others, Maynard reiterates the history of Black slavery in Canada from 1628, when "the first Black enslaved person, Olivier Le Jeune, landed on the shores of what is now Québec" (though the French had already been enslaving Indigenous people), through King Louis XIV's approbation of slavery in 1689, the American Revolution, the War of 1812, and the United States Civil War (Maynard loc. 602ff).

While 1834 marked the official end of slavery across the British colonial holdings—thirty years before the United States ratified the Thirteenth Amendment to abolish slavery—the lawful practice of racial segregation in Canada continued, as it did in the States, through the late twentieth century, and the social, economic, and emotional effects of slavery continue to inform contemporary Black and Indigenous life. "Though formalized Black bondage was officially over, the meaning of Blackness had been consolidated under slavery and remained intact in the post-abolition period," Maynard writes. "In the end, slavery had accomplished more than an economic subjugation, it had created particular meanings of what it meant to be Black" (loc. 817).

Though Canada, particularly after passing the 1793 Act to Limit Slavery (which prohibited bringing *"new enslaved people"* into pre-Confederation Canada [loc. 810; emphasis added]), provided sanctuary for Black enslaved people who survived the journey from the United States South, it was also not "solely a 'sanctuary'" (loc. 735). While approximately 30,000 Black formerly enslaved people came to Canada via the Underground Railroad, "some enslaved Black people actually escaped pre-Confederation Canada to seek freedom in the Northern states in the late eighteenth and early nineteenth centuries" (loc. 735)—part of what Colin A. Thomson (1979) refers to as the "reverse Underground Railroad" (qtd. in Maynard loc. 735).

Atwood's plot of having June and her family attempt to cross the Canadian border echoes classic narratives of the nineteenth-century Underground Railroad, and Atwood makes several references to the "underground" throughout the novel—including as part of Moira's narrative at Jezebel's (a sex-positive-*ish* club for the cultural and political elite), in which Moira details to the snuck-out June (courtesy of the Commander) Moira's nearly successful escape route through the "Underground Femaleroad" (Atwood, *Handmaid's Tale* 315). The Underground Femaleroad emerges again in the last chapter of the novel, "Historical Notes," wherein a scholar, during a 2195 "Symposium on Gileadean Studies," identifies Bangor, Maine's role as "a prominent way-station on what our author [June] refers to as 'The Underground Femaleroad,' since dubbed by some of our historical wags 'The Underground Frailroad.' *(Laughter, groans)*" (372; emphasis in original).

Atwood too references the Underground Railroad and the history of slavery in the United States in her introduction to the 2017 edition of *The Handmaid's Tale*. Responding to FAQs about the novel, Atwood replies to the query "Is *The Handmaid's Tale* anti-religion?" "True, a group of authoritarian men seize control and attempt to restore an extreme version of the patriarchy, in which women (like nineteenth-century American slaves) are forbidden to read" (Atwood, *The Handmaid's Tale* 18). Shortly after, she continues, "In the book, the dominant 'religion' is moving to seize doctrinal control, and religious denominations familiar to us are being annihilated." She cites various oppositional religious factions—the Bolsheviks and the Mensheviks, the Red Guard, the Catholics and the Baptists—before writing, "The Quakers have gone underground, and are running an escape route to Canada, as—I suspect—they would" (19).

At the risk of performing a gendered trope of apologizing for my work, while also secure in the limitations of any scholar's capacity, I feel the need to note that even as my research into the vast material, scholarly and more colloquial, on Atwood and *The Handmaid's Tale* is extensive, it is by no means comprehensive. That is, there are texts that, despite my detailed and more general searches, I have not found; there are likely a few still in the lists saved from the University of Toronto's John P. Robarts Research Library and Google Scholar that, despite my efforts, I have not read. However, these searches have yet to yield a single reference specific to Canada's involvement in the transatlantic slave trade in material related to Atwood or *The Handmaid's Tale*. The closest allusion I have discovered is in Danita

J. Dodson's 1997 interview with Atwood, in which Atwood notes that some of the earliest Canadian literature are accounts by (settler) women (Dodson, "An Interview" 98) and that Canada's diversity—diversity here determined through colonialist intervention—makes it less suspect of Gileadean leanings: "Remember that a third of [Canada] is French speaking. So you might postulate a Gilead in, say, a province of Canada, but it would be hard to do in the whole thing" (Atwood qtd. in Dodson, "An Interview" 100). Because oppression, apparently, only speaks one language. When Dodson presses Atwood about the significance of the history of African American slavery in the United States to *The Handmaid's Tale*, Atwood responds that "it's not *just* African Americans; it's slavery in general. Or, say, oppression in general." She continues: "One of the things that oppressors like to deny, and usually do, to the people that they are oppressing is education" (qtd. in Dodson, "An Interview" 101). The last segregated Black school in Canada closed in 1983; the last residential school closed in 1996 (Maynard loc. 298; Truth and Reconciliation Commission of Canada 105). The history of Black enslavement in Canada remains largely absent in primary, secondary, and post-secondary curricula (see Maynard loc. 556).

And so the future, improbably balanced on stolen land and suppressed histories, becomes, as the tagline to advertisements for Hulu's series read, "a f*ucking nightmare" (see Velocci). In 2018, prominent white Quebecois theatremaker Robert Lepage and his company, Ex Machina, had two productions cancelled on North American stages—the first, *SLĀV*, a collaboration with white singer Betty Bonifassi, an exploration of Black music originally scheduled to premiere at the Montreal International Jazz Festival in which Bonifassi was cast to play Harriet Tubman (see Canadian Press, "Controversial Play"; Canadian Press, "Artistic Freedom"; Nevins); and the second, *Kanata*, a collaboration with Ariane Mnouchkine and Le Théâtre du Soleil, concerning the history of white settlers and Indigenous people in Canada, which instead premiered in Paris (see CBC News; Koustas; G. Hamilton; Nestruck). Though each show approached histories of marginalized and underrepresented people, neither engaged dramaturgical or creative consultation with Black or Indigenous people.

Also in 2018, during the final debate as part of the Canada Reads finale on CBC (during which prominent Canadian cultural celebrities argue the merits of individual books nominated for that year's "Reads"), Jeanne Beker, white television personality, accused Black singer Jully Black of "attacking [her]" when Black "emphasize[d] the distance colonial privilege creates from the reality Indigenous, Black and other people of colour live every day, because [Canadians] have not atoned for our past as a racist, colonial state" (Kaur). Black, who was defending Métis author

Cherie Dimaline's *The Marrow Thieves* (Beker was defending Japanese Canadian author Mark Sakamoto's *Forgiveness: A Gift from My Grandparents*), blogged after the incident, "possibly for the first time on Canadian national television, the daily lived reality of Black women was brought into instant focus" (Black).

The story of white women sublimating the voices, experiences, and histories of Black and Indigenous women, and, as Clarkista Kent writes, the "historical injustices done to [them]," is not new. Karen Crawley alludes to several theorists who have asserted that *The Handmaid's Tale* "is almost a re-enactment of Harriet Jacobs's 1861 *Incidents in the Life of the Slave Girl*, documenting Jacobs's life as a slave, the sexual abuse she suffered, and how she gained freedom for herself and her children" (Crawley 343). Specifically mentioning Maria Lauret's critique of Atwood's novel, Crawley writes the following:

> Atwood's *The Handmaid's Tale* borrows the generic features of the nineteenth-century slave narrative but suppresses its African American origins, displacing political discourse of African American emancipation onto that of white women's resistance to patriarchy, through the appropriation of the trope of oral storytelling and motifs such as the underground railroad (the underground "Femaleroad"), the fugitive trail to Canada, lynching as a public spectacle, and the practice of naming people after their owners (e.g. OfFred). (343; see also Dodson, "Blank White Spaces"; Lauret)

It is especially useful to remember, too, the story of Marie-Joseph Angélique, an enslaved Black woman in Canada who, in 1734, allegedly set Montreal on fire. Afua Cooper writes the following in her extraordinary *The Hanging of Angélique: The Untold Story of Canadian Slavery and the Burning of Old Montréal*:

> The story of Angélique, dramatic and extraordinary as it is, is relatively unknown in Canada. Canadian history, insofar as its Black history is concerned, is a drama punctuated with disappearing acts. The erasure of Black people and their history … is consistent with the general behaviour of the official chroniclers of the country's past. Black history is treated as a marginal subject. In truth, it has been bulldozed and ploughed over, slavery in particular. (Cooper 7)

Robyn Maynard likewise reiterates the stories of enslaved Black women in Canada that have gone untold in the broader history of the transatlantic slave trade and in Canadian history: Lydia Jackson, Hetty, Peggy.… These names echo under the handmaids' whispers in Atwood's gymnasium: "Alma. Janine. Dolores. Moira. June" (Atwood, *The Handmaid's Tale* 23).

HOW (NOT) TO TELL A MAN'S STORY

As well as Atwood is known for her dystopic futures—futures that would seem to bespeak the present moment in no small way—she is just as much, if not more so, an avid historian. The fact that even her forward-looking worlds of civic and social disaster, results of climate change and despots in charge, are predicated on extant technologies—"One of my rules," she writes, "was that I would not put any events into the book that had not already happened … nor any technology not already available" (*Handmaid's Tale* 14)—bears this out. As do the (predominantly white) women appearing at political rallies dressed in the now-familiar red robes of Atwood's handmaids. Further, Atwood has not only addressed lurid cases in Canada's own history (in *Alias Grace* [1996], for instance), she has also situated the historian as a prominent figure in her novels: Tony in *The Robber Bride* (1993) and those present at the "Twelfth Symposium on Gileadean Studies, held as part of the International Historical Association Convention," whose fictional notes conclude *The Handmaid's Tale* (Atwood, *Handmaid's Tale* 369). The glaring absence, then, of any prominent Black (or otherwise racially marked) character and that of the history of enslaved Black people in Canada in *The Handmaid's Tale* makes Atwood's telling of this tale as disturbingly colonialist in its silences as its silences make it disturbingly emblematic of Canada's, and CanLit's, own ongoing colonialist project.

In "Narrative of Power: Historical Mythologies in Contemporary Québec and Canada," David Austin writes, "Locked in a narrative of modernist progress in a society that is, in part, dominated by its physical landscape, Canada's multicultural policy ultimately treats non-whites as a kind of national environment, outside of history and in need of taming" (Austin 22; see also Mackey). The corruption of the physical landscape yields the corruption of the social landscape in *The Handmaid's Tale*, and this story is played out through white women's bodies in the novel and through a sort of post-race #AllLivesMatter women's bodies in the Hulu series, both of which deny the Black and Indigenous women who actually lived this story. "Black women's suffering is used to tell a man's story," writes Roxane Gay in her critique of the film *12 Years a Slave* (2013) (Gay, *Bad Feminist* 229). It is also used, in *The Handmaid's Tale*, to tell a white woman's story—and it is a woman's story set against a man's that spawned UBC Accountable. Margaret Atwood is not the only woman who might question her feminism in this twenty-first-century moment.

Having reread, again, *The Handmaid's Tale* (and watched the first two seasons of Hulu's series available at the time of this writing), I find June to be a sad feminist at best, but certainly a bad one—and not in the way Gay meant. This reawakening of *The Handmaid's Tale*, and of Atwood's foundational (feminist?) role in CanLit, is a moment for readers, students, teachers, and scholars to reawaken as well, and to look to the land, to the histories buried within it, to reimagine a future that might promise rather than withhold.

CRITICAL REFLECTION QUESTIONS

1. In the novel *The Handmaid's Tale*, Atwood constructs June as a fairly passive character, feminist only in retrospect. In the Hulu series, however, June attains an active feminist persona. Do you identify this with the time period between the novel's and television series's releases, or do you think June could have asserted a more feminist agenda in the novel itself? Do you think the series belies or betrays the novel's intentions?

2. Margaret Atwood is perhaps the most internationally acclaimed Canadian author, and it is no small fact that she is a woman. Is it anti-feminist to accuse her of anti-feminism in her actions during UBC Accountable? How do we read her work retroactive to this incident?

3. While Margaret Atwood has spoken publicly at length about the relationship *The Handmaid's Tale* has to the history of slavery in the US, what does her silence about the history of slavery within Canada mean to the broader history of CanLit? How can we, as scholars and readers of CanLit, amplify a history that, for the most part, has remained untold in our art, literature, and curriculum?

NOTES

1. With regard to issues of cultural appropriation by white feminism, specifically referring to Atwood's op-ed, see also Kong; Lee; and McGregor, among many others. With regard to generational tensions between feminists, particularly those arising after *Le Monde* published the open letter critical of #MeToo made infamous by Catherine Deneuve's signature, see Tremonti; Edwards; and Merkin, again, among many others and reflective of a vast array of perspectives. That nearly all my preliminary citations come just from January 2018 also reflects a unique temporal impact and import (and the potential brevity of the impact and import) of these issues when they play through mainstream and social media.

2. See Gay's chapters "The Smooth Surfaces of Idyll," "What We Hunger For," and especially "The Trouble with Prince Charming, or He Who Trespassed Against Us," in which Gay writes,

"The thing about fairy tales is that the princess finds her prince, but there's usually a price to pay. A compromise is required for happily ever after. The woman in the fairy tale is generally the one who pays the price. This seems to be the nature of sacrifice" (Gay, *Bad Feminist* 193).

3.   I find Atwood's conclusion that such a state as she hypothesizes in the *Walrus* would necessarily discredit accusations rather than pose all men as a potential threat not only rhetorically but ethically unstable. Not only is the fact that false accusations comprise only 2 to 10 percent of all accusations—and that is taking into account the discrepancy in how various organizations determine what constitutes "false" in their reporting (see National Sexual Violence Resource Center)—but the threat men pose to women is a position Atwood has taken before herself. In her 1982 Hagey lecture at the University of Waterloo, Atwood recounted the story of asking a "male friend," "Why do men feel threatened by women?" His response: "They're afraid women will laugh at them." Atwood went on to relate that, upon asking "some women students" taking a poetry seminar she was teaching, "Why do women feel threatened by men?" the women responded, "They're afraid of being killed" (Atwood, "Male Character" 674).

4.   There is a lone reference in Atwood's novel to the "Children of Ham" (Atwood, *Handmaid's Tale* 8) and a few more to the "Sons of Jacob" in both June's narrative (320) and the Historical Notes (480ff). The former recites a Biblical reference to Noah's son Ham, and is, as readers are to assume, Gilead's labelling of African American people. They are "resettled" (8). The Sons of Jacob, in contrast, whom Atwood also refers to as Jews, are offered the option of converting or relocating to Israel (320). See Dodson, "Blank White Spaces."

WORKS CITED

Ahmed, Sara. *The Promise of Happiness*. Duke UP, 2010.

Atwood, Margaret. "Am I a Bad Feminist?" *Globe and Mail*, 13 Jan. 2018, www .theglobeandmail.com/opinion/am-i-a-bad-feminist/article37591823/. Accessed 1 Mar. 2018.

———. *The Handmaid's Tale*. McClelland and Stewart, 2017.

———. "Margaret Atwood on the Galloway Affair." *Walrus*, 17 Nov. 2016, thewalrus .ca/margaret-atwood-on-the-galloway-affair/. Accessed 1 Feb. 2019.

———. "Taking a break from being Supreme Being Goddess…" Tweet, 14 Jan. 2018, twitter.com/margaretatwood/status/952583123157516288. Accessed 1 Feb. 2019.

———. "Writing the Male Character." *Second Words: Selected Critical Prose, 1960–1982*, Kindle edition, House of Anansi Press, 1982, pp. 672–701.

Atwood, Margaret, and Susan Swan. "Where We Are Now: A Joint Statement by Margaret Atwood and Susan Swan." *Where We Are Now*, 22 Mar. 2018, wherewearenow2018.ca/. Accessed 1 Feb. 2019.

Austin, David. "Narratives of Power: Historical Mythologies in Contemporary Québec and Canada." *Race and Class*, vol. 52, no. 1, pp. 19–32. *Scholars Portal*, doi:10.1177/0306396810371759. Accessed 1 Feb. 2019.

Bastién, Angelica Jade. "In Its First Season, *The Handmaid's Tale*'s Greatest Failing Is How It Handles Race." *Vulture*, 14 Jun. 2017, www.vulture.com/2017/06/the-handmaids-tale-greatest-failing-is-how-it-handles-race.html. Accessed 1 Feb. 2019.

Black, Jully. "Take It to the Altar: Why I Spoke Up at Canada Reads." *ByBlacks*, 4 Apr. 2018, byblacks.com/main-menu-mobile/opinion-mobile/item/1858-take-it-to-the-altar-why-i-spoke-up-at-canada-reads. Accessed 1 Feb. 2019.

Canadian Press. "Group Opposed to Controversial Play SLĀV Calls for Commitment to Discussion on Race, Diversity." *Globe and Mail*, 11 Jul. 2018, www.theglobeandmail.com/arts/article-robert-lepages-controversial-play-slav-to-continue-run-across-quebec/. Accessed 1 Feb. 2019.

———. "Robert Lepage Says Decision to Cancel SLAV Show 'Direct Blow to Artistic Freedom.'" *Global News*, 6 Jul. 2018, globalnews.ca/news/4316470/robert-lepage-says-decision-to-cancel-slav-show-a-blow-to-artistic-freedom/. Accessed 1 Feb. 2019.

CBC News. "Indigenous Artists Criticize Quebec Director Robert Lepage over New Show." *CBC News*, 14 Jul. 2018, www.cbc.ca/news/canada/montreal/indigenous-artists-robert-lepage-kanata-1.4747228. Accessed 1 Feb. 2019.

Cooper, Afua. *The Hanging of Angélique: The Untold Story of Canadian Slavery and the Burning of Old Montréal.* Harper Perennial, 2006.

Crawley, Karen. "Reproducing Whiteness: Feminist Genres, Legal Subjectivity and the Post-racial Dystopia of *The Handmaid's Tale* (2017–)." *Law and Critique*, vol. 29, no. 3, 2018, pp. 333–358. *SpringerLink*, doi-org.myaccess.library.utoronto.ca/10.1007/s10978-018-9229-8. Accessed 1 Feb. 2019.

Dean, Flannery. "What's #ubcaccountable & Why Are So Many Authors Tweeting About It?" *Flare*, 24 Nov. 2016, www.flare.com/tv-movies/whats-ubcaccountable-what-does-margaret-atwood-have-to-do-with-it/. Accessed 1 Feb. 2019.

Díaz, Junot. "Make Margaret Atwood Fiction Again." *Boston Review*, 29 Jun. 2017, bostonreview.net/literature-culture-margaret-atwood-junot-diaz-make-margaret-atwood-fiction-again. Accessed 1 Feb. 2019.

———. "The Silence: The Legacy of Childhood Trauma." *New Yorker*, 16 Apr. 2018, www.newyorker.com/magazine/2018/04/16/the-silence-the-legacy-of-childhood-trauma. Accessed 1 Feb. 2019.

Dodson, Danita. "An Interview with Margaret Atwood." *Critique: Studies in Contemporary Fiction*, vol. 38, no. 2, pp. 96–104, doi: 10.1080/00111619.1997.10543168

———. "'We Lived in the Blank White Spaces': Rewriting the Paradigm of Denial in Atwood's *The Handmaid's Tale*." *Utopian Studies*, vol. 8, no. 2, 2017, pp. 66–86, scholar.google.com/scholar_lookup?title=Incidents%20in%20the%20life%20of%20the%20slave%20girl&author=Harriet.%20Jacobs&publication_year=1861. Accessed 1 Feb. 2019.

Donovan, Ken. "Female Slaves as Sexual Victims in Île Royale." *Acadiensis*, vol. 43, no. 1, 2014, pp. 147–156. *JSTOR*, https://www.jstor.org/stable/24329582. Accessed 1 Feb. 2019.

Edwards, Stassa. "The Backlash to #MeToo Is Second-Wave Feminism." *Jezebel*, 11 Jan. 2018, jezebel.com/the-backlash-to-metoo-is-second-wave-feminism-1821946939. Accessed 1 Mar. 2018.

Gay, Roxane. "Actually, Margaret …" Tweet, 13 Jan. 2018, twitter.com/rgay/status/952333625894170624. Accessed 1 Mar. 2018.

———. *Bad Feminist: Essays*. Kindle Edition, HarperCollins, 2014.

Gibb, Camilla. "For Those of You Following #ubcaccountable on Twitter…" *Facebook*, 19 Nov. 2016, www.facebook.com/authorcamillagibb/posts/10153887576146540. Accessed 1 Feb. 2019.

Hamilton, Graeme. "Indigenous Consultants Distance Themselves from Robert Lepage Play 'Kanata' over Lack of Native Actors." *National Post*, 17 Jul. 2018, nationalpost.com/entertainment/theatre/indigenous-consultants-distance-themselves-from-robert-lepage-play-kanata-over-lack-of-native-actors. Accessed 1 Feb. 2019.

Hamilton, Sylvia. "Naming Names, Naming Ourselves: A Survey of Early Black Women in Nova Scotia." *We're Rooted Here and They Can't Pull Us Up: Essays in African Canadian Women's History*, edited by Peggy Bristow et al., University of Toronto Press, 1999, pp. 13–40.

Jacobs, Harriet. *Incidents in the Life of the Slave Girl*. Thayer & Eldridge, 1861. *Google Scholar*, books.google.ca/books?id=JZIbpB7SnFoC&lpg=PR15&ots=EC6xAeakB8&lr&pg=PR15#v=onepage&q&f=false. Accessed 1 Feb. 2019.

Jones, Ellen E. "*The Handmaid's Tale*'s Race Problem." *Guardian*, 31 Jul. 2017, www.theguardian.com/tv-and-radio/2017/jul/31/the-handmaids-tales-race-problem. Accessed 1 Feb. 2019.

Kaur, Rachna Raj. "Jully Black is the True Winner of Canada Reads 2018." *Now*, 4 Apr. 2018, https://nowtoronto.com/culture/books/jully-black-canada-reads-2018/. Accessed 1 Jan. 2020.

Kent, Clarkisha. "The Black Woman's Tale: Why Margaret Atwood's Espousal of White Feminist Beliefs Shouldn't Surprise You." *Root*, 18 Jan. 2018, www.theroot.com/the-black-woman-s-tale-why-margaret-atwood-s-espousal-1822138695. Accessed 1 Mar. 2018.

Kestler-D'Amours, Jillian. "Robert Lepage Cancels Kanata Show after Co-producers Withdraw Support." *CBC*, 26 Jul. 2018, www.cbc.ca/news/canada/montreal/kanata-cancelled-after-criticism-indigenous-robert-lepage-1.4762524. Accessed 1 Feb. 2019.

Kong, Stacy Lee. "Yes, Margaret Atwood *Is* a Bad Feminist. Here's Why." *Flare*, 15 Jan. 2018, www.flare.com/news/margaret-atwood-feminism/. Accessed 1 Mar. 2018.

Koustas, Jane. "Brave New World: Robert Lepage and the First Nations Presence." *Quebec Studies*, vol. 59, 2015, pp. 145–170. *University of Toronto*, doi:10.3828/qs.2015.10. Accessed 1 Feb. 2019.

Lalonde, Julie S. "An Open Letter to Margaret Atwood." *Yellow Manteau Blog*, 2016, yellowmanteau.com/julie-blog/210-an-open-letter-to-margaret-atwood.html. Accessed 1 Feb. 2019.

Lauret, Maria. *Liberating Literature: Feminist Fiction in America*. Routledge, 1994.

Lederman, Marsha. "Margaret Atwood to Donate to Sexual-Violence Fund." *Globe and Mail*, 9 Mar. 2018, www.theglobeandmail.com/arts/books-and-media/margaret-atwood-to-donate-to-sexual-violence-fund/article38264853/. Accessed 1 Feb. 2019.

Lee, Jen Sookfong. "On Margaret Atwood and the New CanLit." *Open Book*, 15 Jan. 2018, open-book.ca/News/On-Margaret-Atwood-and-the-new-Canlit. Accessed 1 Mar. 2018.

Le Monde. "*Nous défendons une liberté d'importuner, indispensable à la liberté sexuelle.*" *Le Monde*, 9 Jan. 2018, www.lemonde.fr/idees/article/2018/01/09/nous-defendons-une-liberte-d-importuner-indispensable-a-la-liberte-sexuelle_5239134_3232.html. Accessed 1 Mar. 2018.

Mackey, Eva. "Death by Landscape: Race, Nature, and Gender in Canadian Nationalist Mythology." *Canadian Woman Studies*, vol. 20, no. 2, 2000, pp. 125–130. *ProQuest*, myaccess.library.utoronto.ca/login?url=https://search-proquest-com.myaccess.library.utoronto.ca/docview/217461916?accountid=14771. Accessed 1 Feb. 2019.

Maynard, Robyn. *Policing Black Lives: State Violence in Canada from Slavery to the Present*. Kindle Edition, Fernwood, 2017.

McGregor, Hannah. "Episode 2.1: White Feminists and Listening to Criticism." *Secret Feminist Agenda*, 19 Jan. 2018, secretfeministagenda.com/2018/01/19/episode-2-1-white-feminists-listening-to-criticism/. Accessed 1 Mar. 2018.

Merkin, Daphne. "Publicly, We Say #MeToo. Privately, We Have Misgivings." *New York Times*, 5 Jan. 2018, www.nytimes.com/2018/01/05/opinion/golden-globes-metoo.html?smid=tw-nytimes&smtyp=cur&_r=0. Accessed 1 Mar. 2018.

Mugabo, Délice Igicari. "Rebirth of the Slick: Transformative Justice and New Black Feminist Possibilities in Montreal." Paper presented at the American Studies Association Conference, 2015.

National Sexual Violence Resource Center (NSVRC). "False Reporting Overview." *NSVRC*, 2012, www.nsvrc.org/sites/default/files/2012-03/Publications_NSVRC_ Overview_False-Reporting.pdf. Accessed 1 Feb. 2019.

Nestruck, J. Kelly. "Lepage's Kanata Tells an Aimless, Emotionally Distant Tale." *Globe and Mail*, 18 Dec. 2018, p. A10. *LexisNexis Academic*, www-lexisnexis-com. myaccess.library.utoronto.ca/lnacui2api/api/version1/getDocCui?lni=5V0F-RY21- F06S-31V7&csi=303830&hl=t&hv=t&hnsd=f&hns=t&hgn=t&oc=00240&perma =true. Accessed 1 Feb. 2019.

Nevins, Jake. "Montreal Jazz Festival Cancels Show with White Actors Performing Slave Songs." *Guardian*, 5 Jul. 2018, www.theguardian.com/music/2018/jul/05/slav- montreal-international-jazz-festival-cancelled-racist-songs. Accessed 1 Feb. 2019.

Sears, Djanet. "Play Equity and the Blindspots." *SpiderWebShowPerformance*, 16 Feb. 2016, spiderwebshow.ca/play-equity-and-the-blindspots/. Accessed 1 Feb. 2019.

Silman, Anna. "Junot Díaz Responds to Allegations of Sexual Misconduct and Verbal Abuse." *The Cut*, 4 May 2018, www.thecut.com/2018/05/author-junot-diaz-accused- of-sexual-misconduct-verbal-abuse.html. Accessed 1 Feb. 2019.

Thomson, Colin A. *Blacks in Deep Snow: Black Pioneers in Canada*. J. M. Dent, 1979.

Tremonti, Anna Maria. "Is There a Generational Divide in the #MeToo Movement?" *The Current*, CBC Radio, 16 Jan. 2018, www.cbc.ca/radio/thecurrent/the-current- for-january-16-2018-1.4488140/is-there-a-generational-divide-in-the-metoo- movement-1.4488151. Accessed 1 Mar. 2018.

Truth and Reconciliation Commission of Canada. "Canada's Residential Schools: The History, Part 2 1939–2000." *TRC Findings*, 2015, http://www.trc.ca/assets/pdf/ Volume_1_History_Part_2_English_Web.pdf. Accessed 1 Jan. 2020.

UBC Accountable. "An Open Letter To UBC: Steven Galloway's Right To Due Process." *UBC Accountable Archived Documents*, 14 Nov. 2016, www.ubcaccountable .com/open-letter/steven-galloway-ubc/. Accessed 1 Feb. 2019.

Velocci, Carli. "Hulu Went All-In on This Bold 'Handmaid's Tale' Marketing (Photos)." *The Wrap*, 27 Apr. 2017, www.thewrap.com/hulu-bold-handmaids-tale-marketing/. Accessed 1 Feb. 2019.

Whitfield, Harvey Amani. "Slavery in English Nova Scotia, 1750–1810." *Journal of the Royal Nova Scotia Historical Society*, vol. 13, 2010, pp. 23–40. *ProQuest*, myaccess. library.utoronto.ca/login?url=https://search-proquest-com.myaccess.library.utoronto .ca/docview/881833833?accountid=14771. Accessed 1 Feb. 2019.

York, Lorraine. 2006. "Biography/autobiography." *The Cambridge Companion to Margaret Atwood*, edited by Coral Ann Howells, Cambridge UP, 2006, pp. 78–107.

CHAPTER 5

"Thank You, Spike": Representations of Teen Pregnancy in the Degrassi Franchise

Christine Mazumdar

As much as I loved *School's Out*, why did it have to stop there? I for one, would be content to follow the characters through the remaining arc of their lives. I'm thinking along
the lines of a Degrassi university, a Degrassi Inc., for the former kids entering into
the soul-killing workforce and ultimately a Degrassi retirement community chronicling
the former kids' twilight years to the grave. I'd renounce my American citizenship and
move to Kitchener to be able to watch the continuing saga of Degrassi.

  —*Kevin Smith ("Degrassi Reunion" 1999)*

Before Drake was Drake and Nina Dobrev became a vampire, they were part of
Degrassi Community School, where Joey Jeremiah was "fucking Tessa Campanelli,"
Craig Manning was dating every girl ever (sometimes at the same time), and
somehow Snake became the principal. Spanning four decades, the Degrassi fran-
chise has been one of the most successful and groundbreaking series in Canadian
television history. Producing five series of 22-minute episodes—*The Kids of Degrassi
Street* (1979–1986), *Degrassi Junior High* (1987–1989), *Degrassi High* (1989–1991),
Degrassi: The Next Generation (2001–2015), and *Degrassi: Next Class* (2016–2017)—
the various incarnations of the series have collectively produced over 600 episodes.
Known for addressing controversial youth issues, the series has addressed, among
other topics, teen pregnancy, suicide, eating disorders, self-harm, substance abuse,
gender and sexuality, and racism.

Degrassi is also noteworthy for featuring strong women leads, who, as Michele Byers notes, "actively articulate feminist positions and engage in feminist cultural production. Although they do not necessarily name their project as

feminist, it clearly is and, as such, it offers a good model for its younger viewers" (Byers 207). Tracking various teen pregnancy storylines from each of the Degrassi incarnations, this chapter considers the historical evolution of teen pregnancy as represented in Canadian television. Witnessed through various storylines in the series, I argue that gender stereotypes are heightened in teen-pregnancy story arcs, often leaving the young women to turn to one another for support as opposed to the "fathers to be," who coincidentally (or perhaps not), in the Degrassi universe, demonstrate an alarming trend toward unstable, self-destructive behaviour.

ON AUTHENTIC ORIGINS

> Television networks can take a program that has somewhat liminal textual generic identifiers and sell it as either a documentary or reality program by packaging it in such a way as to appear either more educational/informative or more entertaining/ sensational, or in some cases both.
>
> —Susan Murray, *Reality TV: Remaking Television Culture*

Gender representation on Degrassi is especially significant because of the series's claim to and investment in "authenticity." Created in 1979 by former high school teacher turned television producer Linda Schuyler and writer/director Kit Hood, Degrassi's original premise encompassed several main objectives: to "present television for youth that spoke to young people in a voice that was authentically their own" (Byers 33), to show youth that they are not alone, and to show consequences. Schuyler's Playing with Time Inc. (also founded in 1979) was responsible for each Degrassi series up until *The Next Generation*. The company was groundbreaking for the way that it incorporated the actors into the creative process. In *Whatever It Takes*, Stephen Stohn, the executive producer for *Degrassi: The Next Generation* and Schuyler's husband of 25 years, describes the unique read-through sessions that became a collaboration between the writers and actors. The read-throughs were the first time that the actors saw the script: "They simply read aloud the lines for their respective characters as the lines come up. They've had no time to prepare for how their character 'ought' to be saying the lines, or what emotions they should be portraying" (Stohn 195). Writer Yann Moore would make notes not only on the script but also on the actors' raw response to the words. Stohn explains:

> Following the read-through we have detailed discussions with the actors about their thoughts on the scripts, what they felt worked, what didn't and whether they had personally gone through anything like that themselves.

We then make adjustments to the scripts based on this extraordinarily valuable feedback. It's like having our own focus group. (Stohn 195)

While different aspects of the actors' personalities and real-life experiences at times made it into the script—Pat Mastroianni really did drive a vehicle without a licence as a teen, just like Joey; Neil Hope lost his father in real life just as his character, Wheels, did—other topics unrelated to the actors' experiences, such as Darren Brown's character Dwayne contracting HIV, were produced in conjunction with workshops for the actors. As Brown explained in 1999, people living with HIV and AIDS were brought in to talk to the actors in preparation for the storyline, which, in true Degrassi fashion, was revolutionary, filmed in 1990 amidst the AIDS crisis. Their objective in confronting real-life issues was not to critique behaviour or stigmatize experiences. Rather, as Schuyler states in the 1989 CBC behind-the-scenes documentary *Degrassi: Between Takes*, "our mission is not to stop kids from having sex or doing drugs ... our biggest mandate is to present kids with alternatives for behaviours and it's still up to them which way they are going to choose.... Let them make life choices from an informed base rather than just out of naivety" (*Degrassi: Between Takes*). At Degrassi no subject is taboo, because "if they are talking about it in the halls of the schools, we should be talking about it on Degrassi" (Stohn 156).

One way Degrassi's creators have broached their objectives is through their unique approach to casting—casting non-actors and having teens play teens, unlike other teen dramas that followed (see, for example, the Andrea Zuckerman phenomenon of *Beverly Hills, 90210*, where the actress playing her, Gabrielle Carteris, was over a decade older than her character). In a 1999 Degrassi reunion on the CBC talk show *Jonovision*, Pat Mastroianni—known for playing Joey Jeremiah, the fedora-wearing lead singer of the band Zit Remedy—equated the show's success with its ties to realness and authenticity: "I think that for the most part we were trying to be as real as possible. We weren't trying to be anything we weren't. The stories were real and honest" ("Degrassi Reunion").

In her essay "Degrassi Then and Now: Teens, Authenticity and the Media," Sherri Jean Katz defines "authenticity" in relation to the series: "Authenticity is that quality of perceived believability or realness that makes television viewers buy-in on a fundamental level to what is happening on-screen, even as they are quite aware of the presence of constructed characters and written scripts" (Katz 77). In the Degrassi world, the presence of non-actors or inexperienced actors serves to bridge this gap between storyline and real life. Rejecting a glamourized aesthetic, Degrassi writer Yan Moore describes, "The glamour is right out of basement theatre productions. Most of the kids have never acted before Degrassi and their freshness is part of the show's arc" (*Degrassi: Between Takes*). Authenticity in the original Degrassi series (before other incarnations like *The Next Generation*) was also achieved through the show's budget constraints: "A lot of naturalism comes from a … very small crew" (*Degrassi: Between Takes*). Some scenes had crewmembers using flashlights for additional lighting. The show was not filmed on a set: "it looks like a real school. The hallways and all the sounds. Because it's not a set, this is a real school where we film" (*Degrassi: Between Takes*). As the late actor Neil Hope, who played Wheels, stated in 1989, "we want to be polished, we don't want to be slick" (*Degrassi: Between Takes*). In this way, authenticity is not simply about the faces on screen, but the environment the production was situated within.

While Degrassi's objectives have, for the most part, remained intact throughout its various iterations, as the series has progressed, the non-glam aesthetic and low-budget "naturalism" have shifted. In "Changing Faces" Ravindra N. Mohabeer posits that part of this change comes from the series shifting from the publicly funded CBC, which aired the first three series, to the privately owned CTV, which aired *The Next Generation* (*TNG*), premiering in 2001. *TNG* was eventually moved to MuchMusic and then MTV Canada. Most recently, *Next Class* has been made available on the Family Channel and on Netflix. The response to the shift has not always been seen in a positive light: "(TNG) has come under fire from some fans for not being true to its origins: a glossy visual style that contradicts the low-budget image of the original series, actors that are far too pretty to exist in real life, and characters that, well, aren't Joey Jeremiah" (Mohabeer 101). This shift toward a "glossier" aesthetic is highlighted through the characters' constructed gender expression, costuming, and aesthetic. In the first three series, for example, there was no makeup department at all. *The Kids of Degrassi Street* didn't have the actors wearing makeup; *Junior High* used minimal makeup that the actors did themselves (often sporting their real clothes and hairstyles—yes, that was Spike's real hair!); and *Degrassi High* again saw the actors doing their own makeup. Gender expression was not designed or costumed by a professional, but representative of the people themselves. While the work was scripted, the focus was on projecting an air of the "real." *The Next Generation*, on the other hand, started to show Emma and her friends much more made up than we'd ever seen at Degrassi Community School. Despite the shift, Degrassi has managed to preserve a sense of Canadiana—"We want you to think you could see each of those kids in your own school" (Ellis 122)—by not striving toward the moneyed glam of shows like *Beverly Hills, 90210* (1990–2000).

As such, I consider this notion of "authenticity" to explore the ways in which Degrassi has continually provided a more direct and educational conversation around teen pregnancy and abortion—which is, in no small part, possible because it is a Canadian show rather than a US show. The show privileges or strives toward a more "real" representation of teens and teen experience, but it also uses that depiction as a means to enable a discourse around sensitive and controversial topics that is rarely available on other shows—and frankly isn't available in many spaces for teens, especially in the United States. As Letizia Guglielmo writes in *MTV and Teen Pregnancy*, "In 2000, a Centres for Disease Control and Prevention survey revealed that a "majority of viewers (52%) report picking up health information that they trust to be accurate from prime time TV shows, and 1 in 4 (26%) say that these shows are among their top three sources for health information" (viii). In this case, the show's imperative to depict relatively "real" characters and situations allows it also to create a more inclusive and more provocative social space for teens.

The need for such programing seems particularly relevant at the time of writing this chapter in 2019, when the precarity of women's rights has become ever more apparent in both the US and Canada. Proposals to revise and in some cases drastically alter abortion laws in the US, alongside Doug Ford's 2018 proposal to revert to the 1998 sex-ed curriculum in Ontario (which would remove—among other things—any discussion of consent from student education), are indicative of the ongoing threat to women's bodily rights and the need for alternative modes of education. Indeed, despite how far we have come in Canada, safe and accessible information on abortion and sexual activity can still be put in jeopardy. In April 2019, Alberta Premier Jason Kenney appointed Adriana LaGrange as education minister. While no curriculum changes have been solidified, LaGrange previously acted as president of Red Deer Pro-Life, a group that provided, among other things, anti-abortion presentations in Red Deer schools and has been vocal about a desire to overhaul the NDP's previous curriculum. As Guglielmo writes, "As government funding for comprehensive sex education has continued to decrease since the 1980s, entertainment media has played an increasing role 'in educating the public about significant health issues,' including pregnancy" (vii–viii). With such political rulings and education cuts, shows like Degrassi, which present the very issues the government is attempting to silence, become a stand-in for a more formal curriculum.

TEEN PREGNANCY STORYLINES

These examples from popular culture demonstrate not only our culture's obsession with the maternal body but also our culture's continued objectification of women's bodies and the reduction of those bodies to reproduction even when they have college degrees from prestigious universities and they are running for the highest offices in the country.
—*Kelly Oliver*

Rather than presenting the issue of teen pregnancy as a one-off plotline or developing the story through a secondary character, the series has tackled teen pregnancy
nine times throughout the four-decade span of the Degrassi universe, with characters Spike, Erica, Tessa, Manny, Liberty, Mia, Jenna, Claire, and Lola. Each
storyline has been told in a different way, with various outcomes ranging from
keeping the child, abortion, adoption, miscarriage, instances where the father is
informed, and others where the father is not informed. The consequences of these
life-altering decisions surrounding teen pregnancy are demonstrated throughout
the course of the characters' development at the school: "The issue carries. We've
seen it in all the generations. Teens, teens have babies. They have to deal with being
young and having all this responsibility" ("Miriam McDonald"). Pregnant women
on the series are not simply depicted as the "bad kids" or outcasts. Degrassi successfully demonstrates, unlike other teen series, that everyone can face these kinds
of challenges. Even more noteworthy is the way in which Degrassi allows these
instances to extend beyond a one- or two-episode story arc. Ultimately, teenage
pregnancy is the through line that enables the series to continue over generations.

Spike (*Degrassi Junior High, Degrassi High, Degrassi: The Next Generation*)

One of the most famous storylines from any Degrassi series is Christine "Spike"
Nelson's pregnancy from *Degrassi Junior High* (*JH*), which begins in season one
of the series in the episode "It's Late."[1] It is perhaps the most important storyline
throughout the series, as it is revisited over the span of multiple series and decades, as opposed to simply touching upon it in a 22-minute episode and then not
addressing it again. Degrassi establishes a strong sense of lineage in the storyline of Spike, the daughter of a single mother who gave birth to her at 17. Like
her mother, Spike raises her daughter without a father, all the while finishing
school and establishing a career in hairdressing like her mother. In grade eight, at
age 14, Spike has sex with classmate Shane McKay at Lucy Hernandez's party—
confessing to her mother, "I wanted him to like me" ("It's Late")—which eventually results in the birth of her daughter, Emma. Ultimately, Emma is the catalyst
for the next Degrassi series, *The Next Generation*, which follows her adolescence in
the series's plotline.

Spike's plot is a daring storyline, particularly in the 1980s, when teen pregnancy had rarely been explored on the small screen. In *Degrassi Junior High*, the response from Spike's friends—twins Erica and Heather—and Shane demonstrate
the lack of knowledge surrounding the issue. In "It's Late," after Spike admits to

Erica and Heather that her period is late, she is initially reassured by their naïveté: "If it's your first time, you're okay. You can't get pregnant the first time." Her mother later refutes the claim, stating that "They say one in five girls gets pregnant their first time" ("It's Late"). Meanwhile, when Spike tells Shane that she thinks she's pregnant, he literally exits stage right out the door. He later not-so-subtly asks Joey Jeremiah, "What would you do if you got someone pregnant? It wouldn't be the guy's problem, right?" ("It's Late").

This misogynistic outlook echoes throughout the storyline, beginning with Joey's comment as the episode starts. Shane is making out with Spike at the party when Joey walks up to them, saying, "Can't we all share?" ("It's Late") as he runs his fingers over Spike's shoulder, indicating his desire to make out with her as well. Iris Young notes,

> The culture's separation of pregnancy and sexuality can liberate (pregnant women) from the sexually objectifying gaze that alienates and instrumentalizes her when in her pregnant state. The leer of sexual objectification regards the woman in pieces, as the possible object of man's desire and touch. In pregnancy the woman may experience some release from this alienating gaze. (qtd in Oliver 26)

Although Spike does not seem "liberated" while pregnant, Joey's attitude toward her certainly shifts. In the episode entitled "Trust Me" (one of many to chronical Spike's pregnancy), the school board expels Spike because she "sets a bad example." When Joey is asked about the hypocrisy of why Shane hasn't been kicked out, he replies, "I guess because he's not out to here [*miming a large belly with his hands*]" ("Trust Me"). Joey's comment implies that *the pregnant body* is something to shame, something that should not be seen at his school. Principal Lawrence seems to echo these sentiments as he states offscreen, "pregnant girls aren't allowed at Degrassi" ("Trust Me"). The school board's response and Joey's joke demonstrate both how the onus is placed on the woman to deal with her pregnancy on her own, and also how such isolation extends, as she is punished and not permitted to attend school with her friends. They make her finish grade eight from home, as if she is sick and risks infecting the rest of the student body. All the while, Shane continues at Degrassi without punishment or shaming.

With Shane's lack of support, Spike turns to her mother in "It's Late," realizing that she has no one to rely on. Her mother proclaims that "whatever happens, she is in her corner" and stands firmly by her daughter. While Shane accompanies Spike, with her mother, to the clinic for the pregnancy test results, his relationship with her continues to be strained until it eventually dissolves during the storyline. In "Censored," when rumours begin circulating that Spike may be expelled, Shane does nothing to support or stand up for Spike. It is another young woman, class-mate Caitlin Ryan, who writes an article to get the student body to rally around Spike. In the end, this doesn't change the school board's decision, and Spike says that she doesn't want the attention from Caitlin's article. But the kinship struc-tures of women supporting women is clear. Whereas the boys in the school and the school board itself refuse support and understanding, the positive influence of women effectively challenges the trope of "mean girls" or "cat fights" so often pres-ent on teen series. Women, rather than being pitted against each other, become the faces of empowerment.

Spike gives birth off screen in the season finale of *Degrassi JH* season two, "Pass Tense." The following season, we learn that Spike gave birth to Emma (named for the Emmy award the storyline earned) through 12 hours of labour and a six-week-premature birth, which almost led to Emma's death. Season two of *Degrassi JH* continues to explore Spike's storyline, chronicling her struggles as a single mother. Again, the continuation of this narrative is one that is incredibly rare in television portrayals of young mothers. As a straight-A student prior to giving birth (even during her school-imposed home confinement), Spike describes her grades as suffering. In the holiday episode "Season's Greetings," Spike is forced to care for Emma at school when her child care plans unravel. Shane meets his daughter for the first time nearly half a year after her birth. While this encounter seems to partially shift his attitude, this new outlook comes to an end in episode 10 of season three, "Twenty Bucks," where Shane claims he can't contribute money to child support that month. While Spike is initially understanding of Shane's lack of funds, she later finds out that he has purchased tickets to the "Gourmet Scum" concert. They have a confrontation in which Spike states that she does all the work and that she had really wanted to go to the concert. In the next episode, the two-parter "Taking Off," Shane is seen purchasing LSD at the concert and consuming it. He later does not return home from the concert and his body is found badly injured under a bridge. It is unclear if he fell or jumped. Shane's self-destructive behaviour ends up being his exit from Degrassi Junior High, as he transfers to a school for special needs students, having suffered neurological damage from the fall. Ultimately, he becomes completely estranged from Spike and Emma follow-ing the traumatic and permanent brain injuries he sustains. He truly escapes his responsibilities in fatherhood, as evidenced in *Degrassi: The Next Generation* more than a decade later, when Emma goes searching for him in his long-term care facility.

Amanda Stepto was praised for her honest portrayal of Spike—she was so convincing that "some fans offered to send clothes for the baby" (*Degrassi: Between Takes*). Again, this speaks to the impact of the series, not only in terms of gender representation, but character reception. The illusion of "authenticity" ultimately made the experience *feel* more real for audiences as well. Schuyler describes some of the messages that Stepto and the other teen actors would receive from viewers: "'I really like my boyfriend, should we have sex?' That's what scares me ... you're not teen counsellors. The audience sometimes expects the teens to have knowledge about their characters that they don't have in real life" (*Degrassi: Between Takes*). While Stepto did not have the experience of teen pregnancy in real life, she received messages from fans asking her questions about teen pregnancy and sex. Stepto went on to host a 1992 episode of *Degrassi Talks* (a standalone docu-series following real-life stories of issues addressed in the Degrassi universe) on the topic of sex and teen pregnancy. In the case of Spike,

> viewers, parents, and educators all made their thoughts about the Emmy-winning story line known to the producers of the show. Opinions ranged from complete outrage that such a topic had appeared in a show for young people to heartfelt gratitude that Degrassi had dared address the subject. However, the story line was not seen in all the countries where Degrassi aired—each broadcaster decided for itself whether or not to show it, and many decided not to. (Ellis 137)

Spike's storyline is continued on *Degrassi: The Next Generation*, where we learn of the sacrifices she's made for Emma (not going away to college like her friends) but also that she is successful and happy. She ultimately marries Snake and has another child with him in 2003. Originally, the plot of *The Next Generation* was intended for a new teen soap opera: *Ready, Willing and Wired*, created by the same production company that did the original Degrassi series. One of the original writers on the *Degrassi JH* series, Yan Moore, approached Linda Schuyler:

> I've done the calculations. Emma was born in the final episode of Season 2 of *Degrassi Junior High*, which first aired March 28, 1988. That would make her a bit more than eleven years old now, but by the time we produce a show and get it to air, she'd be thirteen and going to junior high herself. Why don't we keep the stories we've been working on for *Ready, Willing and Wired*, but make the lead character Emma. She and her friends are going to school. Why don't we make that school *Degrassi*. (Stohn 154)

In 2015, Miriam McDonald, who plays Spike's daughter, Emma, on *The Next Generation*, was interviewed, and she discussed the storyline on Adamo Ruggiero's web series, *Straight Talk*:

Ruggiero: I think what's cool about your character is that in the Degrassi, correct me if I'm wrong, but in the Degrassi world, you're like the only, like, teen baby that was kept. And I'm so grateful Spike kept you. Because we would not have Degrassi, like we would not have had this.
McDonald: Thank you, Spike, thank you.
Ruggiero: Let's all thank Spike. ("Miriam McDonald")

McDonald then reveals how, despite being censored in some countries, the storyline was used as an educational tool in her elementary school health class, demonstrating the scope of the storyline:

McDonald: I remember, the only time I had ever seen Degrassi was in health class.... I feel like it would have been the pregnancy episode.
Ruggiero: Isn't that so bizarre? It would have been that episode and then you were the result of that pregnancy.... That's so cool.
McDonald: It's amazing. I mean, now here we are 14 years later. ("Miriam McDonald")

Spike's pregnancy storyline revolutionized the way that teen pregnancy was shown on TV, as the consequences are carried over throughout various seasons, decades, and multiple series. Spike's success can be attributed to her determination, the sacrifices she has made, and her ability to rely on other women (her mother, her friends), despite Shane's absence and escapist behaviour, which also have dramatic consequences.

Manny Santos (*Degrassi: The Next Generation*), "Accidents Will Happen"

Fast-forward to 2004 and into the world of *Degrassi: The Next Generation*, when Emma Nelson's best friend, Manny Santos, also at age 14, finds herself in the same predicament that Spike did in junior high, after Manny loses her virginity to Craig Manning. Manny faces added complications, as Craig had also been involved with Ashley Kerwin during their tryst. Ashley, furious with Craig's betrayal, announces to the school that Manny is pregnant: "these two idiots are pregnant … because it's way too difficult to use a condom" ("Accidents Will Happen: Part 1"). While Craig was the one who lied and cheated, Manny faces the brunt of the shaming and humiliation. Manny apologizes to Craig after revealing her pregnancy to him: "I know you're mad and I'm sorry." Though he says he isn't mad, Craig notably does not apologize to her for his actions.

Recently orphaned Craig suggests, "It's okay. I started thinking about it after you asked me that question yesterday. What if we had it? We could be a little family. All our own" ("Accidents Will Happen: Part 1"). Part 2 of the episode begins with Craig bringing Manny milk at school, presumably to keep her strength up. The couple fantasizes about baby names and having a family together. However, as Manny begins to have doubts, she turns to another woman, Spike, for support and guidance:

Manny: I want to know what being a single mom is really like.

Spike: Maybe like juggling six things all at once, plus all six things are on fire and you're standing up riding a bus and you can't stop for at least 12 years. Lots of women raise kids on their own but doing it at 14 was extra hard. All my friends went off to college, university, Europe, but I stayed home.

Manny: … Craig wants me to keep it.

Spike: And he's always going to be there? Ultimately the responsibility is yours so the decision is yours, no one else's.

Manny: I don't have to do this if I don't want to? ("Accidents Will Happen: Part 2")

Manny's own mother stands by her as well and supports her daughter's decision to have an abortion. However, when Manny confides in Emma about her decision, Emma—influenced by her own conception—is furious with Manny, creating a rift in their friendship:

Manny: Look, I know you think it's wrong.

Emma: And your child would too.

Manny: I'm just trying to do the right thing here, for me, you know, for everyone, I guess. I wouldn't want to give some baby a crappy life with some mom who isn't ready. ("Accidents Will Happen: Part 2")

Manny faces similar complications when she tells Craig. He becomes possessive and aggressive, and even grabs her shoulder: "No, no you're not. Manny stop. No, I won't let you. (*Grabs her by the shoulder*)" ("Accidents Will Happen: Part 2"). Ultimately it is Emma who stands up for her friend and puts Craig in his place:

Craig: Emma, you butt out. What she's doing is wrong.

Emma: I agree with you, okay? If she was just some stranger, I would be furious with her, but she's my friend and it's her choice.

Craig: It's my baby.

Emma: And Manny's body. What about her? ("Accidents Will Happen: Part 2")

Manny ultimately has the abortion. It is a very different storyline from Spike's, in that it does not play out over decades. However, its impact on Manny's life continues beyond these two episodes. We see a shift in her behaviour and style, as she had previously been slut-shamed for her risqué attire. While her mother supports her, Manny goes through a major falling out with her parents in later seasons and moves in with Emma. The abortion clearly has left a lasting impression, particularly on her father. Moreover, her relationship with Emma is affected, growing stronger at times but also leading to fights in their future. Manny's storyline also echoes Spike's in that, once again, the young woman faces the brunt of shaming, rifts with other students, even fear of Craig's reaction. While Shane abandons Spike by not wanting anything to do with her, Craig abandons Manny's well-being through his selfishness and controlling behaviour. Once again it is women that support and care for Manny (Spike, her mother, and Emma). It is noteworthy that while not occurring directly after the storyline, Craig's erratic behaviour culminates in the following seasons when he becomes violent and is diagnosed with bipolar disorder. He, like Shane, although years after the pregnancy storyline, also experiments with drugs. While it is difficult to say how much this pregnancy impacted his mental state, his behaviour during the storyline shows glimpses of erratic behaviour that later consumes his life. In both of these instances—and counter to many teen narratives—there are clear consequences experienced by men, in part for their mistreatment of women. They do not come out unscathed, but suffer emotional and mental health struggles.

Tuffin and colleagues write the following in "The 'Missing' Parent":

Teenage fatherhood sits at the intersection of biological possibility and cultural expectation, and for that reason is peppered with challenges. When a fourteen-year-old boy announces that he is the father of two children this can raise eyebrows as we question social expectations about maturity and parental responsibility. (270)

That both Shane's and Craig's fates on the show are written through neurological damage and mental illness not only plays into the trope of the disappearing teenage father—"Conspicuously absent from most teen pregnancy prevention campaigns, teen fathers—often referred to as 'baby daddies' to further characterize this role as 'other'" (Guglielmo x)—but also implies, dangerously, that mental illness is the punitive result of the teen fathers' actions. Perhaps viewers are meant to believe that Craig's symptoms were in part triggered by the emotional duress he experienced from Manny's decision, but it seems a too simplistic (and not entirely responsible) way to write Shane off of the show. In "16 and Pregnant, Masculinity, and Teen Fatherhood," Jennifer Beggs Weber and Enid Schatz explain that teen fatherhood, while clearly pointing to new familial and financial responsibilities,

> clashes with general expectations of young masculinity in ways that motherhood and femininity do not. This conflict or, at the very least, liminality influences the ways in which teen fathers navigate both fatherhood and masculinity but also the ways in which the labels and definitions of "good" and "bad" dads are constructed on the show and in reality. (127)

Degrassi has yet to flesh out a storyline with both teen parents assuming equal responsibility over time regardless of what decision is initially made about the pregnancy. Ultimately, it remains unclear if Degrassi uses mental illness as a means of writing absent fathers out of their respective storylines, or alternatively if their mental illness might be a means to complicate the oft-erased narratives of fathers, by creating separate storylines that address mental illness in teen culture.

Finally, Manny's storyline was received internationally in a similar fashion to Spike's, with the US opting not to air the episode—an indication of the magnitude of the issue even in the mid-2000s. Kelly Oliver explains:

> Abortion is a controversial issue and on American television, which makes up the vast majority of series that air in Canada and abroad, it is rarely raised, particularly not by mainstream networks (public or private) or in youth programming. When abortion issues do make it to the small screen, the crisis turns out to be a false alarm or characters choose not to have abortions, have spontaneous miscarriages, are wracked with guilt or are severely punished for their choices. (Oliver 199)

Jake Epstein, the actor who played Craig, spoke about the impact the storyline had on him in real life:

Epstein: I remember after Craig impregnated Manny, which happened on the show, people threw condoms at me—

Ruggiero: What?

Epstein: —the day after the episode aired. And like nowadays, I'm like that's amazing, people thought it was real. People, like, connected with it to the point that—

Ruggiero: They chucked condoms at you.

Epstein: Yeah. But at the time, when I was like 17 years old … it was like bullying. I did not like that attention at all. I didn't know how to deal with it. ("Jake Epstein")

Epstein's experience seems to reaffirm Degrassi's connection to authenticity. While nowhere near as lengthy as Spike's storyline, "Accidents Will Happen" remains an iconic episode of *The Next Generation*, even more so because things come full circle for Spike's character as she counsels and supports Manny in a way that no one else on the series can.

Lola Pacini (*Degrassi: Next Class*), "#IRegretNothing"

> Unlike most other teen shows, the cast changes organically.... The ever-changing nature
> of the cast also means that issues and stories can be revisited over the years through the
> eyes of different characters who have different points of view, keeping the storytelling
> fresh. This may be one reason why the franchise has lasted as long as it has. (Stohn 197)

While there are substantial shifts in *Degrassi: Next Class*—the newest Degrassi series jointly produced by Epitome Pictures, DHX Media, and Netflix—similar issues are addressed, albeit in different ways. In 2017, the most recent teen pregnancy storyline on Degrassi occurred with Lola, at 16 years old. Lola's storyline feels very different from any other teen pregnancy on Degrassi, notably because of its purposeful lack of sentimentality. Moreover, the entire storyline occurs in one 22-minute episode.

When Lola becomes pregnant by classmate Miles Hollingsworth III, she immediately knows that she wants to have an abortion. She tries to tell Miles about her pregnancy, but he pushes her away before she has a chance. Lola makes an appointment for an abortion and confides only in her friend Yael, who offers to accompany her to the clinic. Lola is shown inside the procedure room, a first for Degrassi. She has the abortion and returns to class the next day, ready to move on with her life. She doesn't cry, and she doesn't show signs of being upset or being emotionally affected by the experience. During a class presentation, she accidentally reveals her abortion to the class when they see information about abortion on her phone that she uses to load her overhead presentation. Yael consoles her and Lola says she feels guilty for feeling nothing about her abortion. At the end of the episode, Lola is seen talking about her abortion via vlog at school and says she feels no shame or embarrassment. She is supported by her women friends who take her out for ice cream. Miles finds out after the fact. The end.

Once again, the young man is absent, though not necessarily by choice; more significantly, he has also been written as dealing with substance abuse issues and mental illness. The women, again, though, support and stand by each other. Lola's story is particularly significant because it refuses the sentimentality of previous storylines. While Spike, Manny, and other pregnancy storylines during the franchise's history suggest devastating consequences, Lola's reaction seems to signify that there has been a significant shift in the way that teen pregnancy and abortion are portrayed on the small screen.

> From 2009 to 2010, the birthrate among teenage girls in the United States dropped 9 percent. In a nineteen-year period (1991–2010), the birthrate among teenage girls dropped 44 percent. Despite the decline in teen births, the coverage of pregnant teenage girls has increased through a variety of reality television shows, including *Teen Mom* and *16 and Pregnant*. McCarthy explains, "Reality television [serves] as a place where popular culture and social science [overlap] via a realist ideal in which social norms, mechanisms of conformity, ritualized scripts, and modes of interaction [are] put on display." (McClanahan 149)

Likewise, Degrassi's inclusion of an abortion as part of the everyday offers a fresh and often unseen perspective. Moreover, because this episode is available on Netflix, the issue of censorship on network TV does not come into play, making it more accessible and signifying how the topic has been normalized. While Manny's decision to terminate her pregnancy and the arc the show developed around it fundamentally shifted the broader discourse around teen pregnancy and abortion in a way that Spike's and other previous characters' stories on the show could not have, given the show's cultural context and network restrictions, *Degrassi: Next Class*'s handling of Lola's choice, and her decisive, pragmatic approach to it (through its only one-episode duration), is absolutely dependent on Spike's extended character arc.

CONCLUSION

While I address only three of the nine pregnancy storylines here—Spike's, Manny's, and Lola's—the frequency of teen pregnancy on the series and the shifts in those representations are indicative of concurrent changes in societal norms and expectations surrounding teen pregnancy. From a student not being permitted to attend school because of pregnancy to a student vlogging about her abortion online, Schuyler's notion that "nothing is taboo" rings increasingly true. Degrassi's representation of pregnancy on the small screen not only highlights women's experiences, but also contributes to the very normalization and destigmatization that the trajectory depicts.

In 2010, *Degrassi: The Next Generation*'s slogan was "it goes there." Despite the serious and dramatic issues these teens constantly face, though, it is the friendships and support systems that are nothing short of remarkable. Women supporting women, in particular in the pregnancy storylines, echoes Schuyler's initial sentiment to teens, expressing that you "are not alone" (*Degrassi: Between Takes*). While the style of the series may have shifted since its earliest days, Degrassi's core principles seem to have, for the most part, remained intact: "nothing is black and white … it is not always clear what is right or wrong, and … we all are empowered to make choices, but every choice has a consequence. And the consequences are not just events that unravel in the short run; they can reverberate throughout a lifetime" (Stohn 209).

CRITICAL REFLECTION QUESTIONS

1. It is clear that Degrassi's narratives around pregnancy have pushed boundaries and offered perspectives that were otherwise absent from the small screen. Have other issues portrayed on Degrassi had similar effects of "normalizing" once taboo issues? Are there issues that you think the show would still be hesitant to address?

2. Gender stereotypes are often perpetuated in media; at other times pop culture resists tropes and offers alternative frameworks for understanding gendered experiences. With this in mind, how can the absence or instability of the would-be fathers on Degrassi be explained in contrast to the women-supporting-women motif?

3. As Degrassi has progressively become more glam than the original version, how has this notion of glamour impacted its mandate of "authenticity"?

NOTE

1. In a follow-up episode on teen pregnancy and abortion on the show—*Degrassi High*, "A New Start," parts 1 and 2, where Degrassi student Erica finds herself pregnant and contemplating abortion—Spike has a particularly poignant moment speaking to Erica's twin sister, where she describes that abortion was the wrong decision for her, but is right for other people.

WORKS CITED

"Accidents Will Happen (parts 1–2)." *Degrassi: The Next Generation*. Epitome Pictures, season three, episodes 14–15, 2004.

Beggs Weber, Jennifer, and Enid Schatz. "16 and Pregnant, Masculinity, and Teen Fatherhood: Reconciling or Reinforcing Stereotypes?" *MTV and Teen Pregnancy: Critical Essays on 16 and Pregnant and Teen Mom*, edited by Letizia Guglielmo, Scarecrow Press, 2013, pp. 125–140.

Byers, Michele. "Have Times Changed? Girl Power and Third-Wave Feminism on Degrassi." *Growing Up Degrassi: Television Identity and Youth Cultures*, edited by Michele Byers, Sumach Press, 2005, pp. 191–209.

Degrassi: Between Takes. CBC Television, 1989, https://www.youtube.com/watch?v=Sb2437TFOkc.

"Degrassi Reunion." *Jonovision*, CBC Television, 23–24 Dec. 1999.

Ellis, Kathryn. *Degrassi Generations*. H. B. Fenn, 2005.

Guglielmo, Letizia. *MTV and Teen Pregnancy: Critical Essays on 16 and Pregnant and Teen Mom*. Scarecrow Press, 2013.

"It's Late." *Degrassi Junior High*, Playing with Time Productions, season one, episode 11, 1987.

"Jake Epstein." *Straight Talk with Adamo Ruggiero*, 2015, https://www.youtube.com/watch?v=LlouYtxQpW8.

Katz, Sherri Jean. "Degrassi Then and Now: Teens, Authenticity and the Media." *Growing Up Degrassi: Television Identity and Youth Cultures*, edited by Michele Byers, Sumach Press, 2005, pp. 77–95.

McClanahan, Andrea M. "Teenage Fathers: The Disruption and Promotion of the Heterosexual Imaginary." *MTV and Teen Pregnancy: Critical Essays on 16 and Pregnant and Teen mom*, edited by Letizia Guglielmo, Scarecrow Press, 2013, pp. 141–160.

"Miriam McDonald." *Straight Talk with Adamo Ruggiero*, 2015, https://www.youtube.com/watch?v=akXernRwnbI.

Mohabeer, Ravindra. "Changing Faces: What Happened When Degrassi Switched to CTV." *Growing Up Degrassi: Television Identity and Youth Cultures*, edited by Michele Byers, Sumach Press, 2005, pp. 96–112.

Murray, Susan, and Laurie Ouellette. *Reality TV: Remaking Television Culture*. New York UP, 2009.

Oliver, Kelly. *Knock Me Up, Knock Me Down: Images of Pregnancy in Hollywood Film*. Columbia UP, 2012.

Stohn, Stephen. *Whatever It Takes*. Dundurn Press, 2018.

Tropp, Laura. "What's a Baby Daddy to Do? Fathers on the Fringe in MTV's 16 and Pregnant." *MTV and Teen Pregnancy: Critical Essays on 16 and Pregnant and Teen Mom,* edited by Letizia Guglielmo, Scarecrow Press, 2013, pp. 161–176

"Trust Me." *Degrassi Junior High,* Playing with Time Productions, season two, episode 11, 1988.

Tuffin, Keith, et al. "The 'Missing' Parent: Teenage Fathers Talk About the Meaning of Early Parenthood." *Re/Assembling the Pregnant and Parenting Teenager,* edited by Annelies Kamp and Majella McSharry, Peter Lang, 2018, pp. 269–290.

CHAPTER 6

"Thank You for Making Me Feel So Comfortable in Your Home": *Baroness von Sketch* Queering Up Canadian Television

Claire Carter

INTRODUCTION

The *Baroness von Sketch Show* has now aired its third season on CBC television, has secured a viewership in the United States, and has an established relationship with Netflix, notable for being the first all-female feminist sketch comedy show, which was picked up from a hand-videotaped submission. The show is based in Toronto and features four white women as the heart of the comedy troupe, with various supporting actors who often show up across the three seasons, playing different characters. By its nature, the show is made up of a series of skits in each episode, ranging in length and topic from playfully mocking seemingly everyday *common sense* urban behaviours, such as ordering your coffee in the correct hip fashion, to more political commentary on the lack of effective (or any) processing of rape kits by police. Informed by queer and feminist media and popular culture scholars, this chapter focuses on the queering potential of the show through an analysis of several skits that do not simply involve the representation of queer characters but, I will argue, go some way in disrupting heteronormativity and the all-too-often sanitized portrayal of the queer (Gamson).[1] In addition, skits alongside those with explicit queer content, I suggest, engage in a critique of white femininity / the normative feminine ideal, notably the white, cis, heterosexual, able-bodied, and middle-upper-class woman. This ideal is highlighted and made visible, even eccentric, which functions to *trouble* its normalcy and secured or fixed status (Butler).

Queer and feminist media and popular culture scholars have identified phases of queer representation (or lack thereof) over the past century or so, documenting particular themes and changes as a result of societal shifts, notably with respect to increased legal rights and societal acceptance in Western societies. Walters, for example, in her article on the representations of lesbian kinship in the movie *The Kids Are Alright*, documents three phases of gay visibility. The first is "marked by absence, coded or subterranean images or abject stereotypes"; the second, in the 1980s to 1990s, is informed by "social movements, by Hollywood niche marketing, by commodification, by disease," wherein queers were brought out of the closet and into the "highly problematic space of public spectacle"; and the third, most recent phase is that of "banal inclusion, normalization, assimilation, everyday unremarkable queerness, and of course continued abjection" (Walters 918). Doty argues that while representation of queers prior to the 1980s was minimal, there were queer elements and/or storylines that the queer eye could discern and take pleasure in. Queer elements, however, are not just pleasurable, but serve to highlight that seemingly heteronormative texts are "never entirely successful at supressing the complexities of sexual desire and gender identity" (Gamson 346). While it is important to remember that there was a time when queer people had to look for hidden or subtle queer readings within popular representations, the contemporary context contains numerous gay and lesbian and, to a lesser extent, bisexual and transgender characters and storylines. However, Raymond argues, "this new cultural phenomenon should not be uncritically valorized as an unambiguous symptom of heightened cultural tolerance and inclusion" (99). As a result, we need new approaches and forms of analysis for the vast number and different forms of queer representation currently available (Raymond).

Gamson's discussion of the two different approaches to queer representation is useful here: the minority model and the queering model. In brief, the minority model subscribes to the notion of identity as fixed and stable and promotes increased visibility of queer people as a fundamental means to improve their social standing and diminish discrimination (Gamson). The objective is to promote more positive representation, to increase visibility, and to challenge stereotypical representations that function to reinforce negative beliefs about queer people. The queer model is based in queer theory and as such views identities as fluid and multiple (Gamson). As a result, it is not sufficient to have positive images of queer people within mainstream heteronormative culture; the objective is to *queer* culture and disrupt heteronormativity. These two approaches emerged alongside the gay and lesbian rights movement and were responding not only to an increase in number but also a change in the form of representations of queers in various media (Gamson). Walters's more recent critique identifies two tropes that inform contemporary representations within popular culture, namely same-sex marriage and a resurgent biological essentialism through, for example, the embracing of slogans such as Lady Gaga's *Born This Way* (918). While the first of these appears to some as positive societal movement (though this is debated, and hence why I use *some*), the second is in stark contrast to the queer model and its objective of queering mainstream culture. Walters suggests that these tropes have led to media-friendly forms of representation that involve "an erasure of feminist and queer critique of gender normativity and the nuclear family" (919). Critically, she argues that the "mainstream visibility of the unthinkable possibility (gay marriage) hinges on mainstream invisibility of a more unthinkable possibility (feminist, queer families), and helps to bolster the liberal, assimilationist models of 'acceptance' and tolerance of queers" (Walters 919).

The *Baroness von Sketch Show* is a mainstream Canadian television show and is not identified or promoted as queer, but all of the troupe play queer characters in various skits and almost every episode involves a skit with some explicit queer content as well as more general queering effects. This was intentional, as the one queer identified member, Carolyn Taylor, articulates: "As a queer woman, it was very important to me that there be gay content" (Karr), in large part, Taylor argues, because it is "an aspect of female experience that is all-too-often glossed over, even in media coverage of the show" (Kuitenbrouwer). While comedic, the *Baroness von Sketch Show*'s playful queer critique is not about offering up more positive representations of queerness or making queers more palatable or normal for mainstream society. Rather, the show actively critiques heteronormativity, making visible everyday heteronormative social norms, and in doing so, ascribes to the notion that "queerness should challenge and confuse our understanding and usage of sexual and gender categories" (Doty xvii). This is supported by Onstad, who suggests in their *New York Times* review that "the series over all runs on a casual gender fluidity, where drag and gay characters are part of the comedy and an unabashed raunchiness often tilts queer." The show thus supports a universalizing lens, as the relationship between gender, sex and sexuality, and queer affect is positioned as "an issue of continuing, determinative importance" for all viewers, not only queer or LGBT audiences (Sedgwick 1). Further, inherent in this form of queer critique in the show is increased visibility of the intersection of race and, to a lesser extent, class and ability upon which heteronormative femininity depends (hooks; Skeggs).

It is notable that the show is produced by a national crown corporation, the CBC, and that Canada has a vested interest in promoting itself as a progressive liberal nation, in part through reference to LGBT rights (Rayter). There are undoubtedly elements of the show that can be read as contributing to this national mythology, but as several reviewers have articulated, *Baroness* often pushes the CBC out of its comfort zone and engages in a mockery of the normative middle-class white

Canadian. Notably, Kuitenbouwer states, "that this ground-breaking queer feminist comedy sketch show finds its home on the CBC, typically a platform for safe, bland comedy and drama, is the perfect paradox—proof that if you develop a show that trades on authenticity, and that celebrates the gritty, uncomfortable truth of women's lives, people will flock to it." Further, many skits engage directly with feminist killjoy moments (Ahmed), calling attention to sexual harassment, homophobia, violence against women, and institutional and everyday sexism. Feminists are "typically represented as grumpy and humourless," as unable to take a joke or receive a compliment, "often as a way of protecting the right to certain forms of social bonding," locker room talk, for example (Ahmed). When feminists draw attention to racist, sexist, transphobic, or ableist commentary or behaviours, they are said to *kill the joy* or ruin the happy occasion, thereby disrupting social relations. The resultant bad feelings are attributed to feminists, rather than the person and/or institution actively discriminating and causing harm (Ahmed). However, as I will demonstrate in an analysis of several skits, *Baroness* "manages to be wildly funny while enacting a form of social protest" (Kuitenbouwer) and blatantly disproves long-standing stereotypes that neither women nor lesbians are funny (Onstad).

THE COTTAGE

I begin with one of the show's most well-known skits, "The Cottage," as it is exemplary of both elements of critique that I argue are at play—or have potential in the show. "The Cottage" involves three scenes—morning, afternoon, and evening—of the first day that five white presumed urbanites are on retreat at a cottage for the weekend. The characters are the host heterosexual couple and their guests: a lesbian couple and another (potentially) single woman.

The opening scene features Brian (the husband) bringing out Caesars for everyone to drink at breakfast, and while there is some pause to consider whether it is too early to drink, the soon to be common refrain of the skit, *we're at the cottage*, entices everyone to take a glass. Happy to have convinced all of the women to have a drink, Brian says "Atta girls," to which one of the women retorts, "It's women." Her partner leans in and says to her, "Just let it slide, we're at the cottage." The refrain *at the cottage* thus comes to demarcate the space (and time) as one beyond or free from the oft-labelled common-sense, politically correct standards of everyday life: drinking anytime and not calling out derogatory comments. The heterosexual couple exchange a kiss, after which the lesbian couple look at each other somewhat sheepishly and then lean in for an awkward peck. Immediately, the husband/Brian reacts, saying "Oooh, okay." His wife shoots him a look, to which he responds, "I've only seen that in the movies. I'm sorry." What was already seemingly awkward has now become a focal moment of breakfast. The wife teasingly scolds Brian and then says to the lesbian couple, "I'm sorry, you kiss whenever you want, *we're at the cottage*." One of the women responds, completely deadpan, "Thank you for making me feel so comfortable in your home." The delivery of this comment makes evident that she feels exactly the opposite. This exchange is significant as it illustrates the inclusion of queerness as acceptable only within the confines "of the cottage" and connects queer intimacy with the other behaviours deemed abnormal in everyday life mentioned above. Further, the kiss is far from the lesbian fantasy Brian is undoubtedly referring to (I've only seen that in movies), such that even an attempt to act like the other couple present and exchange a morning kiss becomes both a stand-in for the stereotypical fantasy of two women kissing that heterosexual men are all presumed to desire, and is then granted permission only because they are "at the cottage." But rather than let the skit end the scene on that note, the queer gets the last word, asserting her discomfort. The use of discomfort and awkwardness in this scene is strategic and central to the troupe's comedic critique throughout the show. The effect of this, I suggest, is that the audience is made aware of the discomfort the couple experiences, and in this way the skit calls attention to the existence of heteronormativity. Rather than just being a skit that happens to include a lesbian couple as some of the characters and thereby normalizing the queer within mainstream television, this scene takes it a step further and calls attention to the discomfort experienced by queers within heteronormative society and intimate spaces (Raymond; Gamson).

The third scene in this skit, the evening, continues in this vein but offers a broader critique of a presumed heterosexual male fantasy. The five characters are all lounging, and the suggestion of going into the hot tub is offered up. Once again, the refrain *we're at the cottage* is invoked around the idea of smoking marijuana and of going naked in the hot tub, leading to a playful go-round about the unfolding evening: "have a little smoke-y"; "drink a little vodk-y"; "have a little soak-y." Brian/ the husband finishes this sequence by beginning to gyrate and state, "and then it's BOOM BOOM BOOM in the hot tub, BOOM BOOM BOOM in the hot tub, BOOM BOOM BOOM in the guacamole, BOOM BOOM BOOM in the chips," getting more pronounced in his movement with each refrain. Each of the women starts to react to his actions and it becomes quickly apparent that he is on his own with respect to the potential orgy he is imagining. When Brian notices the reactions, he says, "too far," to which the women all assert, "way too far." Brian/the husband tries to invoke *we're at the cottage*, but this time to no avail; the limitations of this space/the cottage are delineated and the heterosexual male fantasy is *off limits*.

Thus, while "The Cottage" begins by setting the stage that normal rules of engagement or socialization can be left at the door—*we're at the cottage*—it ends by asserting that there are limitations to allowable discretions or deviations. This scene functions to highlight the imposition of heterosexuals' discomfort and tolerance of queerness/queer intimacy on queer people and ridicules, albeit in great comedic fashion, the oft assumed willingness of women to satisfy male fantasies.

Further, the eccentric and exaggerated pronouncement *we're at the cottage* seems to playfully mock the white middle-upper-class settlers, portraying them as somewhat juvenile and insecure. The stage of the cottage is central to the skit, as the ability for white settlers to retreat to a cottage is only possible because of the displacement and forcible resettlement of Indigenous peoples across much of cottage country in Ontario. Cherie Dimaline documents these forced movements with respect to her family history, from Drummond Island to the shores of the bay near Penetanguishene to the now town of LaFontaine (Douglas). In this reading—and to be clear, the skit does not explicitly reference Indigenous peoples, treaties, or colonization—whiteness is, to some extent, made visible and odd. Dyer articulated that "representation of whiteness … in mainstream film is difficult partly because white power secures its dominance by seeming not to be anything in particular" (141), that is, whiteness is "invisible, everything and nothing" (146). In "The Cottage," whiteness is central to the characters and to the success and acceptance of the skit's narrative, and as a result it becomes—somewhat—visible.

GOLD STARS, GAY BOOK CLUB, AND GENDER ROLE PLAY

In several scenes, the *Baroness von Sketch Show* draws in queer viewers through the use of lesbian/queer explicit language and insider knowledge that not only are rare within mainstream popular culture, but also serve to grant queer viewers the last laugh, disrupting the dominance of heteronormativity for a moment. One scene, which is quite short, features two women chatting while cycling beside each other down the street. One woman asks, "So if a lesbian who has never slept with a man is called a gold star, a straight woman who has only slept with a man is …?" to which the other, presumably queer woman responds, "missing out," and then turns off the street onto another road. The reference to "gold star," a known—and not without contention—referent within queer lingo, is undoubtedly a shout out to queer viewers, but the playful assertion that there is not a comparable, positive concept for straight women who have only slept with men privileges queerness over heteronormativity. Moore's analysis of the Showtime series *The L Word* reveals that within several sex scenes in the first two seasons, straight sex is found "not to measure up" to queer sex. One of the scenes Moore cites involves Jenny, having watched through the fence two women have sex in the pool next door, recount the incident to her boyfriend, Tim, while he endeavours to keep pace with the sequence of events. Tim, however, cannot keep up. The other scene involves two characters, Alice and Dana, having sex and Alice's request for more fingers. Moore argues that the scene and request highlight the knowledge and ability of queer partners to meet their lovers' needs not only through providing more girth but also through the use of different positions and forms that challenge the primacy of the "penis as a primary tool for fucking" (139). I include a brief mention of Moore's analysis of these scenes here, as the "Gold Star" skit serves a similar function, but notably within the context of a non-queer-specific television show; in "Gold Star" queers are portrayed as desirable, whereas straight women are missing out.

In the skit "Gender Studies," which has a sequel in the third season, we are introduced to a comedic discussion of key concepts within queer theory by the reading of group members, some of whom are local Canadian queer celebrities. This skit features the group in the midst of discussion when the host's partner enters the room and initiates small talk with various forms of incorrect language, from calling it a "gay book club," to calling them girls, women, guys, and finally, folks. This skit seems delightfully intended for queer viewers, especially those of an academic and/or nerdy persuasion; how often does Butler get thrown around in conversation on mainstream television? The situating of this skit in the midst of several others in the episode, however, indicates that it is not intended *only* for queer viewers and that there is a creative effort to engage straight viewers in queer culture, as well as to illustrate the ability of queers to poke fun at them/ourselves. As an example, the skit involves a debate about whether it was the partner who called her lover "baby" because she got "unconsciously caught in the ideological crush of the linguistic grid" or if it was "Rachel who responded to the interpolating call of baby" who acted inappropriately. This skit thus represents both a queering of mainstream television by drawing attention to language and gender politics, as well as momentary normalization of queer content in an episode that features a range of issues and characters.

The show directly engages with stereotypes about queers that are typically found in mainstream media, including two skits that play on the gay friend dynamic, which engage in a comedic critique that privileges and normalizes queer experiences. The first, "Straight Women Who Flirt with a Lesbian," is from the first season and takes place in a bar. Two friends are chatting and one of them says that two of her friends from work will be joining them and not to judge them, as they don't know any gay people. The friends arrive and immediately the two women direct their focus on the "lesbian" friend, Trish, and endeavour to convince her that they are allies by telling her that they boycotted the Sochi Olympics. Two aspects of the dialogue are particularly noteworthy, as they illustrate the ridiculousness of the interaction—and ignorance of the straight women—but also because, by contrast, the queer appears normal and rational. In the first, Liz, one of the women, says, "If I could go back in time, I would totally be gay," to which Trish responds, "You don't have to go back in time, you can be gay now," causing Liz to laugh hysterically. The second begins with the other woman, Donna, coming up close to Trish and asking her if she wants to kiss her, to which Trish says no. The woman persists, saying, "Because I want you to know something, I am really fluid like that and I'm really open" (said with a push up of her chest toward Trish). Trish says again, "I don't want to kiss you," and Donna responds, "But if you wanted to, you could." Liz chimes in and mocks her friend, saying, "Donna, don't be an idiot, just because she's a lesbian doesn't mean she wants to kiss every woman in the bar." Sensing some acknowledgement, Trish thanks her, only to have Liz remark, "but you want to kiss me." While both of these moments are going on, Donna and Liz are both constantly moving; it is as if their bodies are buzzing, making them seem eccentric and a bit outlandish in their performance of straight sexuality. Donna and Liz are acting out common stereotypes and assumptions about gay people, which, it seems, they think will be perceived as progressive and supportive. The scene, however, almost comes across from a queer perspective, making visible the awkwardness and ignorance of this straight effort, and effectively disrupts any notion of queers as eccentric or abnormal.

The other skit, "Lesbian Friend," is in the third season and similarly draws attention to processes of othering that queers experience within everyday encounters. Walking along the street, a woman passes a friend from work who is with her mother, to whom the friend says, "Oh mum, this is my lesbian friend I was telling you about, remember." Upon hearing this, the lesbian friend says, "Well, I am a friend from work," and again, the woman says, "Yeah, my lesbian friend from work." The qualifier *lesbian* is obviously highlighted, suggesting that perhaps the friendship wouldn't exist if she weren't a lesbian and therefore of social cachet and/or value to the woman. Engaging with this dynamic, the lesbian friend says, "Oh okay, I am so sorry, I didn't realize we were doing introductions based on who we have sex with. Fun game, okay. Mrs. Thompson, you know Ellen [her daughter], but maybe you didn't know that she mostly dates guys that look exactly like her dad. I think it's weird, but you raised her, so what are you going to do? See you at work, gotta run," and leaves the two a bit stunned. This exchange is reminiscent of the Heterosexual Questionnaire, a series of questions that are typically asked of queer people, but in this instance are reversed and asked of heterosexual people, such as "What do you think caused your heterosexuality? Is it possible your heterosexuality is just a phase? Why do heterosexuals place so much emphasis on sex?" (Rochlin). This brief skit enacts this very reversal and highlights practices of othering by identifying someone based upon one aspect of their identity and their difference from the norm (read: white male heterosexual able-bodied middle-upper class), in this case being a lesbian. As with the questionnaire, the skit utilizes comedic effect to highlight this practice, making it both visible and tangible, but also more palatable; it is not an angry (though anger can be very productive) calling out of an offensive action but rather a reversed gesture that makes evident the ridiculousness of introducing someone "by who they have sex with."

A final example of explicit queering/queer content I want to discuss takes place in one of the skits in the episode "It's a Garment of Liberty," in season two. The skit is set in a park, where two separate couples sit on either side of a park bench, and opens with the queer couple exchanging a few kisses before showing a discussion taking place between the heterosexual couple across the bench about doing the dishes. The exchange, about equitable responsibility for domestic chores, is familiar; the woman says, "When your friends come over … I end up doing the dishes," to which the man replies, "That's why I bought you a dishwasher so it wouldn't be so hard." The discussion becomes a bit more heated; the woman states, "It would just be nice if you could help out more," and the man more assertively responds, "Honey, I bought you a dishwasher; I don't know what more I can do." The couple on the other side of the bench stop kissing and, looking a bit exacerbated by the unfolding conversation, one of them gently says, "Um excuse me, I don't mind if you engage in heteronormative gender role play, but do you have to do it out here in the park?" The other partner adds in, "Yeah, maybe keep it for the privacy of your own home," to which a final comment is made by the queer couple: "There's children here." Like the short skit referenced above, this one directly calls attention to heteronormativity and reverses the ascriptions of "abnormal" and "deviant," typically made about queer people, onto the heterosexual couple. Viewers are tricked, as what is undoubtedly a very familiar debate about domestic chores between heterosexual couples becomes, in this skit, "gender role play" and thought to be indecent for public audiences, turning this familiar interaction on its head and marking it as abnormal and perverse. Again, this critique of heteronormativity is strategically done using comedic effect, so that audiences are not at first aware of the depth of the critique, laughing at the absurdity of a common debate being cast into the place usually held by queer couples, wherein abnormal, deviant behaviours should be kept hidden within the privacy of their homes. After all, it was not so long ago that a queer kiss on mainstream television required a warning before its airing, whereas heterosexual intimacy was deemed acceptable and viewable (Skerski). Thus, the intimacy—kisses—between the queer couple adds weight and sets the appropriate stage for the critique of heteronormativity the skit enacts.

QUEERING NORMATIVE WHITE FEMININITY

I now turn the focus of my analysis of the *Baroness von Sketch Show* to another aspect of its queering potential, namely its eccentric and exaggerated representation of normative white femininity. The skits "Dry Shampoo" and "Red Wine Ladies" are two of the show's most well known and are illustrative of my argument about heterosexual femininity. Following this, I will end the chapter with a discussion of their skit on yoga in the episode "It's a Garment of Liberty," which offers the show's most direct and pointed critique of whiteness.

"Dry Shampoo" features a group of white women who regularly meet for lunch, seemingly set up as a toned-down play on the regular friend lunches on the HBO show *Sex and the City*. The skit unfolds over several different lunches, with the increasing absurdity of one character's behaviour as she arrives late to meet the other women. Her lateness is attributed each time to a different personal incident, which intensifies with each rendition, from catching her husband cheating, to legal battles surrounding the ensuing divorce, to her personal retreat into the woods and encounter with a bear, to, finally, her husband taking custody of their children. The friends' astonishment at each new proclamation is followed by a compliment on how great her hair looks, leading the woman to declare her secret, dry shampoo. The woman in question has long brown hair with perfect soft curls that cascade over her shoulders and down her back—a central feature of ideal feminine beauty (Bordo). The increasing intensity of the woman's personal situation is matched by the corresponding intensity of the size of her hair and pronouncement of her love of dry shampoo to the extent that, in the final scene, she pulls out two cans and continuously sprays the area around her hair while bellowing. The comedic message of the skit is that, when life is too busy for you to have a moment to yourself, to take care of yourself, there is dry shampoo to help you out. The undercurrent to this is that above all else, women's appearance is of utmost importance; even when life is falling apart all around you, you can have great-looking hair. While the skit could be said to offer a mild critique of the beauty demands of femininity (Bartky), I think there is a further element about whiteness at play. Similar in some ways to my critique of "The Cottage" earlier, this scene works in many ways *because* the women are all white. The intersection of class—they are all able to meet regularly for lunches with each other, illustrating flexible work schedules and/or leisure time—with race is central to the performance of heterosexual femininity within the skit. Caucasian standards of beauty continue to inform representations of ideal femininity that dominate mainstream media, which reinforces historical constructions of femininity as unattainable for women of colour and working-class women (Banks; Bordo; hooks; Rice; Skeggs). While race is not directly referenced, my reading suggests that white heterosexual femininity is the focus of the skit's ridicule, casting it as eccentric and exaggerated and yet with an air of familiarity about the love and commitment many women have for their beauty products (Bartky; Bordo).[2]

"Red Wine Ladies," similar to "Dry Shampoo," features the four white women out at a restaurant, though instead of having lunch, this time it is a girls' night out. The skit, which has another iteration in the second season, follows the women's conversation and interaction over the evening and multiple bottles of wine. As the women toast each other with their first glass, they say, "To us and those who want to be like us, us, us, us," as they look each other in the eyes, saying "eyes, eyes, eyes." The dialogue includes disdain and frustration at being a mother, drunken assessment of the quality of the wine, declarations of love for each other, and playful mocking of one of their efforts to flirt with the waiter while wearing Spanx for a dress. This skit could easily just be read as a silly or humorous depiction of the four women getting progressively drunker, but I think there is more going on. The opening refrain, "To us and those who want to be us," stands in contradiction to the ensuing silly, insecure, and somewhat awkward behaviour, but is also revealing of the women's racial and class status. Skeggs argues that for working-class women, ascriptions of *carer* or *mother* are avenues to respectability, and similarly, clothing choices are far from trivial; rather, they reflect knowledge about distinctions between "style and fashion, between looking good and looking tarty, between looking feminine and looking sexy" and involve substantial labour (103). In "Red Wine Ladies" both of these key attributes and/or means to access respectability are playfully mocked—being a mother is lamented and one is able to wear a supportive undergarment as one's outfit without scrutiny or social sanction. The skit's success is tied to a normative construction of femininity that is race and class specific, but this construction is also highlighted and made visible, at first by being presented as secure and desired—"To us and those who want to be us"—but then, as the skit unfolds, is found somewhat eccentric and ridiculous.

The final skit I want to discuss I will call "Yoga," as it features a yoga class and is the show's most obvious and direct critique of whiteness. In brief, the skit opens with the four main characters preparing for a yoga class at the back of the studio room when a presumed South Asian woman enters and sets up her mat in the middle of their row. Immediately, the four women assume that she is the teacher and begin copying her warm-up stretches. Confident in their assumption, the women take turns addressing this woman; from applauding her wisdom and teaching style of being in amongst the students, to sharing how wonderful and inspiring one of their trips to India was, to thanking her for her presence in the space. The assumption that she is not from Canada—that she is potentially from India, is apparent in this exchange and serves as a referent for the common racist practice of asking people of colour where they are from, thereby demarcating that they are not *from here*. This form of questioning functions to secure Canada as a white nation that racial "Others" have immigrated to and makes invisible settler relations of forced occupation and displacement of Indigenous peoples. In response to the white woman referencing her four-day trip to India, the woman says, "I'm from Brampton," while looking somewhat confused by the attention and assumptions the white women are enacting. The white woman cannot register that she has referenced a suburb of Toronto and is steadfast in her belief that she is from India, and so replies, "Oh I didn't make it that far south," as if Brampton is in India. Beginning to catch on as the actual teacher (a white woman) arrives, the woman is asked by one of the women if she offers private lessons, to which she responds with a bit of a smirk, "Sure, twenty bucks, out back." The skit is not subtle or indirect in its mocking of whiteness, in particular white middle-upper-class femininity, of which appropriation of yoga has become quite a central feature. Similar to the show's critiques of heteronormativity, this skit represents the white women as ignorant and slightly ridiculous yuppies, and through them offers a satire of white femininity. While this skit is the most obvious in its portrayal of cultural appropriation and white middle-upper-class women's ignorance self-imagined as enlightened and/or progressive politics, the show sustains a critique throughout its three seasons of normative femininity, and notably the centrality of whiteness to that ideal. In Munoz's introduction to *Disidentifications*, he states that the fact that the vast majority of publications in queer studies "treat race as an addendum, if at all, indicates that there is something amiss" (11). Extending his analysis to popular culture, arguably the same could be said with respect to the vast majority of queer popular culture; race is treated as an addendum, if represented at all. Within the *Baroness von Sketch Show*, the few characters of colour appear to be *add-ons*, playing supporting and not central characters. Instead, the show's focus with respect to a racial analysis appears—thus far—to have been a purposeful and sustained parody of white femininity.

The *Baroness von Sketch Show* has become one of the CBC's most successful shows, which, given that it is an all-female comedy troupe that engages with degrees of feminist critique, makes it worth paying attention to. There are numerous examples that make the show stand out and consumable for a range of viewers, from humorous calling out of sexist advertising to the online dating *dick pic* phenomenon. This chapter has argued that while the cast and topics they engage with are noteworthy on their own, it is the show's well-crafted comedic critique that lends itself to a queering potential. Strategies of reversal in the "Lesbian Friend" and "Gender Role Play" skits, eccentric and exaggerated representations of whiteness, and incorporating queer language and politics make visible dynamics that are often invisible and/or left out of mainstream popular culture. The show features four white women enacting characters and/or storylines of white middle-upper-class women, something that is undeniably all too commonplace on television. Within that context, I suggest that there are queering moments, moments that disrupt stereotypes and representations of queers and moments that mock white femininity in ways that make it tangible and visible. My hope for season four is that the troupe will take this potential further, de-centring whiteness in ways they have so effectively de-centred heterosexuality.

CRITICAL REFLECTION QUESTIONS

1. How might *queering* mainstream television act both as a means of resistance and as a way to co-opt or popularize queer aesthetics and politics?
2. Is the *Baroness von Sketch Show*'s strategy of making whiteness visible as central to the ideal of femininity in mainstream media effective or does it re-centre whiteness?
3. Identify another Canadian series that represents queer characters. Taking an intersectional approach, consider how this compares to *Baroness*.

NOTES

1. Of importance, my argument about the queering potential of the show refers to the critique of heteronormativity and heteronormative white femininity. In some skits, cast members dress up and act as characters of another sex, which, in my reading as a cis settler queer woman, is done to highlight everyday sexism and critique normative masculinity (notably, cat-calling by male construction workers). However, these representations of (assumed) cis-identified women dressing up as another sex could be read as cissexist and transphobic. In addition, my argument about the queering potential of making whiteness visible is inherently tied to my positionality as a white settler.

2.   It is important to note the significant relationship of hair to one's gendered identities within both Black and queer communities. Banks's work, as well as many others, argues that for Black women, what is deemed desirable with respect to hair is "measured against white standards of beauty" (2; see also Johnson). For queer women, hair is often critically tied to visibility as a lesbian/queer woman, notably short and androgynous in style (Jones; Rooke). Black and/or queer women are defined against the hairstyles associated with white middle-class femininity portrayed in "Dry Shampoo."

WORKS CITED

Ahmed, Sara. *The Promise of Happiness.* Duke UP, 2010.

Banks, Ingrid. *Hair Matters: Beauty, Power, and Black Women's Consciousness.* New York UP, 2000.

Baroness von Sketch Show. Canadian Broadcasting Corporation, 2016.

Bartky, Sandra. "Foucault, Femininity, and the Modernization of Patriarchal Power." *Writing on the Body: Female Embodiment and Feminist Theory*, edited by Katie Conboy et al., Columbia UP, 1997, pp. 129–154.

Bordo, Susan. *Unbearable Weight: Feminism, Western Culture and the Body.* University of California Press, 1993.

Butler, Judith. *Gender Trouble: Feminism and the Subversion of Identity.* Routledge, 1990.

Doty, Alexander. *Making Things Perfectly Queer: Interpreting Mass Culture.* Minnesota UP, 1993.

Douglas, Carla. "Indigenous Writers in Canada: Interview with Author Cherie Dimaline." *Publishing Perspectives*, 3 Nov. 2017, https://publishingperspectives.com/2017/11/indigenous-writers-canada-interview-author-cherie-dimaline/. Accessed 7 Feb. 2019.

Dyer, Richard. *The Matter of Images: Essays on Representation.* Routledge, 1993.

Gamson, Joshua. "Sweating in the Spotlight: Lesbian, Gay and Queer Encounters with Media and Popular Culture." *Handbook of Lesbian and Gay Studies*, edited by Diane Richardson and Steven Seidman, Sage, 2003, pp. 339–354.

hooks, bell. *Black Looks: Race and Representation.* South End Press, 1992.

Johnson, Elizabeth. *Resistance and Empowerment in Black Women's Hair Styling.* Ashgate Publishing, 2013.

Jones, Lucy. "'The Only Dykey One': Constructions of (In)Authenticity in a Lesbian Community Practice." *Journal of Homosexuality*, vol. 58, no. 6–7, 2011, pp. 719–741.

Karr, Andrea. "The Women of the Baroness von Sketch Show: Our Most Embarrassing Moments." *Canadian Living*, 21 July 2016. https://www.canadianliving.com/life-and-relationships/culture-and-entertainment/article/

the-women-of-baroness-von-sketch-show-our-most-embarrassing-moments. Accessed 5 July 2019.

Kuitenbouwer, Kathryn. "The Viral Appeal of Baroness Von Sketch." *The Walrus*, 28 July 2016. https://thewalrus.ca/the-viral-appeal-of-baroness-von-sketch. Accessed 5 July 2019.

Moore, Lisa. "Getting Wet: The Heteroflexibility of Showtime's *The L Word*." *Third Wave Feminism and Television: Jane Puts It in a Box*, edited by M. L. Johnson and I. B. Taurus, 2007, pp. 119–146.

Munoz, Jose Esteban. *Disidentifications: Queers of Color and the Performance of Politics.* University of Minnesota Press, 1999.

Onstad, Katrina. "The Baronesses Are Coming! And Filling a Comedy Gender Gap." *The New York Times*, 28 July 2017. https://www.nytimes.com/2017/07/28/arts/television/the-baronesses-are-coming-and-filling-a-comedy-gender-gap.html. Accessed 5 July 2019.

Raymond, Diane. "Popular Culture and Queer Representation: A Critical Perspective." *Gender, Race, and Class in Media: A Text-Reader*, 2nd edition, edited by Gail Dines and Jean M. Humez, Sage, 2002, pp. 98–110.

Rayter, Scott. "Introduction: Thinking Queerly About Canada." *Queerly Canadian: An Introductory Reader in Sexuality Studies*, edited by Maureen FitzGerald and Scott Rayter, Canadian Scholars' Press, 2012.

Rice, Carla. "Out from Under Occupation: Transforming Our Relationship with Our Bodies." *Canadian Woman Studies*, vol. 14, no. 3, 1994, pp. 44–51.

Rochlin, Martin. "The Heterosexual Questionnaire." *Gender and Women's Studies in Canada: Critical Terrain*, edited by Margaret Hobbs and Carla Rice, Canadian Scholars' Press, 2013, pp. 197–198.

Rooke, Alison. "Navigating Embodied Lesbian Cultural Space: Toward a Lesbian Habitus." *Space and Culture*, vol. 10, no. 2, 2007, pp. 231–252.

Sedgwick, Eve Kosofsky. *Epistemology of the Closet*. University of California Press, 1990.

Skeggs, Beverly. *Formations of Class and Gender: Becoming Respectable*. Sage, 1997.

Skerski, Jaime. "From Prime-Time to Daytime: The Domestication of Ellen Degeneres." *Communication and Critical/Cultural Studies*, vol. 4, no. 4, 2007, pp. 363–381.

Walters, Suzanne Danuta. "The Kids Are Alright but the Lesbians Aren't: Queer Kinship in US Culture." *Sexualities*, vol. 15, no. 8, 2012, pp. 917–933.

PART III

IN SHINING ARMOUR: COPS, ROBBERS, AND SUPERHEROES

CHAPTER 7

The Case of the Missing Detectives: Canadian Crime Films and the Absent Female Sleuth

Andrea Braithwaite and Olga Marques

INTRODUCTION

Canadian crime films and characters can shape how we understand issues like national identity, gendered power dynamics, and crime. Canadian pop culture seems full of female investigators. Professor and sleuth Joanna Kilbourn has appeared in Gail Bowen's series of bestselling novels, the officers on Global TV's hit *Rookie Blue* (2010–2015) cop drama were predominantly women, and CBC's *Frankie Drake Mysteries* (2017–present) follows Toronto's first female private eye and her crime-solving colleague, Trudy, through Hogtown's Roaring Twenties. Yet such figures are absent from mass-market Canadian crime films. This lack of representation has significant implications for what crime and justice mean in Canadian media culture. What roles *do* women play in Canadian crime films when they aren't represented as agents of justice? In the contemporary Canadian films *Bon Cop, Bad Cop*; *Bon Cop, Bad Cop 2*; *Gunless*; and *No Clue*, crimes revolve around their female characters but cannot be resolved by them. These are more than just fictional storylines in feature films. They present, represent, and reiterate persistent understandings about crime, victims, and vengeance—*gendered* and *raced* understandings.

The roles women play in crime films go hand in hand with our ability—or inability—to account for the full range of gendered violence in contemporary Canadian culture. As Homi Bhabha reminds us, we can see "nation as a form of narrative—textual strategies, metaphoric displacements, sub-texts and figurative strategems" (2). By exploring how crime films function as forms of knowledge production, we can learn more about how they contribute to our understandings of Canada and Canadian culture. Canada's past and present cultural policies make this connection clear: Canadian film is frequently envisioned as a vehicle for presenting Canada to itself and to the world. In recent popular Canadian crime films, these representations are also often organized around gendered experiences of crime and justice. They offer audiences leading men whose masculinity is defined by their heterosexuality—by their desires more than their actions. These desires are complemented by female characters who are most often assigned the role—and identity—of victim. Those who aren't victims become nearly unknowable as women, because they do not conform to common pop culture stereotypes of appropriate femininity. Such "metaphoric displacements" (Bhabha 2) also make it more difficult to recognize Canada's most vulnerable populations. In these ways, contemporary Canadian crime films (re)produce a limited and limiting vision of gender, race, and justice.

CRIME FILMS AS KNOWLEDGE PRODUCTION

Pop culture can have far-reaching influences on public understandings of crime and criminal justice. Its dramatic and stylized representations of policing and the criminal justice process have changed how the public perceives police investigations and criminal trials to proceed. While all media forms depict criminal justice and incarceration, film is many people's primary source of information about these topics (Rafter 417). Crime films are an important area of study, as they reflect, refract, and shape popular notions about crime and also serve as an arena for public discussions about crime and as a nexus illuminating points of dissention in society.

The media is fascinated by crime and criminal justice. In Canada in particular, crime fictions frequently display a "preoccupation with law and order, which reflects the long-standing notion that Canada was founded on an ethic of 'peace, order, and good government'" (Sloniowski and Rose xiii). In the absence of actual lived experience or educational knowledge of crime (through the study of criminology, for instance) media representations are often the only exposure that the average person has to the criminal justice system and its processes (Welsh et al. 459). The media is therefore critical in shaping the public's views, perceptions, and understandings of criminal justice and incarceration (Muraskin and Domash; Surette), and is a central source of information when people formulate opinions about criminal justice practices and policies. For example, representations of race in crime films help cultivate societal beliefs of, and a culture of fear around, an "inherently" violent Black culture, which has paved the way for zero-tolerance policing and other practices like identity checks that disproportionately target Black males (Covington).

Media representations can also shape and inform public sentiment on, and heighten fear of, crime (Dowler; Muraskin and Domash; van den Bulk). Media representations affect our interpretations of crime as a social problem (Pfeiffer et al.), in part by depicting certain types of crime as commonplace, such as violent crimes perpetrated by strangers, regardless of the dearth of such events in actual crime data (Muraskin and Domash). And despite significantly lower crime and victimization rates, Canadians express more fear of crime than their American counterparts (Dowler et al. 839). These patterns in our perceptions of, and beliefs about, crime and justice speak to the influence that media representations—whether information or entertainment—have in shaping the ways we understand and experience our social worlds. Whether fictional or based on actual accounts of criminal events, representations of crime across media sources often blur boundaries between fiction and reality, and can cultivate fraught, even inaccurate, perceptions of crime, victims, and criminals (Cuklanz and Moorti; Gerbner).

LEGISLATING CANADIAN FILMS AS DISTINCT

Canada's past and present cultural policies also see a connection between media representations and the ways we think or feel—in this case, the ways we think or feel about Canada. Ryan Edwardson refers to Canada's long history of legislating media as Canadianization: "turning a federation into a nation" (5). Canadian media, including film, has long been charged with acting as points of cultural difference between Canada and the United States: examples of national sensibilities as well as protections against American influence.

These anxieties have been particularly pronounced when it comes to film. The foundational 1951 Massey Report, for instance, decries American media for its "inferior cultural standards" (47). The culmination of a two-year inquiry into the state of the arts in Canada at the time, the Massey Report—formally known as the Royal Commission on National Development in the Arts, Letters and Sciences—articulates some key concerns about American media's reach and popularity, and about the role that film could and should play in Canada's own media landscape. Its conviction that films offer their audiences useful material for making sense of, and identifying with, the world around them was crystallized in the 1950 National Film Act, which directed Canada's National Film Board (NFB) to "produce and distribute and to promote the production and distribution of films designed to interpret Canada to Canadians and to other nations" (National Film Board of Canada).

As the Massey Report makes clear, however, only certain *kinds* of films should be used for these purposes. In order to maintain Canada's cultural specificity, the

Massey Report stands behind the NFB and its prioritization of the documentary form, arguing that "only a national organization protects the nation from excessive commercialization and Americanization" (58; see also Gittings). In comparison, today's media and media policy discourse demonstrate cultural industrialism: "treating culture as a commodity" (Edwardson 20). This is reflected in an increased emphasis on commercial viability in Canada's cultural policies. The economic realities of living in Hollywood's shadow necessitate a close attention to potential strategies for attracting an audience both domestically and internationally. As Edwardson explains, "Cultural activities were increasingly conceptualized and operationalized in accordance with industrial precepts.... Much of the content coming out of cultural industrialism, then, was made as similar as possible to foreign works in order to make it of interest to distributors" (242). Canadian audiences have become habituated to American filmmaking and film genres; Canadian inflections of these now-familiar forms are an increasingly common strategy. Another, as Edwardson describes, is the use of a high-profile Canadian actor, a "model that emphasized celebrities, marketing, name recognition, and so forth in selling Canadian content" (244).

We can see these approaches in many of the films discussed here. *Gunless* (a western starring Paul Gross, star of the hit TV series *Due South*, among many other film and TV projects); *Bon Cop, Bad Cop* and *Bon Cop, Bad Cop 2* (buddy films featuring Quebec film and TV mainstay Patrick Huard and Stratford Festival regular Colm Feore); and *No Clue* (a film noir spoof with comedian and TV star Brent Butt) all situate successful Hollywood genres within a Canadian context and use Canadian celebrities as part of their presumed appeal. They are also all, more broadly, crime films: "films that explore as a central theme crime and its consequences in Canadian society" (Kohm et al. 3). To do so, these films frequently draw upon established crime genre conventions, including common discourses of gender, race, and power.

REPRESENTING GENDER AND RACE IN CRIME FILMS

In pop culture, women victims are frequently blamed or made responsible for their own victimization if they fall outside hegemonic, patriarchal, classed, white, Victorian visions of the *ideal victim*. This is especially true for women victims of sexual violence, whose background, appearance, sexual history, and actions afterwards are frequently subjected to media and public scrutiny. *The Accused* is one of the most infamous film narratives of victim-blaming; a narrative pattern that remains familiar 30 years later in, for instance, Canadian media coverage of radio personality Jian Ghomeshi, charged with four counts of sexual assault and one count of overcoming resistance by choking. He was acquitted on all charges, not because it was determined that the alleged attacks did not happen (given the legal threshold of guilt "beyond a reasonable doubt") but rather because of the actions and demeanour of the alleged victims during the alleged timeframe of the attacks, in the time/years afterwards, and at trial, as well as their "lack of reliability and credibility" (Kingston). As Ken Dowler, Thomas Fleming, and Stephen L. Muzzatti explain, our understanding of an event as *criminal* and therefore of a woman as a *true* victim is "contingent on the victim's social status: victims must be judged as innocent, virtuous, and honourable" (841). We also see this in "missing white woman syndrome" (Sommers 278): cases of (attractive) white women and girls who have gone missing receive greater news media coverage and coverage intensity than racialized women and girls. In Canada, much attention has been drawn to the lack of media coverage (and when present, the prominence of tropes of "respectability" and "degeneracy") of missing and murdered Indigenous women and girls in general, and serial killer Robert Pickton's murders of six Indigenous women specifically (Jiwani and Young 895).

Popular films also often rely upon racialized and gendered representations of those who work in the criminal justice system. For instance, Black police officers are significantly less likely to play the lead "heroic cop" role in cop films (Wilson and Henderson). Black cops are instead most often portrayed as sidekicks, buddies, or comedic relief—from early examples like *Beverly Hills Cop* to more recent films like *Cop Out* (Gates; Wilson and Henderson). When they *do* appear as central crime fighters, like in the *Bad Boys* franchise, Black cops are often represented as professionalized and polished at work, and as dedicated family men at home—to contain and subdue Black male sexuality and masculinity (Ames; Gates; Sexton).

Portrayals of women in policing often maintain and reiterate hegemonic masculinity and femininity. Tracking representations of women cops across pop culture, Cara E. Rabe-Hemp argues that "depictions of women in masculine roles violate collective gendered beliefs and are commonly dealt with by presenting women either as villainous, weak, and insane" or alternately "as caretakers and not 'real' cops" (134). Similarly, Neal King, in his analysis of cop films, finds that women are visually excluded from the most serious forms of police combat. Sherrie A. Inness highlights how hints of women's toughness or strength in pop culture are routinely mitigated by an overwhelming narrative attention to the relationships these women have with men, and a heightened emphasis on their sexuality and femininity. These limited and gendered representations pervade contemporary Canadian crime films as well. In these films, women serve in only a handful of capacities: as an actual or potential sex partner, a likely victim of crime, and/or a mysterious "Other."

SWOON-WORTHY HEROES

Both *Bon Cop, Bad Cop* (*BCBC*) and *Bon Cop, Bad Cop 2* (*BCBC2*) use women to visually and narratively remind the audience of the male protagonists' virility. This is a common trope in buddy cop films, which spend most of their time showcasing the increasingly close and caring relationship between the two male leads (see Ames; Fuchs). Women appear primarily as reassurance that these heroes are properly heterosexual and therefore properly masculine (King). In the *BCBC* films, they also help establish the particular *kinds* of masculinity of each protagonist, encouraging us to see regional differences as cultural ones as well (Braithwaite 137).

For instance, part of how we understand David Bouchard as not just a cop but as a *Quebecker* is through his gleeful lasciviousness—a stereotype rooted in early and pulpy Hollywood films about Canada (Berton). While still friendly with his ex-wife, Suzie, "les filles" (other women) are part of Suzie's litany of reasons why the two of them are no longer married. This distinguishes him from staid Ontario officer Martin Ward, who is single because he is so unexciting that his ex-wife left him for another man. Although Ward appears interested in Suzie, we never see the two of them alone together; Bouchard, meanwhile, goes home with Ward's sister, Iris, for some exuberant and bilingual sex.

Iris has no further role in the film afterwards, one of the many ways *BCBC* reminds us that its protagonists are both deeply (hetero)sexy men. Most of the women in minor roles have a hard time keeping their cool around either Bouchard or Ward; the administrative assistant at a private airport can barely stop smiling at Bouchard long enough to check her records for the information he seeks, while a bartender, Rita, makes numerous sexual overtures to Ward moments after he walks in. That these characters' primary function is sexual is reinforced by the coroner's offhanded comment when Rita is found dead: he notes that Rita backwards sounds like "elle tire" (she pulls)—a Quebec colloquialism for sex work.

BCBC2 continues this pattern. Bouchard is now working undercover in a car theft ring that uses a strip club as its business front; the mise-en-scène regularly comprises nameless, faceless women engaged in an array of sexualized performances. Although Bouchard has reconciled with Suzie, his work keeps them apart, and when they do manage to sneak in a video call, the parts to which we are privy verge on explicit as the couple share their fantasies—a reminder that even though Bouchard has settled down he is still the same rapacious Quebecker we met in the first film.

Sexual fantasies serve a similar purpose in *No Clue*. As part of its satire, hero Leo Falloon lacks the confidence and charisma of film noir figures but still ends up captivated by Kyra, a beautiful, enigmatic woman claiming to need his help and protection. She is searching for her brother, Miles, and worries he might be in danger; her eyes well up with tears and her bottom lip quivers as she confesses her fears. Leo is drawn to this damsel in distress and promises to help and, despite being a salesman of advertising tchotchkes, he doesn't correct Kyra's assumption that he's a private eye in order to spend more time with her. While he insists to his friend Ernie that "she just seemed genuinely lost, like she really needed help," he starts and ends the conversation with breathless descriptions of her appearance: "She's unbelievable. A stone cold gorgeous dish full of red hot fox meat that was set under a hottie lamp until it was smokin'" and "She isn't pretty, she's a smoldering tower of nuclear hottitude."

Leo is not only powerfully attracted to Kyra, but also to the potential for heroic deeds that the role of detective promises. The film noir narrative is often "structured around a testing of the hero's prowess … how he measures up to more extensive standards of masculine competence" (Krutnik 86). While Leo may not appear to have these traditional trappings of film noir masculinity—he panics and bolts at the sight of broken glass and blood, and he tries to postpone the investigation so that he doesn't lose his spot in his building's laundry room schedule—his intense sexual desire for Kyra reminds the audience that he is still a "real man," a heterosexual man.

DAMSELS IN DISTRESS

Leo's desire for Kyra also creates a connection between them that amplifies the emotional impact of Kyra's victimization. Although Kyra appears frightened and helpless when she first appears in Leo's office, he soon discovers she is actually an accomplished professional thief searching for her mark and not her brother. When he spies her efficiently dispatching a rival in a dark alleyway, his anxiety about her behaviour is so powerful he can't stop himself from vomiting. These seemingly askew gender roles—the violent woman and vulnerable man—are righted during the film's climax, which returns Kyra to the role of victim.

Kyra's clever strategizing and physical prowess, on display throughout the first half of the film and key to her years of success as a professional thief, somehow vanish when she and Leo spy a crooked cop escaping on a yacht under cover of darkness. Gun tucked into her belt, she slips into the water and swims out to the boat; she is too busy searching the ship to be stealthy and is easily overwhelmed when her gun doesn't work. Her combat skills, once so effective they made Leo nauseous, seem to have deserted her. This inevitable, if improbable, vulnerability offers Leo the opportunity to save the day. His salesman knowledge of lesser-quality key fobs proves useful when he tosses the cop's keys overboard and they quickly sink, buying them enough time to be rescued and giving him the status of noir hero, for "it is through his accomplishment of a crime-related quest that the hero consolidates his masculine identity" (Krutnik 86). This experience also seems to change Kyra's plans for her future: she decides to leave thieving behind in order to stay in Vancouver with Leo, a choice flagged as both transformative and romantic when Frank Sinatra's "Look at Me Now" swells in the background.

Jane, the feisty female lead in 2010's *Gunless* undergoes a similar transition from impudent to imperiled. A woman working alone on the Canadian frontier, Jane is fiercely determined to make her fledgling farm a success. When the Montana Kid shows up, bedraggled from a run-in with the gang of American outlaws on his trail and looking for a new gun to use in retribution, Jane offers him the broken one she has in storage in exchange for his help erecting a windmill. She has no patience for his personal vendetta and places little stock in his tales of a life of violence; while he works off his debt she insists he behave like an upstanding member of this new settlement.

We learn more about Jane's past when the Montana Kid finds her on her rooftop after a frustrating day of setbacks setting up an irrigation system. She confesses she feels safe there: the rooftop used to be her refuge from her husband, who would often get drunk and abusive. When he eventually decided that she was "not worth the effort to beat," he simply left. Like *No Clue*, *Gunless* deliberately devises an emotional denouement that relies upon women's victimization. While the absence of Jane's husband could be explained in any number of ways—perhaps he set out to find his fortune in the gold rush or perished due to illness or injury—the choice to script him as an abusive alcoholic ensures that Jane is understood first and foremost as a victim.

This framing also sets up the film's climax, in which the gang of American outlaws eventually track down the Montana Kid and threaten to start slaughtering townsfolk unless he gives himself up. Jane, determined to protect her community, picks up the pistol he had been fixing and strides off to face the gang's leader—an instance of the "unexpected twist" trope used to explain women wielding guns in Western movies (Billson). Afraid for her safety, the Montana Kid intervenes and argues for a non-violent resolution; the outlaw quickly tires of such grandstanding and proclaims that Jane "ain't worth the bullet," echoing the words of her abusive husband. While the Montana Kid's impassioned plea that Jane is indeed worth a bullet is played for laughs, this scene is telling for its inadvertent honesty about the worth of women to crime stories: their narrative significance lies in their shootability. In this genre, women are worth more dead or dying than they are as active agents in how their stories unfold.

THE UNKNOWABLE WOMAN

Not all women make genre-appropriate victims. Just as crime films are often concerned with constructing particular masculinities, they also rely upon specific kinds of femininity as well, and women who fall outside of the kinds of femininities we are used to seeing in heroines and victims become unreadable and unknowable *as* women. The women in the films discussed here have a few key characteristics in common: Suzie, Iris, Kyra, and Jane are all white, blonde, slender, and well-off. Even with the differences in genre (buddy cop films, film noir, western) and in the stories' time periods (from the mid-1800s to the early 2000s), what it means to be a woman—and to be a victim—is imagined in remarkably consistent ways.

Other prominent female characters help establish ideas of appropriate and inappropriate femininities through their differences from the heroines. *No Clue* features Reese Horne, the daughter of video games magnate Terrance Horn. In a clear nod to film noir's characteristic femme fatale—"a mysterious, alluring, enigmatic female character … who poses a threat to the male protagonist, using her sexual powers to entrap and lure him to his downfall"—Reese drinks martinis, chain-smokes, and makes her sexual interest in Leo explicit (Kuhn and Westwall 158). She easily adapts her persona to her surroundings: coquettish when she's in a sleazy dive bar, paranoid and defensive when she's at her father's office, flirtatious and possessive when other women are around. These traits combine to mark Reese as outside the borders of acceptable or attractive femininity: her demanding, changeable behaviour is presented as too much for Leo, especially in comparison to Kyra's more conventional appearance and concerns.

Alternative forms of femininity appear in *BCBC2* as well. Now working for the RCMP, Ward has a team of experts at his disposal—including tech guru MC. Brash and crude, her ribald jokes often make as little sense to Bouchard and Ward as the technical issues she deftly handles. Their confusion at her demeanour and at her facility with technology is conveniently assuaged when MC unexpectedly discloses her doctor's diagnosis that she has unusually high levels of testosterone. This changes the tone of Bouchard and Ward's responses: from two older men unfamiliar and perhaps uncomfortable with women excelling at historically male-dominated fields to a validation of their discomfort with her behaviour by suggesting it's so "unfeminine" it may actually be a result of biologically male hormones.

Much like how the Montana Kid's argument that Jane is "worth shooting" is presented as comedic, MC's revelation of her hormone test results is also a punchline. This framing explicitly reduces a spectrum of sex and gender identifications down to an exclusionary binary: masculinity versus femininity. Characters like MC and Reese are "othered" in this way—exceeding (and reifying) the boundaries of culturally acceptable femininity. This sort of othering—"good" and "bad" femininities—stands in for the actual diversity of Canadian women and obscures important issues like race and class. In *Gunless*, for instance, those at the greatest risk of assault, abuse, and a violent death are the predominantly Chinese itinerant railway workers. Travelling great distances for low-paying, highly hazardous work, these labourers—and, as in *Gunless*, their families—were often reviled on the basis of race and treated as less than human. In *Gunless*, they (not Jane) experience multiple forms of physical violence on screen and are in the most immediate peril during the climactic shootout; one is even strung up to be hung. And yet the narrative focuses on Jane's past abuse and present potential danger as the most affective; the threat to the town's Chinese population is background violence. This pattern is particularly important to recognize when thinking about the gendered dimensions of crime and victimization in Canada. Poor and non-white, particularly Indigenous, populations—groups most likely to be othered in everyday life—are the most vulnerable, yet are largely absent in *any* role in these mass-market films.

CONCLUSION: CRIME, EH!

Spectacles of crime, dynamic visual and symbolic representations, are exceptionally powerful means of conveying messages about justice, authority, deviance, and identit(y)(ies). Public conceptions of crime and criminality are created and maintained in part by the imagery we find on our screens. These images and symbolic cues are not without bias: they often present the most sensational aspects of crime and strategically depict people and issues that tap into normative or hegemonic ideals and stereotypes. This is particularly problematic when we take into account the meanings imbued into gender and sex by the media—from properly heroic masculinities to appropriately vulnerable femininities. One way these typologies become normalized and socially inculcated is through their reiteration in film. Stereotypes of gender and race saturate media portrayals of criminality, victimization, and even criminal justice employees.

Yet Canadian crime films are just one pop culture presence. Forms like fiction and television offer additional sets of strategies for narrating gender, crime, and nation. The prominence of non-white and women detectives in these spaces suggests that, beyond film at least, "the Canadian imaginary is comprehensive and diverse" (Sloniowski and Rose xvi). With Telefilm Canada (the country's film financing program) prioritizing gender parity and diversity in feature filmmaking, Canadian crime films may soon follow (telefilm.ca). Looking across Canada's media landscape can reveal the range of stories we tell ourselves about gendered experiences of crime and justice, as well as the stories and voices still missing from this narrated nation.

CRITICAL REFLECTION QUESTIONS

1. What are the differences between TV and film that make us more likely to find women detectives in Canadian TV shows than in Canadian movies? What changes—in Canadian culture, Canadian media, Canadian politics— might increase the number of women detectives on the big screen?
2. How can prominent raced and gendered imagery in Canadian media impact our understandings of criminality and victimization?
3. Can you think of any Canadian crime stories featuring non-traditional representations of women? How do these stories differ from more familiar representations of gender and crime? What can we learn from these differences?

WORKS CITED

The Accused. Directed by Jonathan Kaplan, 1988.

Ames, Christopher. "Restoring the Black Man's Lethal Weapon: Race and Sexuality in Contemporary Cop Films." *Journal of Popular Film and Television,* vol. 20, no. 3, 1992, pp. 52–60.

Bad Boys. Directed by Michael Bay, 1995.

Bad Boys II. Directed by Michael Bay, 2003.

Berton, Pierre. *Hollywood's Canada: The Americanization of our National Image.* McClelland & Stewart, 1975.

Bhabha, Homi. "Introduction: Narrating the Nation." *Nation and Narration,* edited by Homi K. Bhabha, Routledge, 1990, pp. 1–7.

Billson, Anne. "Jane Got a Gun—But Most Women in Westerns Still Don't." *The Guardian,* 21 April 2016, https://www.theguardian.com/film/2016/apr/21/jane-got-a-gun-most-women-in-westerns-dont

Bon Cop, Bad Cop. Directed by Erik Canuel, 2006.

Bon Cop, Bad Cop 2. Directed by Alain Desrochers, 2017.

Braithwaite, Andrea. "*Bon Cop, Bad Cop*: Fighting Crime Across the Two Solitudes." *Screening Justice: Canadian Crime Films, Culture and Society*, edited by Steven Kohm et al., Fernwood, 2017, pp. 132–148.

Cop Out. Directed by Kevin Smith, 2010.

Covington, Jeanette. *Crime and Racial Constructions: Cultural Misinformation About African Americans in Media and Academia*. Lexington Books, 2011.

Cuklanz, Lisa M., and Sujata Moorti. "Television's 'New' Feminism: Prime-Time Representations of Women and Victimization." *Critical Studies in Media Communication*, vol. 23, no. 4, 2006, pp. 302–321.

Dowler, Ken. "Media Consumption and Public Attitudes Toward Crime and Justice: The Relationship Between Fear of Crime, Punitive Attitudes, and Perceived Police Effectiveness." *Journal of Criminal Justice and Popular Culture*, vol. 10, no. 2, 2003, pp. 109–126.

Dowler, Ken, et al. "Constructing Crime: Media, Crime, and Popular Culture." *Canadian Journal of Criminology and Criminal Justice*, vol. 48, no. 6, 2006, pp. 837–850.

Edwardson, Ryan. *Canadian Content: Culture and the Quest for Nationhood*. University of Toronto Press, 2008.

Fuchs, Cynthia J. "The Buddy Politic." *Screening the Male: Exploring Masculinities in Hollywood Cinema*, edited by Steven Cohan and Ina Rae Hark, Routledge, 1993, pp. 194–210.

Gates, Philippa. "Always a Partner in Crime: Black Masculinity in the Hollywood Detective Film." *Journal of Popular Film and Television*, vol. 32, no. 1, 2004, pp. 20–29.

Gerbner, George. "Cultivation Analysis: An Overview." *Mass Communication and Society*, vol. 1, no. 3–4, 1998, pp. 175–194.

Gittings, Christopher E. *Canadian National Cinema: Ideology, Difference, and Representation*. Routledge, 2002.

Gunless. Directed by William Phillips, 2010.

Inness, Sherrie A. *Tough Girls: Women Warriors and Wonder Women in Popular Culture*. University of Pennsylvania Press, 1999.

Jiwani, Yasmin, and Mary Lynn Young. "Missing and Murdered Women: Reproducing Marginality in News Discourse." *Canadian Journal of Communication*, vol. 31, 2006, pp. 895–917.

King, Neal. "Generic Womanhood: Gendered Depictions in Cop Action Cinema." *Gender and Society*, vol. 22, no. 2, 2008, pp. 238–260.

———. *Heroes in Hard Times: Cop Action Movies in the U.S.* Temple UP, 1999.

Kingston, Anne. "What Jian Ghomeshi Did." *Macleans*, 30 March 2016, https://www.macleans.ca/news/canada/what-jian-ghomeshi-did/

Kohm, Steven, et al., editors. *Screening Justice: Canadian Crime Films, Culture and Society.* Fernwood, 2017.

Krutnik, Frank. *In a Lonely Street: Film Noir, Genre, Masculinity.* Routledge, 1991.

Kuhn, Annette, and Guy Westwall. *A Dictionary of Film Studies.* Oxford UP, 2012.

Massey, V. "Royal Commission on National Development in the Arts, Letters and Sciences 1949–1951." *Library and Archives Canada*, 1951, https://www.collectionscanada.gc.ca/massey/h5-400-e.html

Muraskin, Roslyn, and Shelly F. Domash. *Crime and the Media: Headlines vs. Reality.* Pearson Prentice Hall, 2007.

National Film Board of Canada. "Mission and Highlights." http://onf-nfb.gc.ca/en/about-the-nfb/organization/mandate/

No Clue. Directed by Carl Bessai, 2013.

Pfeiffer, Christian, et al. "Media Use and its Impact on Crime Perception, Sentencing Attitudes, and Crime Policy." *European Journal of Criminology*, vol. 2, 2005, pp. 259–285.

Rabe-Hemp, Cara E. "Female Forces: Beauty, Brains, and a Badge." *Feminist Criminology*, vol. 6, no. 2, 2011, pp. 132–155.

Rafter, Nicole. *Shots in the Mirror: Crime Films and Society.* Oxford UP, 2006.

Sexton, Jared. *Black Masculinity and the Cinema of Policing.* Palgrave Macmillan, 2017.

Sommers, Zach. "Missing White Woman Syndrome: An Empirical Analysis of Race and Gender Disparities in Online News Coverage of Missing Persons." *Journal of Criminal Law & Criminology*, vol. 106, no. 2, 2016, pp. 275–314.

Sloniowski, Jeanette, and Marilyn Rose. "Introduction." *Detecting Canada: Essays on Canadian Crime Fiction, Television, and Film*, edited by Jeanette Sloniowski and Marilyn Rose, Wilfrid Laurier UP, 2014, pp. xi–xxiv.

Surette, Ray. *Media, Crime and Criminal Justice: Images and Realities*, 3rd edition. Thomson-Wadsworth, 2007.

Telefilm Canada. "Telefilm Canada Releases its Latest Gender Parity Statistics for Feature Film Production." *Telefilm Canada*, 19 June 2018, https://telefilm.ca/en/news-releases/telefilm canada-releases-its-latest-gender-parity-statistics-for-feature-film-production-funding

van den Bulk, Jan. "Research Note: The Relationship Between Television Fiction and Fear of Crime. An Empirical Comparison of Three Causal Explanations." *European Journal of Communication*, vol. 19, no. 2, 2004, pp. 239–248.

Welsh, Andrew, Thomas Fleming, and Kenneth Dowler. "Constructing Crime and Justice on Film: Meaning and Message in Cinema." *Contemporary Justice Review*, vol. 14, no. 4, pp. 457–476.

Wilson, Franklin T., and Howard Henderson. "The Criminological Cultivation of African American Municipal Police Officers: Sambo or Sellout." *Race and Justice*, vol. 4, no. 1, 2014, pp. 45–67.

CHAPTER 8

Succubi, Synthetics, and Clones, Oh My!: Myths of Multiculturalism and Gender Equity in Canadian Science Fiction and Fantasy

Laine Zisman Newman

I was lost for years. Searching while hiding. Only to find that I belong to a world hidden from humans. I won't hide anymore. I will live the life I choose.

  —*Bo*, Lost Girl *(Opening Credits)*

Finally learning the truth of my origins has caused me to reconsider who and what I am. I learned that I am special, in a good way … I was designed for more, to be more.

  —*Android*, Dark Matter *(Season three, episode 11)*

My story is an embroidery with many beginnings and no end, but I will start with the thread of my sister Sarah who stepped off the train one day and met herself.

  —*Helena*, Orphan Black *(Season five, episode 10)*

JOURNEYING TO BELONG: GENDER AND MULTICULTURALISM IN CANADIAN SCI-FI

I've always loved science fiction. I'm captivated by women-led sci-fi series that unapologetically refuse expectations of feminine fragility. I binge seasons, enticed by the plots that feel relatable, despite their impossibility. I love the way characters' powers and exceptional strength blend with the everyday. Despite the differences from my own daily life, I see my experiences and struggles mirrored in their battles, love triangles, and kinship structures. But the more I reflect on my favourite women heroes, the more I recognize that even as they engage in socially progressive characterizations of their protagonists, they also maintain an exceptionalist nationalism that ultimately serves rather than disrupts the neoliberal status quo.

Three sci-fi/fantasy series, produced or co-produced in Canada, demonstrate intersections of gender, identity, and nationhood through asserting "strong female protagonists" who embrace their exceptionality while struggling to conform. *Lost Girl* (2010–2016), *Orphan Black* (2013–2017), and *Dark Matter* (2015–2017) each sees their protagonist arriving in a new environment, seeking belonging and answers, trying to find themselves and navigate their differences in a new world. Their journeys toward heroism are continually positioned as a choice to pursue goodness, selflessness, and belonging. While not all of these series situate their plots and characters within Canada, they all maintain and perpetuate national ideological norms of multiculturalism and inclusivity in Canada. By centralizing empowered women heroes, these series propagate a neoliberal conception of difference as productive by positioning some bodies, who abide by accepted norms, as proper respectable citizens, at the expense of other less conforming subjects. By promoting gender norms, universalizing race, and erasing Indigenous presence, these series create futurities in which some women can and do succeed, but only if they properly align with national norms and values (Duchastel de Montrouge 1). The series' focus on identity, belonging, and "respectability" mirrors national objectives of inclusion and multiculturalism: Be different, but fit in.

This argument builds on Cath Duchastel de Montrouge's 2013 paper on *Lost Girl*, which utilizes Jasbir Puar's conception of homonationalism[1] to read the series's depiction of human/Fae (non-human) relationships. I develop Duchastel de Montrouge's analysis of difference in *Lost Girl* and extend it to other series to consider how Canadian science fiction is ideally situated to feign resistance and progress while maintaining the need for conformity and belonging. In addition to depicting stereotypical gender norms, these series collectively also exist in a terra nullius post-race society devoid of settler colonialism—or with a heightened, fictionalized settler colonialism that erases Indigenous presence in the country.

I focus specifically on series with strong women protagonists whose strength is exceptionalized through their non-human status. Bo in *Lost Girl* is Fae, a broad classification for non-human beings; Two (a pseudonym for the protagonist Portia's character, taken on in the first episode when she can't remember her real name) in *Dark Matter* is an illegal synesthetic creation, an experiment in creating a being that can withstand injury, but who has a strong proclivity to violence; and Sarah in *Orphan Black* is one of (at least) nine clones who is yet distinct from most of her clone siblings: she is able to biologically reproduce and is a mother to a young daughter.

I begin by outlining a brief history of Canadian multiculturalism and inclusion and then consider why Canadian sci-fi's success centralizing narratives of strong women might be a tactic to feign inclusivity and gender equity without enacting real change. The second half of this chapter focuses on examples from the three series, exploring representations of belonging and gender identity, race and whiteness, and queer sexualities.

NOTES ON FITTING IN: MULTICULTURALISM, INTEGRATION, AND CONFORMITY

In a paper on multiculturalism prepared by the Parliamentary Information and Research Service, Laurence Brosseau and Michael Dewing explain the term in the context of Canadian initiatives and identity:

> As sociological fact, multiculturalism refers to the presence of people from diverse racial and ethnic backgrounds. Ideologically, multiculturalism consists of a relatively coherent set of ideas and ideals pertaining to the celebration of Canada's cultural diversity. At the policy level, multiculturalism refers to the management of diversity through formal initiatives in the federal, provincial, territorial and municipal domains. (1)

Multiculturalism as described here is about presence, shared ideologies in relation to national culture, and formal policies to enact the "management" of diverse populations. Randy Besco and Erin Tolley complicate a simple narrative of Canadian perception of multiculturalism, noting that "perhaps as many as one-third [of Canadians] have clearly negative views. Another third are what we call 'conditional multiculturalists'" (291). They explain, "Conditional multiculturalists support multiculturalism, but not if it means distinct culture or values: 70–80 percent of Canadians say, 'ethnic groups should blend into Canadian society,' and 65 percent believe that 'too many immigrants are not accepting of Canadian values' (Environics Institute 2015)" (303).

Instead of simply assuming that a Canadian approach to belonging centralizes differences and inclusivity, multiculturalism must be explored within the context of not only "diversity" but also race and privilege. In her discussion of homonationalism, Puar contends that "multiculturalism is the accomplice to the ascendancy of whiteness, reproducing the biopolitical mandate to live through the proper population statistics; channeled through the optics of gender and class are their attendant attributes and valuations of longevity, illness, health, environment, fertility, and so on" (27). Inclusivity and diversity are predicated upon the implicit privileging of those who align closest to national norms. People of colour, Indigenous, disabled, and otherwise marginalized individuals are invited into this multicultural home, as long as they benefit these communities, adhering to normalized practices and favouring national values. You can be different, but not too different. In this way inclusivity and diversity are, as Sara Ahmed aptly puts it, "by invitation only" (148).

Multiculturalism is an oft-cited Canadian commitment, founded on a desire to create a nation that is identifiably "inclusive" and "diverse." However the articulation and visibility of multiculturalism on screen, through casting choices, is not necessarily indicative of national policies or laws. Indeed, as the following section argues, even behind the screen, inclusivity and equity are significantly less successful than casting and storylines might suggest.

BEHIND THE SCREEN: EQUITY IN CANADIAN SCI-FI

Canada has a noteworthy history of producing sci-fi and fantasy series, both for a Canadian and international audience. In a 2014 *Huffington Post* article, D. K. Latta clearly maps the histories of sci-fi in Canada, following a past trend of co-production with the United States to a present proliferation of sci-fi being produced in the country. Beginning in the late 1990s, there was an increase in Canada-US co-productions of sci-fi series, including *StarGate*, *Andromeda*, *Earth: Final Conflict*, *TekWar*, and *Poltergeist: The Legacy* (Latta). A national push to film in Canada and subsequent financial incentive through tax credits and grants made co-production and international joint ventures (IJV) all the more attractive (Tinic 56). While Canadian presence and geographies were historically ambiguous or erased in the plotlines—most of the narratives were set in the United States or referenced the United States, and the majority featured American actors—they nonetheless set the groundwork for other sci-fi (co-)productions like *Bitten*, *Dark Matter*, *Orphan Black*, *Lost Girl*, and *Continuum* in the early 2000s (Latta), all of which, quite remarkably, have women leads. At this point, Canada has the precedent, production capabilities, and skilled crew to develop, create, and distribute new series in the genre and continue to produce works that centralize women heroes and protagonists.

While some celebrate Canada's gender equity through women's roles in these series, such an "accomplishment" must be understood within the context of labour equity in the broader television and entertainment industry. Equitable television is not simply about who stars in the series, but also who maintains leadership and control over them. A May 2019 study showed that women's work in writing, directing, and cinematography still has not surpassed the 25 percent mark (Golick and Daniels 10). The series analyzed in this chapter further support these statistics. While all showcase women leads, these series do not possess correspondingly equitable employment in development and production. For example, despite the leading women, the shows have very few women directors. Throughout their seasons, 18 percent of *Lost Girl* episodes were directed by women, 10.2 percent of *Dark Matter* episodes were directed by women (Abbott 214–215), and only 6 percent of *Orphan Black* episodes were directed by women.[2]

These statistics are further complicated by racist realities in the industry. While there has been some increase in white women's work in leadership roles in creative industries, women of colour are not receiving the same increase in opportunities or employment, and Indigenous women's participation has actually dropped. The 2019 study found that while the percentage of women in key creative TV roles increased by 11 percent from 2014 to 2017,

> Over four years, out of 3,206 contracts, 47 went to women of colour. In 2017, 1.81% of TV contracts went to women of colour. Women of colour made up less than 2% of writers, 0% of cinematographers and 5% of directors.… No Indigenous women worked on any of the 24 series studied in 2017. Between 2014 and 2017, Indigenous women received only 0.69% (22 of 3206) of contracts studied. (Golick and Daniels 6)

Media literacy necessitates that we not only actively decode gender on screen but also critically ask why these narratives might increase in popularity, if labour practices off screen don't reflect the same commitment to gender equity. As series producers and writers continue to sell narratives, they target stories to increase and maintain viewership. Given that women make up one of the largest demographics of viewers in Canada (Telefilm Canada 17), it seems plausible that the increase in women protagonists might be not (only) fuelled by a desire for gender equity, but also aimed to market their programming to the largest viewer demographic.

While Canadian sci-fi series do possess the potential to develop feminist-queer characters and subvert expectations of strength and womanhood, such depictions cannot be taken as wholly productive or positive, and must be understood within national frameworks of "acceptable" identities, sexualities, and gender.

"WHEN YOU DON'T KNOW WHO YOU ARE": RECURRING THEMES OF IDENTITY AND BELONGING

The three series I focus on here all emphasize the characters' search for identity and belonging, seeking normalcy and happiness amidst chaos. Just as Canadian multiculturalism seemingly asks us to retain our individuality as we come together as a nation, these women, too, support the idea of being yourself and finding yourself against all odds. But being one colourful piece of a mosaic nonetheless requires you to fit within the puzzle. Difference is tolerable, indeed even praise-worthy, so long as your difference still allows you to conform. Each series centralizes a lost past in the protagonists' origin story and an emphasis on a new present. We watch our heroines leave their pasts behind, promoting the idea that despite a troubled yesterday, hard work and commitment today will allow them to not only succeed tomorrow, but to save the world.

In *Orphan Black*, Sarah Manning's backstory animates her present: a rebellious and absent teenage mom, Sarah was raised in a foster home and has a history filled with sex and drugs before the series narrative begins. In episode one, when she returns to get her life on track and find her daughter, she quickly discovers that she is not like everyone else, when she happens to see one of her identical clone sisters in a train station. Through the five-season series, we follow Sarah and four other central clone sisters (all played by Tatiana Maslany) as they work to discover their clone origins and how that dictates their presents and futures. It is not only the clones who seek their origin stories, but also Sarah's queer foster brother, Felix, who, despite kinship with his foster family and Sarah, laments his upbringing in the foster care system, not knowing his blood origins.

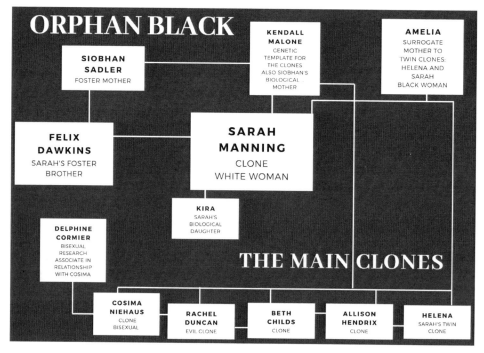

Figure 8.1: *Orphan Black*—Relevant Characters and Their Relations
Note: The character webs included in this chapter provide an overview of characters pertinent to the analyses, but do not necessarily highlight all key figures in each series.

Lost Girl is a series about a young bisexual (or, perhaps more appropriately, pansexual) succubus—who feeds on and gains strength from sexual intimacy—navigating the world of the Fae, learning to understand her species and control her sexual appetite, and negotiating her sexual and polyamorous desires in a monogamous world. The series's opening credits make evident the emphasis on identity:

Life is hard when you don't know who you are. It's harder when you don't know what you are. My love carries a death sentence. I was lost for years. Searching while hiding. Only to find that I belong to a world hidden from humans. I won't hide anymore. I will live the life I choose.

And finally, *Dark Matter* is a Syfy series, based on a comic book of the same name, that follows six space travellers who awaken in the first episode from a cryogenic sleep without any memories of the past or who they are. They name themselves numbers (One through Six), based on the order in which they awoke. Alongside the six amnesiac travellers is also an Android who controls the inner workings of the ship and provides exposition and information to the crew. Throughout the series, all of the characters (even the Android) grapple with the revelations of past identities and how they inform, predict, or resist futures. In the second episode, after the Android reveals the crew members' true identities to them, the Android questions "Two" (now revealed to be a criminal named Portia Lin):

Android: Should I continue my attempts at data recovery? [pause] Portia—
Two: Don't call me that. No computer file is going to tell me who I am. Call me Two. ("Episode 2," season one, episode two)

In the premiere episode of the series, Two refuses her past and reclaims identity through an act of self-naming. Ultimately, Two's identity is complicated further, as it is later revealed that she is not the human Portia Lin, but a synthetic creation made in a lab, named Rebecca. This discovery further compels Two to discover her essential nature.

While this search for identity and belonging provides the women protagonists opportunities to self-define who they are, their journeys toward self-realization do little to challenge or redefine gendered expectations. The search for who you are in these series is directly linked to what you are. Part of what makes these women characters so remarkable is that they are all strong and capable leaders, but they are exceptionalized through their super-human abilities. They are not like ordinary women. And even with their super-human status, in each portrayal their strength and species do not impede upon the depiction of gendered stereotypes related to caregiving, motherhood, and (heteronormative) romance. The women are often love-crazy, occasionally irrational, and frequently reliant upon men (even while they themselves are physically and emotionally strong). By supporting these normalized gendered tropes, these shows do not subvert or resist the status quo but instead implicitly naturalize it.

In her work considering the homonationalist and ableist ideologies of *Lost Girl*, Duchastel de Montrouge argues that "despite being a show about a bisexual, polyamorous succubus who lives at the margins of the Fae and human world, who is superficially presented as a rebel to the established world order … *Lost Girl* is very much a normative, heterosexual tale about the importance of maintaining the dominant hierarchy" (Duchastel de Montrouge 8). Indeed, in *Lost Girl*, Bo is not only depicted as "lost" and in need of guidance and leadership from the male characters but literally in need of healing from men, namely her on-again-off-again love interest, a werewolf Fae named Dyson. When Bo is hurt, she has sex with Dyson, who is strong enough to sustain her orgasms and have aggressive sex with her, enabling her to heal herself. Bo's other love interest, a woman named Lauren, a human scientist and physician for the Fae, is not able to safely heal her without being put at risk. Where sex with Dyson is free, fun, and healing, sex with Lauren is gentle and hesitant.

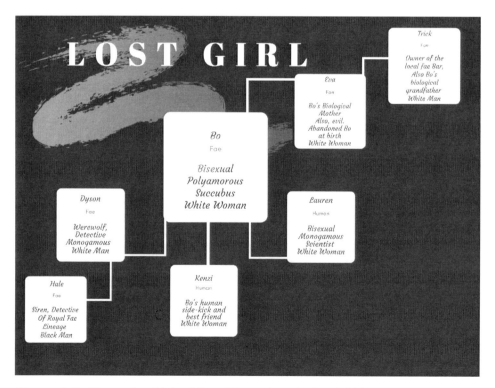

Figure 8.2: Character Web of Key Characters in *Lost Girl*

Orphan Black seemingly addresses the privileging of strong men by making many of the characters smart, cunning, and powerful women. Ultimately, however, as the series continues, we find that the exceptional clone women exist in relation to a male counterpart. These men, "castor clones," are part of a military operation, further constructing an idealized masculinity founded in violence and aggression. While *Orphan Black* challenges essentialized readings of identity, it simultaneously upholds dominant gender expectations by depicting feminine qualities like care and motherhood as a privileged redemptive practice, juxtaposed with the expectations for men to be aggressive, powerful, and, in the case of fathers, absent. Men's aggression, violence, and dominance is expected, maintained in power hierarchies, and naturalized as unescapable, whereas the women characters' strength and leadership is positioned as a result of troubled pasts, further exceptionalizing rather than normalizing their abilities.

Indeed, in sci-fi series, video games, and comics, women's heroism and drive often stem from traumatic events. Such a trope ultimately works to show that women's power comes from their pain. Abuse, control, abandonment, and manipulation are consistently positioned as an inevitable gendered reality, but even more troubling, they are positioned as realities that we (women) benefit from. Leigh Alexander explains: "It seems that when you want to make a woman into a hero, you hurt her first. When you want to make a man into a hero, you hurt … also a woman first." All three series productively create community care networks, friendships, and chosen families, but the heroines' individual traumatic pasts are what compels them to start to take on the pain of others—our traumas are justified through how we overcome them and what they enable us, as individuals, to do. While *Lost Girl*, *Dark Matter*, and *Orphan Black* all work to present empowering, positive images of women, they emphasize that their success overcoming the odds is fuelled by their pain.

RE: WHITES: REWRITING RACISM AND SETTLER COLONIALISM IN POST-RACE FANTASY WORLDS

Narratives in science fiction and fantasy frequently address isolation, discrimination, and difference through metaphors and imagined hierarchies. However, the parables presented remove *real* histories and current experiences of racism from the story. Racism that precludes colour and that erases the histories and present of white supremacy does little to address actual racism—in effect making history irrelevant and oppression circumstantial instead of systemic. Elisabeth Anne Leonard argues, "By far the majority of sf deals with racial tension by ignoring it" (254). While these series might imagine themselves to be constructing a post-race world, as audience members we nonetheless view the characters and plots from our own perspectives. We consume, interpret, and decode explicit racist tropes and white privilege on screen, even, or especially, when they are implicit. These problems are compounded by the overwhelming whiteness of the industry itself.

Dark Matter has arguably the most "diverse" cast of the three shows, and race is continually positioned as a non-issue in their universe. This could be perceived as refreshing and perhaps even positively aimed toward redressing discrimination. However, the perpetuation of stereotypes and appropriation and swapping of cultural histories demonstrates a post-racial dynamic that works to erase rather than solve racism. For example, one recurring character, Four, played by Alex Mallari Jr., is depicted as being from Japanese royal lineage. However, Mallari Jr. is Filipino, a casting choice worthy of critical consideration. The creator of the series, Joseph Mallozzi, shares part of the casting call for the character, describing Four as follows: "Possessed of a quiet strength and dignity that belies an exacting ruthlessness. The part is written as male but could be female. Written as Asian but can be open to all ethnicities." Four is stereotypically stoic, expressionless, and wields a

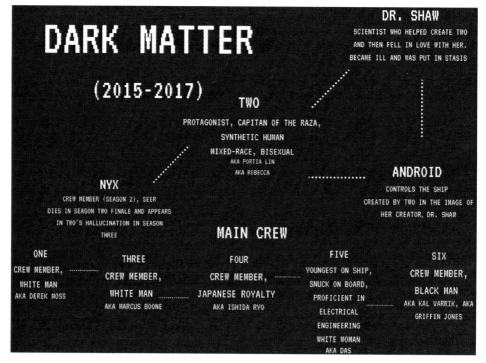

Figure 8.3: *Dark Matter*—Relevant Characters and Their Relations

sword. Being written "as Asian" shows how distinctly a character's race is encoded into their depiction while also, via the casting of a non-Japanese actor, furthering the assumption that all Asians are the same, thus generalizing experiences (as well as stereotypes) and histories. While including racialized bodies, like multicultural ideologies, the show does not do the hard work of understanding how culture, customs, and identities are intertwined.

Conversely, with an overwhelmingly white cast, *Lost Girl* uses speciesism to address issues of oppression and privilege. Humans are often oppressed by the Fae—who see themselves as markedly superior. Racism is erased entirely in this equation. Indeed, the one Black recurring character on the series, Hale (played by K. C. Collins), comes from a royal lineage: a family who has "lived behind their privileged lives for centuries" ("The Girl Who Faed with Fire," season two, episode 17). Even his character's full name, "William Haley François Santiago," seems to allude to his pretentious, privileged standing. Although Hale's depiction might at first appear to make space for privileged racialized subjectivity, his Black family's prejudice and discriminatory treatment toward (white) humans actively erases the specificity of anti-Black racism and violence. This plays out particularly well in scenes between Hale's Black family and Kenzi, Bo's white woman sidekick. Race is never mentioned in their interactions, but Kenzi, a seemingly able-bodied, cisgender white woman, is recast as the Other, repeatedly ostracized and bullied for being human. In season two's episode "The Girl Who Faed with Fire," Kenzi's voice is literally taken away by Hale's sister: a white woman being silenced by a Black woman. This plot point furthers the colour-blind racism already in the episode as it violently rewrites the persistent ways in which Black women are over-whelmingly silenced by white women in daily life. Throughout the episode, the reversal of power dynamics between white and racialized characters does not il-luminate real-life systemic racism. Rather, it actively invalidates experiences of anti-Black racism and identity in favour of keeping white audiences comfortable in their evasion of accountability.

Finally, in *Orphan Black*, the representation of the clones as simultaneously sin-gular and universal, unique and omnipresent demonstrates how their differences (as clones) exceeds (or erases) their racial white privilege. Their white skin stands in for everyone. Indeed, clones appear from all over the world, each with identical likeness: whiteness is emphasized and neutralized through its global presence. One clone who stands out as particularly appropriative of diverse cultures is Cosima. With long dreads, Cosima "is introduced onscreen both to the audience and to main protag-onist clone Sarah … dressed in a skirt evocative of southwestern American Indian textiles and traditional weavings," a costume choice that recurs throughout the series

(Byrd 135). Through the geographies they span, and their hairstyles, languages, and cultures, the white clones' whiteness is effectively neutralized.

Creating a post-race world is also about creating a land that is atemporal, ahistorical, terra nullius. Cameron Greensmith and Sulaimon Giwa note that, by labelling territories and lands "terra nullius," unclaimed or empty, "settlers can understand themselves as the proper inhabitants and owners of Indigenous lands.… [T]he logic of settler colonialism is sustained through the elimination of Indigenous peoples as a consequence of historical processes that continue to inform the present" (132). While marked as fictional, sometimes futuristic or outside linear time, all three series detach their realities from colonial histories, creating fictions of slavery and colonization that are disconnected from Indigenous realities in this country.

Jodi Byrd compellingly argues that *Orphan Black* extends settler colonial violence as it

> reproduces dispossession at the site of an appropriative and fetishized Indigeneity that stands in as sign for the violences that have been imposed on the individual settler by the state.… Despite being filmed in Toronto and set in an imagined BBC America imperial commonwealth between the United States and Canada, the show never explicitly acknowledges the presence of Indigenous peoples at all, even though the themes of the series center on the gendered and sexualized violences endemic to settler societies that have resulted in thousands of missing and murdered Indigenous women throughout North America. (Byrd 134–135)

Similarly, while *Dark Matter* grapples with what it would mean for those with power to colonize space, it erases Indigenous peoples from the conversation. Mallozzi explains:

> The world we created is a world in which multinational corporations have transformed into multi-planetary [corporations]. They're the ones with the money, so they're the ones that are able to build the ships. They're the ones that are able to go out and colonize space, essentially to find planets in order to exploit their planetary resources. (Mallozzi, as quoted in Cofield)

"Colonized space" positions colonialism as a land claim, not a displacement and genocide of real peoples. And even whilst this is a fictional narrative, it nonetheless has an impact on how we understand colonialism. We are made to reflect on the dangers of technology and power but not on the impact of colonization on the first peoples of a land. Inviting settler viewers to associate colonization as a geographical issue, not a human one, actively disconnects colonization from historical and current violence against Indigenous populations.

That is not to say that Indigenous characters or storylines are absent from all of the series. Indeed, in an episode of *Lost Girl* entitled "Can't See the Fae-Rest" (season two, episode 11), the plot revolves around "Batibat,"[3] who are portrayed as peaceful tree-inhabiting creatures who become violent and murderous when someone tries to cut from their tree. In the episode, a Batibat named Maganda vengefully attacks someone who has taken her tree. While the actress who plays this role, Pamela Matthews, is a Cree woman from the Sachigo Lake First Nation, her character's specific origins remain unnamed. She is defined by her tree-status: her tree is her home and her identity; she is depicted as dirty, impoverished, violent, with broken English and a profound connection to nature. While her claim to land is articulated, her claim to the land the other characters reside on is not. Acknowledging Indigenous presence through ethnically ambiguous characters like Maganda is in the service of rewriting histories to accommodate a guilt-free settler presence. Bo demands that the Fae who stole Maganda's home give it back—but by detaching colonization from the human narratives or Canadian geography, settler viewers (and indeed the show's main cast) are not expected to do the same.

Maganda: Hundreds of years, my tree, waltzing with the clouds, waving to the rain. Every leaf grew in my heart. It was home. It was my heart. It was a castle for my grandchildren and now it's gone.
Bo: I'm so sorry. It won't be the same. But your tree will be yours again.
[Maganda reaches for hug; Bo recoils]
Bo: Oh no, that's okay, I don't need a hug.

Bo, the white saviour, saves an impoverished and victimized Other and demands justice, while remaining entirely unaccountable for destruction to Indigenous lands in Canada. Bo gives settler audiences what they need: gratification and absolution without accountability or sacrifice. She offers the possibility of restitution of land and the true pleasure of heroism without asking us to be accountable for our own complicity in a system that continues to disenfranchise Indigenous women. In her final rejection of a physical embrace, Bo maintains a familiar power dynamic in which the settler is positioned as superior. Her refusal to give Maganda a hug solidifies Maganda as different, as less than, as dirty, and perhaps most potently, as undesirable.

REPRODUCING WHITENESS: AT THE INTERSECTIONS OF RACE, GENDER, AND MOTHERHOOD

It is not simply that *Lost Girl, Dark Matter,* and *Orphan Black* erase racialization and settler colonial violence but that they actively reproduce and universalize whiteness. One of the primary intersections of race and gender in all three series is the depiction of women as caregivers and mothers—seemingly compensating for a lack of parental presence and support in the leading women's own lives—always in connection to and toward the reproduction of whiteness.

As noted, in *Orphan Black* one obstacle in casting the clones as "every woman" and as globally present is their physical appearance. How does a white body come to represent every*body*? The universalization of the clones through their diversification occurs early in the series through a brief story arc in the ninth and tenth episodes of season one, when Sarah and her twin sister Helena's "birth mother" is revealed. Amelia—a Black woman who is from South Africa and was paid to act as a surrogate—works to racialize the clones while eliding the issues of a singular (white) body being unproblematically classified as the neutral global body. Laura Harrison argues the following:

> New reproductive technologies appear to offer an alluring promise of the deconstruction of racial difference via a postmodern explosion of the possibility that includes white children born of non-white parents. Theoretically, this mingling of "different" blood and bodies suggests that racial difference is a social construction rapidly losing cultural currency, yet the material evidence of the value placed on white and non-white labor in this reproductive arena suggests otherwise. (262)

Indeed, as Harrison ultimately asserts, the role of the non-white surrogate de-values the surrogate's potential as "mother" and casts non-white bodies in roles of service that are "convenient and non-threatening for white consumers" (262). While Amelia does take on the role of "mother," she does so only briefly, and she is replaced by a biological white mother, Kendal, later in the series.

Amelia's entrance and her brief narrative are in the service of developing and diversifying our leading characters while universalizing whiteness and reproducing white subjecthood. The clones are universal not in spite of their whiteness, but because of the neutrality and mobility whiteness affords them. Indeed, as white women, they are even able to take up space in a Black womb, unaffected by the Blackness that envelops them. They become global and universal in the space they take up.

In *Lost Girl*, Bo's own search for her biological mother emphasizes mother-hood as integral to shaping one's sense of self. Bo's ability to care for her kinship network and to enact maternal love and support is evident in the very first episode of the series, as she clearly demonstrates a desire to foster love and care for her (new) human friend, Kenzi. Bo saves Kenzi in the opening scene of the series and, in episode two, when she and Kenzi enter a space marked for Fae patronage only, Bo adopts Kenzi as her own:

Bo: Where I go, she goes.
Trick: You're claiming her?
Bo: Yes.
Trick: The girl is with her. Understand, she's your responsibility from this point on.
    ("Where There's a Will, There's a Fae," season one, episode two)

This marks a clear solidification of Bo as mother, which becomes increas-ingly important as Bo searches for and then tries to relocate her own biological mother. Bo's maternal presence in Kenzi's life allows her to act as the caregiver that she seeks, persistently saving Kenzi against the odds and claiming her as her own.

Two's relationship to motherhood and reproducing whiteness in *Dark Matter* is perhaps the most complicated. Two is described on the Syfy website as "fiercely protective" of her crew and, indeed, she certainly maintains a maternal presence on the ship (particularly for Five, the youngest woman on board). She also, we come to find, has created (albeit not biologically) another crew member. In season three, Two discovers—and this part can get a little bit convoluted—that prior to board-ing the ship and losing her memory, Two *created* the Android who maintains the ship's central controls. The Android is in fact a replica of Dr. Irena Shaw (played by Zoie Palmer, who coincidently also plays Lauren on *Lost Girl*), who is Two's creator. Two and Dr. Shaw had a romantic relationship before Dr. Shaw became ill and was put in stasis. Without her love, Two creates the Android to look exactly like Dr. Shaw. A strange and complicated mix, perhaps alternatively described through the lineage of Dr. Shaw creating a synthetic human (Two) and falling in love with her, only to fall ill and have said synthetic (Two) create a robot in her image. Two then loses her memory and forgets any of this had happened. Impor-tantly, while Two is of mixed race, Dr. Shaw is a white woman.

A focus on fertility, motherhood, and mothering should not be perceived as isolated from discussions of multiculturalism. Indeed, Puar connects reproduction to attributes of successful multiculturalism and white privilege, associating it with the persistence of privilege, securing futurities, and the capacity to succeed. Puar explains:

> Following Rey Chow's statement that biopolitics is implicitly about the ascendancy of whiteness, the terms of whiteness cannot remain solely in the realm of racial identification or phenotype but extend out to the capacity for capacity: that is, the capacity to give life, sustain life, promote life. (200)

In all three series, reproduction and motherhood typically emerge through the reproduction of white subjecthood: Two reproduces the Android in Dr. Shaw's white image; Amelia, a Black woman, reproduces Sarah and her sister Helena's white bodies (with only a fleeting presence in the series herself); and Bo reproduces whiteness by saving and then claiming Kenzi as her chosen white child.

In each series, the figure of "mother," biological or technological, is rendered distinct from naturalized heterosexual intercourse. Reproduction of race is not predicated upon normalized cisgender pregnancy, but on the capacity for the characters to attach to and reinforce white presence, demonstrating how racial privilege is (re)produced through biopolitical practices and "heroic" gestures of protection.

QUEER AS IN JUST LIKE YOU: HOMONORMATIVITY AND HOMONATIONALISM

While motherhood might be detached from a cis-heterosexual imperative, and indeed makes room for queer sexualities, even queer subjectivities can further encode and extend heteronormative mores. Queer storylines in these series, though often celebrated as intentionally progressive, ultimately depict queer identities as dangerous, fleeting, and conditional. Queer sexuality on all three series is perhaps not radical, but radically surveilled and contingent.

The first time Two's bisexuality is alluded to in *Dark Matter* is in the first episode of season three, when Two is trapped and losing consciousness. Two hallucinates saying goodbye to Nyx—a fellow crew member who dies in the finale of the second season. The lucid hallucination unfolds:

Two: Who was I to think that *we* should be the ones to change things?
Nyx: Just because you failed doesn't mean it wasn't right to try. The old Portia wouldn't have. But you are different, you are a better person.
Two: Being better is so much harder.... You're not even real.
...
Two: I'm sorry we didn't have more time to get to know each other.

Nyx: Me too.

Two: I'm going to miss you. [Pause] We're not going to make it.

Nyx: Goodbye

[The camera cuts to a slow motion close-up of the two kissing, their lips lightly press against each other.]

Even in the context of a fictional futuristic universe, a hallucination is needed to make space for the first moments of queer visibility. This kind of queer baiting,[4] where death precludes the possibility of the characters ever pursuing a relationship, is an empty representation that keeps queer potentiality present, but at a distance. The kiss is only made possible after the assertion "you're not even real." The next time Two's bisexuality comes into focus is in episode 10 of season three, when we discover her previous romantic relationship with her creator, Dr. Shaw. Two has no memory of Shaw or their history and no attraction to her in the present. Again, it is a romance that ended before it even began. So, while it seems evident that Two is bisexual, the context of her same-sex encounters show resistance to depicting a fully fleshed out queer relationship onscreen.

In *Lost Girl*, Bo's sexuality is tied to her livelihood and her safety. Sex is both what saves her (literally what has the capacity to heal her as a succubus) and what plagues her (her sexual impulses can kill others if she is not careful). While her (bi)sexuality is celebrated, the practices that define her differences are persistently positioned as necessitating restraint. She must get injections to curb her sexual hunger; she must attain her love interest; she must learn to be monogamous. Her polyamorous desires are depicted as excess: too much, too wild, too risky. Happiness, particularly in season two, is directly linked to Bo's pursuits of men and her ability to successfully restrain her sexual appetite and deny her polyamorous orientation. Even more worrisome, her relationship with her opposite-sex partner has more freedom, more physical power, more release—whereas her same-sex relationship requires more tender and concentrated care and supervision. Her same-sex relationship is quite literally not enough for her. Rather than celebrating bisexuality, this is a cautionary tale not to pursue it too vehemently. Aligning with a national Canadian ethos for same-sex rights and equality, the series often positions successful inclusivity as conformity. Bo must learn to be like everyone else, simultaneously celebrating and curbing her own sexual identity.

In *Orphan Black*, Cosima's relationship with her sometimes-partner Delphine, another woman who is a scientist, and whose work is deeply embedded in a multi-season plot, is tumultuous and engaging. While all the relationships in the series might possess intricate deception, and betrayal, what makes Cosima and Delphine's love story all the more tragic is the addition of sickness and threat of death. Cosima's character is literally *dying*. This plot point oddly mirrors the famed pulp novels of the 1950s and 1960s (see, for example, *Spring Fire*, by Marijane Meaker, under the pseudonym "Vin Packer"), which increased visibility for lesbians even as they worked to moralize, condemn, and warn against lesbian identities and experiences (Stenson 46). Indeed, while Cosima is ultimately saved—through her own scientific discoveries—we nonetheless spend five seasons watching her slow demise. Delphine is similarly stereotypically portrayed.[5] She is manipulative, untrustworthy (Serafini), and, as with many depictions of bisexuals, positioned as a new recruit: someone who fell for the person, not their gender or anatomy. Such a trope positions bisexuality as fleeting and contextual. As Victoria Serafini notes, "The word 'bisexual' is only used once in *Orphan Black*, when Delphine admits to Cosima, 'I have never thought about bisexuality [until you kissed me]. I mean, for myself.… But as a scientist, I know that sexuality is a spectrum'" ("Entangled Bank," season one, episode eight).

The stunted discussion of bisexuality and the reproduction of persistent stereotypes and tropes around sexuality do little to progress radical queer subjecthood, instead propagating long-standing myths and concerns about living a queer life. The proper queer subject in all three series is the subject who is present but not disruptive.

REFUSING A STANDING OVATION: EXPECT MORE

Lost Girl, *Dark Matter*, and *Orphan Black* have each been applauded for their inclusion of strong women leads. Their characters are capable and heroic, demonstrating agency and resistance against the powers that control them. However, it is these characters' privileges and conformity that enable them to flourish. Even when series seemingly project progressive narratives that cheer on the underdog, such plotlines can nonetheless align with a feigned myth of inclusivity. Jodi Byrd argues that neoliberal gestures toward multiculturalism and inclusivity often work by privileging some subjects—deemed worthy beneficiaries of the state—at the expense of more deviant others (127). Villains, whether they take the form of zombies, "underfae," or the "big bad" of the season, confirm that there is such a thing as too different. Sci-fi series create new worlds but nonetheless justify the structures and power hierarchies in ours—showing a palatable version of resistance that naturalizes mainstream social and political structures and norms.

The argument I make here is not an isolated one. I use these three series as case studies to offer a framework to decode other science fiction series in the context of Canadian nationalism and multiculturalism. When we witness strong women heroes and leaders, there is no doubt much to celebrate. The collective support, community, and kinship structures in these series encourage positive strides toward gender equity. And yet media's mechanisms to incorporate the appearance of progressive political messages, whilst not simply maintaining but perpetuating the status quo, should not be ignored or trivialized. Rather than focusing on the positive attributes in women-led series or seeking the silver lining, I opt to unapologetically argue: We need not be satisfied with the bare minimum. Recognizing that inclusion is not resistance, we can and should expect more from Canadian television.

CRITICAL REFLECTION QUESTIONS

1. If mainstream television is driven in part by sales and viewership, can it effectively construct narratives that enact real change and resist national norms? What other modes and mediums might be used to effectively put pressure on inequitable systems and power structures?
2. If many sci-fi series take place in unknown futures and non-distinct places (or even in outer space), what makes Canadian sci-fi distinctly "Canadian"? How might these series erase Canadian specificity, and what are the effects?
3. This chapter focused closely on settler colonialism, racism, and gender. Watch one episode or season of a Canadian sci-fi series and consider how representations of disability and class complicate or extend the argument presented in this chapter.

NOTES

1. Puar defines how homonationalism is a "brand of homosexuality [that] operates as a regulatory script not only of normative gayness, queerness, or homosexuality, but also of the racial and national norms that reinforce these sexual subjects" (2).
2. It is significant to note, as Stacey Abbott's 2018 study on women and sci-fi demonstrates, that while numbers for women directors remain quite low, there is "a shift towards a growing proportion of women directing [sci-fi] television, albeit largely Caucasian women, thus highlighting continued issues for women of colour in the industry" facilitated by fewer episodes per season and pressure from cast and crew in the industry (229).
3. The Batibat (alternatively called the Bangungot in Tagalog folklore) is actually based on a demon in Ilocano folklore, considered vengeful and often represented as a fat woman in the trees. This is another instance, then, of appropriating cultural references and applying them to a white narrative, erasing histories, context, and cultural specificity.
4. While the term *queerbaiting* has had a variety of definitions (see, for example, Goldyn; Hubbs), in this context I refer to the ways in which popular culture adds homoerotic or more overt (but still ambiguous) queer allusions to "bait" or drawn-in queer viewers without any possibility or assertions that the same-sex characters will romantically or sexually pursue a real relationship.

5.   Interestingly, we can draw many similarities between Delphine in *Orphan Black* and Lauren in *Lost Girl*. Both scientists are portrayed as particularly untrustworthy and take advantage of their love interest on multiple occasions, while professing their love. Such a stereotypical portrayal of smart queer women is certainly not novel but might be worthy of further exploration.

WORKS CITED

Abbott, Stacey. "The Art of Interpretation: Women, Directing and SF Television." *Science Fiction Film & Television*, vol. 11, no. 2, 2018, pp. 203–231.

Ahmed, Sara. *Willful Subjects*. Duke UP, 2014.

Alexander, Leigh. "What Did They Do to You?: Our Women Heroes Problem." *Gamasutra*, 11 June 2014, https://www.gamasutra.com/view/news/219074/What_did_they_do_to_you_Our_women_heroes_problem.php.

Besco, Randy, and Erin Tolley. "Does Everyone Cheer? The Politics of Immigration and Multiculturalism in Canada." *Federalism and the Welfare State in a Multicultural World*, vol. 198, 2019, pp. 291–319.

Brosseau, Laurence, and Michael Dewing. *Canadian Multiculturalism*. Library of Parliament, 2018.

"Built, not Born." *Dark Matter*, directed by Melanie Orr, Prodigy Pictures and Dark Horse Entertainment, 2017.

Byrd, Jodi A. "'Variations under Domestication': Indigeneity and the Subject of Dispossession." *Social Text*, vol. 36, no. 2, 2018, pp. 123–141.

"Caged Fae." *Lost Girl*, directed by Paolo Barzman, Prodigy Pictures in association with Shaw Media (Showcase), 2013.

Cofield, Calla. "Travel Via Clone: 'Dark Matter' Creator Talks SyFy's Newest Series." *Space.com*, 11 June 2015, https://www.space.com/29617-dark-matter-show-creator-interview.html.

Duchastel de Montrouge, Cath. "Friendship, Family and Community: A Crip Reading of the Fae/Human World of Lost Girl or Friendship and Family (f)or the Nation-state: Lost Girl as Fae/Human Homonationalist Discourse." *Popular Culture Association of Canada*, 2013.

"The Dwarf Star Conspiracy." *Dark Matter*, directed by Steve DiMarco, Prodigy Pictures and Dark Horse Entertainment, 2017.

"Episode One." *Dark Matter*, directed by T. J. Scott, Prodigy Pictures and Dark Horse Entertainment, 2015.

"The Girl Who Faed with Fire." *Lost Girl*, directed by Brett Sullivan, Prodigy Pictures in association with Shaw Media (Showcase), 2012.

Goldyn, Lawrence. "Gratuitous Language in Appellate Cases Involving Gay People: 'Queer Bating' from the Bench." *Political Behavior*, vol. 3, no. 1, 1981, pp. 31–48.

Golick, Jill, and Amber-Sekowan Daniels. "On Screen Report." *Women in View*, May 2019.

Greensmith, Cameron, and Sulaimon Giwa. "Challenging Settler Colonialism in Contemporary Queer Politics: Settler Homonationalism, Pride Toronto, and Two-Spirit Subjectivities." *American Indian Culture and Research Journal*, vol. 37, no. 2, 2013, pp. 129–148.

Harrison, Laura. *Brown Bodies, White Babies: The Politics of Cross-Racial Surrogacy.* NYU Press, 2016.

Hubbs, Nadine. "Bernstein, Homophobia, Historiography." *Women and Music: A Journal of Gender and Culture*, vol. 13, no. 1, 2009, pp. 24–42.

Latta, D. K. "The Rise of Canadian Fantasy/Sci-Fi TV." *HuffPost Canada*, 21 Mar. 2014, https://www.huffingtonpost.ca/dk-latta/canadian-tv-science-fiction_b_4628046.html.

Leonard, Elisabeth Anne. *Race and Ethnicity in Science Fiction. Cambridge Companion to Science Fiction.* Edited by Edward James and Farah Mendlesohn, Cambridge UP, 2003, pp. 253–263.

Mallozzi, Joseph. "The Dark Matter Rollout Continues! Introducing Alex Mallari Jr. as FOUR!" *Joseph Mallozzi's Weblog*, 14 May 2015, https://josephmallozzi.com/2015/05/14/may-14-2015-the-dark-matter-rollout-continues-introducing-alex-mallari-jr-as-four/.

Packer, Vin. *Spring Fire.* World Distributors, 1966.

"Pilot—Part Two." *Dark Matter,* directed by T. J. Scott, Prodigy Pictures and Dark Horse Entertainment, 2015.

Puar, Jasbir K. *Terrorist Assemblages: Homonationalism in Queer Times.* Duke UP, 2018.

Serafini, Victoria. "Bisexual Erasure in Queer Sci-fi 'Utopias.'" *Transformative Works and Cultures*, vol. 24, 2017.

Stenson, Linnea A. "'Drifting on an Unfriendly Sea': Lesbian Pulp Novels and the Creation of Community." *Lambda Nordica*, vol. 9, no. 1–2, 2003, pp. 45–56.

Telefilm Canada. *Audiences in Canada: Trend Report*, 2015.

Tinic, Serra. "Where in the World Is Orphan Black? Change and Continuity in Global TV Production and Distribution." *Media Industries Journal*, vol. 1, no. 3, 2015.

"Where There's a Will, There's a Fae." *Lost Girl*, directed by Gail Harvey, Prodigy Pictures in association with Shaw Media (Showcase), 2011.

CHAPTER 9

Nelvana of the Northern Lights: White Goddess or Inuk Superheroine?

Chris Klassen

INTRODUCTION

It is 1941 and the world is introduced to a novel concept: a superheroine who is a demi-goddess from an "exotic" locale. No, it is not Wonder Woman. It is Nelvana of the Northern Lights, daughter of the god Koliak and a mortal woman from the isolated beauty of the Arctic. Nelvana was introduced four months before Wonder Woman, not in the growing American comic book industry, but in Canada, not a location typically associated with comic books. However, the circumstances of World War II pushed Canadians into the comic book industry, and one of the most successful was Nelvana, a powerful and independent woman.

It would be easy to claim Nelvana as a Canadian feminist, or proto-feminist, icon. This is certainly the tone of the 2013 Kickstarter campaign to reprint the original comics that ran from 1941 to 1947. However, the power of her strength and determination are mitigated by her relationship to the North and the Inuit. For decades Nelvana was understood to be a white goddess revered by the Inuit she protects. In 2013 Hope Nicholson and Rachel Richey suggested that the fictional Nelvana was inspired by a real Inuit woman and thus should be understood as an Inuk superheroine. This chapter is an exploration into the differences between these interpretations of Nelvana's identity, in light of the continued colonial context of the nation of Canada. Nelvana, as a Canadian superheroine, fights for the well-being of the nation of Canada. As such, she stands with the government and its policies, both foreign and domestic. I argue that whether we understand her as a white goddess or an Inuk superheroine, Nelvana's role in maintaining Canada's interests in the North make her an agent of the colonial nation regardless of her racial categorization.

My analysis comes from my position as a white settler trying to make sense of my role and responsibility in the decolonizing process. I cannot speak for Inuit understandings of Inuit identity, nor have I found any published Inuit interpretations of Nelvana. However, as a settler Canadian, I am implicated in the colonial and national project reinforced within the Nelvana comic books. Whether Nelvana is Inuit or white, her representation of the idea of Canada, as will be explained through this chapter, has consequences for settler Canadians and Indigenous Peoples, albeit in differing ways.

Nelvana of the Northern Lights

The Canadian comic book industry really began in the 1940s, when the Canadian government under Mackenzie King passed the War Exchange Conservation Act. This act was designed to limit importations of non-essential items, such as American comic books, during the war, in order to preserve currency for wartime materials. Faced with the lack of American comic books, a number of Canadian publishers and artists began creating Canadian comics. Some of these were simply reiterations of the American stories. However, the development of Canadian originals boosted the industry and provided new, patriotic figures for Canadians young and old to enjoy. As Alan Walker points out, "the two most consistent traits of Canadian comic books are their purposeful Canadianism and their patriotic attitudes towards the Second World War" (14). Of these Canadian originals, the first to specifically embody a heroic Canadian identity was *Nelvana of the Northern Lights*, first published in 1941.

Nelvana was created by artist Adrian Dingle in conversation with his friend, Group of Seven artist Franz Johnston. According to Dingle, Johnston introduced the idea of a Northern goddess after his journeys in the Arctic region. He told Dingle a legend about a "powerful Inuit mythological figure—an old woman called Nelvana," (Bell 5) who was a frightening, crone-like character. Dingle and Johnston altered the image of Nelvana to one of a young, attractive, and benevolent protector goddess. She was revered by the Inuit but, due to World War II, was compelled to journey south to be more involved in the war effort. Here she takes on the alter ego of Alana North, an indication that she is the personification of the North.

Most interpretations of Nelvana understand her as following in the "white queen" tradition initially associated with H. Rider Haggard's *She* of 1886. *She* is the story of a couple of British men who venture into the jungles of Africa, where they encounter a vicious people who are ruled by a white queen named

Ayesha, commonly referred to simply as "She" or "She-who-must-be-obeyed." The idea of a white ruler, whether mortal queen or immortal goddess, of tribal people was appealing to many Europeans and Euro-North Americans who accepted the Victorian racial notion that whites were superior rulers to all others. To make this white ruler a woman allowed for further visual titillation in early comic books, particularly in the tradition of minimal clothing. The first of these was *Sheena, Queen of the Jungle*, which was first published in 1937 as the first comic book with a female lead. After this, many comic book writers took inspiration and created various jungle queens. Common traits in this trope are a character who is beautiful and immortal, with a name ending in -*a* (such as Ayesha or Sheena), who "ruled over 'primitive' peoples (often lost races)" (Bell 7). The name ending in -*a* is also a trait of female embodiments of nationhood, such as Britannia. John Bell, Canadian comic book historian, puts these characteristics together to name Nelvana as a personification of Canada as the North, reflective of a (white) Canadian "rule" over the Indigenous peoples who are in awe of the power and beauty of the Canadian nation. For Bell, Nelvana "was very much a white goddess—not an Inuit" (7). Jason Dittmer and Soren Larsen further articulate this relationship between Nelvana, as embodiment of Canada, and the Inuit:

> The character of Nelvana of the Northern Lights herself embodies and constitutes both the categories of a colonial, white South, a colonized, aboriginal Arctic North, and the Canada that purports to unite them. It is notable that Dingle felt the powerful Inuit mythology of Nelvana needed to be whitened in order to fit the genre conventions. This simple act recast the Inuit demi-goddess as an agent of southern supremacy over the Arctic North. (60)

Nelvana of the Northern Lights was published from 1941 to 1947. After the war ended, American comic books were once again available in Canada, and the Canadian comic book industry was unable to compete with the glossy, coloured stories from south of the border. In 1995 Canada Post issued a series of stamps to commemorate the early days of Canadian comics. They included Nelvana in that series. It took, however, until the new century for the *Nelvana of the Northern Lights* comics to be accessible to the public again.

The Kickstarter Campaign

In 2013, Hope Nicholson and Rachel Richey started a Kickstarter campaign to re-publish the *Nelvana of the Northern Lights* comic books in a single volume. Richey had encountered some copies of the comic at Library and Archives Canada and was fascinated with the stories that seemed to have been forgotten. At this point the copyright for Nelvana was in the hands of Michael Hirsh and Patrick Loubert. Hirsh and Loubert had bought all the existing copies, including copyright, and other comic book paraphernalia from Commercial Signs of Canada, owned by John Ezrin, in 1971. They then went on to found, along with Clive S. Smith, an animation company that they named after Dingle's superhero. Nelvana is a highly successful company with such titles as *Max and Ruby*, *Babar*, and *Franklin* in its lineup.

Along with finding surviving copies of the comic book to reprint, Nicholson and Richey did some research on the origins of the series. In a conversation with Dingle's son, Christopher, they came to the conclusion that the Nelvana that Franz Johnston encountered was not part of some Inuit mythology, but was actually a living woman (Beaupré). To support this theory, they drew on a 1973 interview with Dingle by David Sim, where Dingle says there was a picture that Johnston showed him of a toothless old woman who was, supposedly, Nelvana (see Sim). Nicholson and Richey took their research to the North (figuratively, not literally) and discovered the name *Nelvana* was not uncommon in Inuit contexts and there were at least two figures they believed could have been the Nelvana of Johnston's acquaintance (or possibly the grandmother these women would have been named after).

Nicholson and Richey argue that if Nelvana of the Northern Lights is based on a real Inuk woman, then she cannot be thought of as a "white queen or goddess" figure. Her Inuk identity, they argue, makes her even more powerful an image of Canadian female heroism. While they recognize that the representation of the Inuit in the comic is simplistic, stereotypical, and sometimes cringe-worthy, ultimately, they believe "most people we've talked to have been extremely proud that Canada's first superheroine is Inuk!" (Beapré). To this date, there have not been any published analyses of Nelvana by Inuit scholars, artists, fans, or critics.

What is so appealing in Nelvana that Nicholson and Richey wanted to reprint the whole series as an inspiration of Canadian heroic womanhood? No doubt about it, Nelvana is an impressive female character. While dressed in the typical revealing outfit of a 1940s superheroine, Nelvana rarely, if ever, relies on men to help her (the exceptions being her brother, near the beginning of the series, and her father, the Northern Lights God, Koliak). She has one marginal romance and works with a male sidekick without any romantic entanglements. She is largely an independent woman with physical and mental strength. That she was first published in 1941 (four months *before* Wonder Woman was introduced in the United States) is astounding. As a woman, she could certainly be an inspiration of our time. The feminist magazine *Herizons* certainly thought so when they published Nicole Rubacha's review of the Kickstarter product (see Rubacha 2014). However, we are not only our gender. As an Inuk woman, as claimed by Nicholson and Richey, there are other complications that require considering the relationship between the Inuit (and other Indigenous peoples) and the Canadian government and non-Indigenous Canadians, in the context of colonialism.

THE INUIT, THE NORTH, AND CANADIAN IDENTITY

Is Nelvana a white goddess or an Inuk superheroine? While these are quite different interpretations of her identity, the implications they each hold may not be as different as Nicholson and Richey suggest. Both situations are embedded within the relationship between the Inuit and the North, and the Canadian government and the South. In general, Canadian comic books of this era were largely about nationalism. Bart Beaty suggests that as the first specifically Canadian superhero, "Nelvana draws upon a number of classic stereotypes of Canadian identity, including a close association with the land and an opposition to mass—or more precisely, American—culture" (430). Beaty points to the 1996 Canada Post comic book stamps as a reinforcing of superheroic Canadians as nationalist heroes. That said, can a Canadian nationalist superhero be Inuit in any way that the Inuit would recognize and claim her? Are the Inuit themselves recognized as embodying Canadian identity? Using an Indigenous, in this case Inuit, character to stand in for Canadian identity seems to whitewash the colonial experience the Inuit have had and continue to have.

In the American context, Richard C. King points out that there are problems of using Indigenous characters in popular culture to somehow appease white settlers' concerns about nationalism and colonialism:

> For amusement, education, and profit, artists and others take Native Americans and remake them as they please. Removing Indianness—or better fragments of it—from context, they reimagine American Indians in alien forms, according to Eurocentric ideals, fears, and preoccupations. In settler states like the United States and Canada, audiences and artists alike have understood this process of appropriation to be appropriate; rarely have they considered the impact of such images or sought the input or interpretation of Indigenous peoples. (215)

This is reminiscent of Shippewa storyteller Lenore Keeshig-Tobias's critique of Canadian authors and artists appropriating Indigenous stories in the cultural appropriation debates of the early 1990s. In a *Globe and Mail* essay, Keeshig-Tobias calls out Canadian authors who "would rather look to an ideal native living in never-never land than confront the reality of what being native means in Canadian society" (A7). If we apply King's and Keeshig-Tobias's concerns to Nelvana, we can see that whether she is white or Inuit she *operates* as an agent of the Canadian government. This is the same government that was in the process of trying to "get rid of the Indian problem," a process articulated by Duncan Campbell Scott only a couple of decades before World War II and the publication of *Nelvana of the Northern Lights* (McDougall). Ten years after *Nelvana of the Northern Lights* was published, this same government forced a relocation of 92 Inuit from Inukjuak (in Northern Quebec) and Mittimatalik (in what is now Nunavut) to a couple of High Arctic locations. Canada wanted these Inuit to establish Canadian sovereignty in the High Arctic and promised improved living conditions. These improved living conditions did not materialize, and the people were left to their own devices in an even harsher climate than they had been accustomed. "The Inuit High Arctic relocations are often referred to as a 'dark chapter' in Canadian history, and an example of how the federal government forced changes that fundamentally affected (and continues to affect) Inuit lives" (Madwar). It is this nation that Nelvana embodies. When Nicholson and Richey praise Dingle for creating his superheroine based upon an Inuk woman, they are essentially accepting a white colonial definition of Inuit womanhood as representative of Canadian identity. Is this really better than (or different from) a white goddess figure?

To some extent it comes down to the question, as articulated by Comanche scholar and musician Cornel Pewewardy in his study of First Nations people in comic books, "Who has the power to define whom?" When it comes to Canada, Canadian identity, and the North, the Inuit have had very little opportunity to define themselves, at least in a way that is recognized by the Canadian government. While Nelvana may stand with the Inuit, as her "Eskimo" people (using the language from the original comic, and 1940s settler culture), her embodiment of Canada has implications. Samantha Arnold evaluates some of these implications in her study of Nelvana and her relationship to Canada's northern foreign policy. Arnold writes, "Nelvana's adventures tell us something important about how the relationship between northern peoples and the south has been imagined—and I argue, still is" (95). It is the "still is" that becomes particularly relevant to analyzing the Kickstarter campaign.

Arnold highlights how Canadian northern policy is tied to both resources and foreign policy. Canada's north is part of the circumpolar region and, as such, Canada is part of the Arctic Council that also includes Denmark, Finland, Iceland, Norway, Russia, Sweden, and the United States. At the time of the writing of *Nelvana of the Northern Lights*, however, Canada's north was a potential site of invasion from the Germans and the Japanese. In the comic book, Nevlana is first invoked by the Inuit to find out why all the fish and game are missing. It turns out to be a plot by Germans trying to sneak in to bring the war to Canada. Nelvana saves the day and continues to fight for the safety of not just the Inuit but Canada as a nation. The assumption here is that to fight for the good of the Inuit and the good of the nation of Canada are the same thing. Also implied is the idea that for the Inuit to live in peace in their traditional ways, they must be protected by Canadian agents who know what is best for them. The comic book never suggests that the lack of game may, in fact, be related to the fur trade that the Canadian nation was built upon.

Nelvana uses her superpowers to help the Inuit, but she also allies with a white RCMP officer, Corporal John Keene, stationed in an isolated cabin, and utilizes Western technologies (such as radio) to get her job done. Eventually she goes south herself and works under cover with the RCMP as Alana North, secret agent. In most references to the Inuit, they are contrasted with Nelvana and the Canadian government, who use "advanced" science and technology, as opposed to "primitive" hunting and gathering. The Inuit, in these stories, are passive beneficiaries of Western science and technology. Arnold suggests that current Canadian northern policy, as opposed to that in the 1940s, would challenge this dichotomy of advanced civilization versus primitive people, at least in theory. She claims the Canadian government and Canadian scientists are increasingly saying that Indigenous traditional knowledge (particularly Indigenous traditional environmental knowledge) is an important part of understanding the North. However, it is easier to give lip service to Indigenous knowledge than it is to respect it as another way of legitimately viewing the world. Overall, says Arnold, Indigenous traditional knowledge has been judged, and still is, largely by the standards of Western science. She writes, "Perhaps the clearest indication of the extent to which science sets the terms of engagement between TK [traditional knowledge] and science is the overwhelming tendency to frame the issue as one of how to *integrate* TK into western science" (102). In other words, traditional knowledge is reduced to data. But Indigenous traditional knowledge is not just *what* is known, it also involves what *can be* known and *how* it is known. If traditional knowledge is solely data, then the Indigenous participants in the dialogue are not allowed to participate as equals; they are more like participants in a study or consultants. Traditional knowledge is not allowed to challenge or disrupt Western science.

For Arnold, both in the 1940s stories of *Nelvana and the Northern Lights* and in current Canadian northern policy, southerners are the experts and the Inuit are only given token mention with little specificity, blending different Indigenous cultures and knowledges together in a simplistic fashion. "A scientific gaze on the North prevails" (Arnold 104). The significance of this is that the paternalism reflected in the 1940s *Nelvana of the Northern Lights* is still at work in present-day northern Canada. If this is the case, we must put an Inuk Nelvana as personifica-tion of Canada in that context. An Inuk woman who represents Canada cannot also represent the Inuit.

The desire to see Nelvana as both Canadian and Inuit is perhaps tied to the persistent cultural construction of Canada *as* the North. Canadians have a ten-dency to romanticise the North and their ability to endure its hardships, even though the vast majority of Canadians have never gone past the 60th parallel. Sherrill Grace says it well when she writes, "The history of southern Canadian sentimentalizing indifference is, in fact, a history of civil imperialism: the 'North' is valuable insofar as we can exploit its resources, one of which is its seemingly endless capacity to generate resonant (and marketable) images of a distinct Canadian identity—without our having to go there or face its realities" (2). This image of Canadian identity results in such things as inukshuks for sale in airports from Vancouver to Halifax as specifically Canadian memorabilia for tourists. Very few of those tourists actually visited any Inuit.

CONCLUSION

The desire for a strong female character that Canadians can be proud of and look to for further inspiration is an understandable desire for young Canadian women in the twenty-first century. That Nicholson and Richey prefer an interpretation of Nelvana as Inuit instead of a white goddess figure is also understandable. The colonial relationship between Canada and the Inuit is not conducive to an inter-sectional feminist vision; celebrating an Inuk superheroine could be seen as an anti-racist and perhaps postcolonialist move. However, Canada is not postcolonial. As a nation we have barely acknowledged our colonial history, never mind recog-nizing our continued colonial present. Even if Nelvana was inspired by an actual Inuk woman, she was put to the task of reinforcing Canadian governmental con-trol over the North.

So, should the *Nelvana of the Northern Lights* comic books be tossed onto the trash heap of unpleasant history? No, of course not. She is part of Canadian popular culture and as such needs to be understood in order to understand Canadian identities of the 1940s, and perhaps later in continued fan responses. We use her as a feminist icon, though, to our peril, unless we are comfortable with a white colonial feminism. I am not.

CRITICAL REFLECTION QUESTIONS

1. Why might it have been important to create Canadian superheroes in the 1940s?
2. What does the popularity of a "white queen or goddess" figure in comic books imply about race and gender?
3. What is the significance of Nelvana being interpreted as an Inuk superheroine rather than a white goddess?

WORKS CITED

Arnold, Samantha. "Nelvana of the North, Traditional Knowledge, and the Northern Dimension of Canadian Foreign Policy." *Canadian Foreign Policy Journal*, vol. 14, no. 2, 2008, pp. 95–107.

Beaty, Bart. "The Fighting Civil Servant? Making Sense of the Canadian Superhero." *American Review of Canadian Studies*, vol. 36, no. 3, 2006, pp. 427–439.

Beaupré, Maddy. "Interview with Hope Nicholson and Rachel Richey of the Nelvana of the Northern Lights Kickstarter." *Women Write About Comics*, 2013, https://womenwriteaboutcomics.com/2013/10/interview-with-hope-nicholson-and-rachel-richey-of-the-nelvana-of-the-northern-lights-kickstarter/. Accessed 20 Jan. 2019.

Bell, John. *Guardians of the North: The National Superhero in Canadian Comic-Book Art*. National Archives of Canada, 1992.

Dingle, Adrian. *Nelvana of the Northern Lights*. Edited by Hope Nicholson and Rachel Richey, Ideas and Design Works, 2014. [reprinted from 1941–1947]

Dittmer, Jason, and Soren Larsen. "Aboriginality and the Arctic North in Canadian Nationalist Superhero Comics, 1940–2004." *Historical Geography*, vol. 38, 2010, pp. 52–69.

Grace, Sherrill. "Representing North (or Greetings from Nelvana)." *Essays on Canadian Writing*, vol. 59, 1996, pp. 1–4.

Haggard, H. Rider. *She: A History of Adventure*. Longmans, 1886.

Keeshig-Tobias, Lenore. "Stop Stealing Native Stories." *Globe and Mail*, 26 Jan. 1990, A7.

King, Richard C. "Alter/native Heroes: Native Americans, Comic Books, and the Struggle for Self-Definition." *Cultural Studies Critical Methodologies*, vol. 9, no. 2, 2009, pp. 214–223.

Madwar, Samia. "Inuit High Arctic Relocations in Canada." *The Canadian Encyclopedia*, 2018, https://www.thecanadianencyclopedia.ca/en/article/inuit-high-arctic-relocations. Accessed 19 Jan. 2019.

McDougall, Robert L. "Duncan Campbell Scott." *The Canadian Encyclopedia*, 2008, https://www.thecanadianencyclopedia.ca/en/article/duncan-campbell-scott. Accessed 19 Jan. 2019.

Pewewardy, Cornel. "From Subhuman to Superhuman: Images of First Nations Peoples in Comic Books." *Studies in Media & Information Literacy Education*, vol. 2, no. 2, 2002, pp. 1–9.

Rubacha, Nicole. "Nelvana of the Northern Lights: Meet the Canadian Superhero Who Predated Wonder Woman." *Herizons*, Summer, 2014, pp. 16–19.

Sim, Dave. "Living in a World of Fantasy: *Cerebus* Creator Dave Sim Talks with Canadian Comic Book Pioneers Adrian and Pat Dingle and Bill Thomas." *AlterEgo*, vol. 3, no. 26, 2004, pp. 27–29. [reprint from 1973]

Walker, Alan. "Historical Perspective." *The Great Canadian Comic Books*, edited by Michael Hirsh and Patrick Loubert, Peter Martin Associates, 1971, pp. 5–21.

PART IV

TAKING CHARGE: RECASTING POP CULTURE
THROUGH PARTICIPATORY MEDIA

CHAPTER 10

Instapoets and YouTube Stars: Second Generation Immigrant Young Women Reimagining the Canadian National Narrative

Anuppiriya Sriskandarajah

INTRODUCTION

If nations are imagined, national narratives set the parameters. The Canadian national narrative has been partly constructed and propagated through a narrow framing of what constitutes the Canadian literary canon. Historically, those who have defined the Canadian national narrative for the most part have been white, heteronormative, middle class, and male. The formation of the national narrative from its inception has been based on the erasure of differences. For example, hegemonic cultural texts describe early Canadian life mostly as devoid of Indigenous Peoples. These cultural outputs construct worlds whereby Indigenous Peoples "have already been removed" (Calder 87). These erasures continue to be reproduced in the mainstream Canadian literary and media traditions. Though a few notable "diaspora" authors, like Michael Ondaatje, Shyam Selvadurai, Rohinton Mistry, and Joy Kogawa, have attained prominence, they too remain of a particular class and age. Their works mostly cater to a white gaze. When diverse voices are incorporated into the traditional Canadian national narrative cultural texts, their works often focus on life in other parts of the world, migration, or the struggles of integration into Canadian society. Feelings of Otherness juxtaposed with a "true" sense of Canadianness remain central to their storytelling. This can be attributed to both the authors' genuine interests and to publishing houses that continue to determine which stories are worth sharing. Longing for integration and the desire to belong become the reoccurring trope.

Publishers and media producers act as important gatekeepers for what becomes accepted as a part of the established Canadian national narrative. In this chapter I advocate for the rearticulation of which mediums are used to constitute the Canadian national narrative and whose voices are incorporated. The redefinition of the national narrative must go beyond incorporating voices of those on the margins in existing hegemonic institutions that continue to have the power to dictate the composition of the national narrative. I argue that the use of social media as a way to share narratives diverges from traditional systems and challenges conventional ways of dissemination. In this chapter I argue that if we want to expand what constitutes the Canadian narrative we need to change where we listen to these voices. I contend that the advent of social media has the potential to change the composition of the Canadian national narrative. Changing what constitutes the Canadian national narrative cannot be done by only adding new voices to old formulas, whereby we continue to work within the established parameters. Social media allows for centring content produced on the margins. Although still seen as outside the purview of "real" art, what I partly aim to do in this chapter is illustrate that works produced on social media platforms like YouTube and Instagram must be recognized as constituting an element of the mainstream Canadian national narrative.

I intend to do this by focusing on a web series created by a young Punjabi Canadian woman, Ms. Mutta, titled *Anarkali*, named after the lead character. The web series, in its third season, follows the lives of a young woman in her twenties and her friends as they navigate life, love, and everyday realities as second generation immigrants. What makes web series different compared to their mainstream TV counterparts is that these stories are written, produced, and performed by the young racialized women themselves. These stories are unapologetically about them and for them. However, with an average of 60,000 to 75,000 views per episode (which typically range from 7 to 10 minutes) we can glean that through their particularities these stories become universal.

SOCIAL MEDIA: THE RESERVOIR OF THE NEW NATIONAL NARRATIVE

> Since the creation of the printing press, publishers have enjoyed a pre-eminent role in the development of national literatures, playing a key role in the mediation and consecration of literary works—in other words, in canon formation. They decide which texts are deemed valuable …
> —Iribarren 321

According to Kuusela (128), when it comes to cultural production there has been a "rise of the so-called participatory culture" via social media. Participatory culture provides for those traditionally on the margins the opportunity to produce and share their works. Jenkins (141) argues that participatory culture in the production of cultural texts is not necessarily novel. However, digital technology has allowed participatory culture to become normalized. Social media has minimized barriers associated with more traditional avenues of dissemination, like production companies and publishing houses.

The long maintained power of publishers and production companies as the gatekeepers of the national narrative is being partially displaced by new media. Studying digital media allows us to not only canonize voices on the margins but also to meta-analyze the processes of canonizations. European scholars have made the case that because digital media is in its infancy we will be able to examine the process through which things become canonized (Backe 4). The technological revolution of the past few decades has undeniably changed the character of life. For some, the use of technology remains to be seen as neutral and utilitarian, ignoring the social context of the use of technology. Pfaffenberger (qtd. in Berry and Goodwin 910) states that "to use technology" is to articulate a "social vision."

In 2017, YouTube was the most popular website after Google, both globally and in Canada. It is the most widespread video sharing website (Alexa qtd. in Raby et al. 497). YouTube has allowed young people to create and share their art globally (Raby et al. 497). Sites like YouTube are particularly unique and engaging for young people because they merge creation and dissemination with social networking. These spaces allow for creators to link and distribute content in participatory ways not possible through traditional media (Chau 72).

Social media allows users to create and share original works. The Internet has enabled writers and content creators to connect with others, form communities, and publish original content (Berry and Goodwin 925). It allows creators to bypass traditional gatekeepers that restrict sharing of works, like traditional publishing houses or production houses. Platforms like YouTube and Instagram enable artists on the margins to share their works and to be received by millions of people outside traditional art spaces. For example, Instagram accounts like @arthoecollective and @girlgazeproject showcase art that is submitted by women and racialized women (Caldeira et al. 27). Here they are able to represent themselves the way they want to be seen, defying stereotypical depictions. In this way, representations on these platforms act as a form of everyday activism (Vivienne and Burgess 365).

SOUTH ASIAN CANADIANS AND THE CANADIAN NATIONAL NARRATIVE

It is important to consider that the producers of cultural texts that constitute what can be deemed part of the South Asian Canadian national narrative are tremendously diverse, representing the many internal divergences that exist within the categorization of a people. Though there is a shared narrative amongst those who identify as having roots in the subcontinent, it is not without recognizing the enormous heterogeneity that exists within the literary and cultural outputs. Pirbhai (9) captures these tensions in her attempt to define *South Asian Canadian*:

> A diasporic or ethnic category, emerged from a seemingly fraught polemic: on the one hand, it was seen to be a productive marker of socio-religious and ethnocultural affinities; on the other hand, it was seen to be a multiculturalist invention, shaped for the expedience of a nation attempting to accommodate a vast and unruly influx of new immigrants connected to an equally vast and unruly place, the Indian subcontinent.

These might have been the impetus for mainstream definitions of the South Asian Canadian cultural outputs. However, they are fraught with added tensions that recognize that certain narratives are generally missing, including stories from Kashmir, Bhutan, and Bangladesh (Pirbhai 14). South Asian Canadian as a category is further complicated when we consider those who trace their roots to South Asia through the Caribbean or East Africa (Pirbhai 14). As Pirbhai (20) so concisely states, "ethno-national and diasporic specificities must continue to inform our reading of South Asian Canadian identities."

South Asians have settled in Canada for more than a century. However, in the national imaginary their existence seems to be only cemented after the reconfiguration of the historically race-based system of migration to the current point-based system in the 1970s (Pirbhai 6). In the 1980s and 1990s, we begin to see the emergence of works that could be considered a part of the South Asian Canadian national narrative constituted by first generation immigrants (Pirbhai 9), including seminal works like Rohinton Mistry's *A Fine Balance*, Michael Ondaatje's *Anil's Ghost*, and Shyam Selvadurai's *Funny Boy*. Common themes of these writers include the experiences of South Asian Canadians' pre-migration life, the struggles of post-migration life, and/or their transnational connections (McGifford qtd. in Pirbhai 12).

Unlike those that make up the traditional South Asian elements of the Canadian national narrative, *Anarkali* is unapologetically "Canadian," setting it apart from these other works. The young women featured in this web series are not questioning their "Canadianness" but rather taking their rightful place in the Canadian imaginary. They do not lament over the struggles of integrating into Canadian society but rather question power structures that constrict their everyday lives. These are narratives that are pervasive and need to be part of the Canadian national narrative. Themes explored in this chapter include traditional expectations versus contemporary realities, body as discourse, colourism, agency, constructions of South Asian femininity, notions of Canadianness, and intercultural relations within the context of Canadian multiculturalism as explored through the web series.

Anarkali

Anarkali, the title character, is a hopeless romantic inspired by the Bollywood movies she watches. However, unlike the lives portrayed by Bollywood actresses, Anarkali's love life is more complex. Her life is shaped by the realities of living as a second generation immigrant woman in Canadian society. The story begins with Anarkali's boyfriend of nine years ending their relationship, two months before their big Indian wedding. The show unfolds from this point, allowing viewers to watch how a twenty-something second generation Punjabi Canadian woman in an ethnic enclave in Brampton, Ontario, navigates finding love and constructing herself in the process. *Anarkali* unabashedly tackles gender, race, sex, and the second generation's relationships with immigrant parents. The women show no qualms about smoking weed, drinking alcohol, and talking about sex, sex tapes, and abortions.

The opening scene of *Anarkali* sets the tone for the show. The scene is set in a local coffee shop, where Anarkali's best friends Roop and Dil are having a lively conversation:

Roop: Indian girls don't do open relationships.
Dil: I am Indian and I do them. (*Anarkali*, season one, episode one)

The conversation at the coffee shop foreshadows the issues that the series explores and how unapologetically it examines these issues. These issues are not hidden under metaphors or subtle glances but rather directly unpacked for the viewers. The opening conversation is a clear example of the many ways the series disrupts common tropes of South Asian femininity as submissive and sexually passive. South Asian women are stereotypically portrayed as victims of their sexuality. They are generally shown to be lacking the agency to exert their desires. South Asian culture is often portrayed as a culture where familial honour rests on the protection of South Asian women's sexuality. However, *Anarkali* unsettles the notion that South Asian women's sexuality is sacred and in need of protection by centring South Asian women's desires and the multiple ways they explore their sexuality.

"SO HOW DARE YOU MOCK YOUR MOTHER"

The struggle between first and second generation relations is by far not new in the Canadian diasporic literature. However, what sets *Anarkali* apart is its ability to capture the nuances of these realities. The web series covers the ambiguity of being second generation Punjabi in Ontario, Canada. For example, when discussing Anarkali's aversion to the idea of an arranged marriage, it is not without later showing viewers her cousin's successful arranged marriage.

The intergenerational struggle is best captured by the relationship between Anarkali and her mother. Soon after the end of Anarkali's relationship with Prince (her boyfriend of nine years), her mother begins a quest to make sure Anarkali is married by what she deems a respectable age. There is a constant tension and negotiation between satisfying community expectations and individual desires. Anarkali feels her choices in whom she dates, at what age she marries, how she dresses, and how she chooses to spend her time are to be determined by and for herself. However, her mother constantly reminds her of the importance of fulfilling community expectations. Her mother is particularly compelled to meet these community expectations because of the stigma associated with raising her child alone after the death of her husband. Her mother has to navigate her own pressures of living in both an Indian and Canadian patriarchal society whereby the death of her husband fuels her fear that Anarkali will not be raised with "Indian values." As the mother of a prospective arranged-marriage suitor states, "We were a bit hesitant to come see your daughter, because you know in this country growing up without a father it is very hard to keep Indian values" (*Anarkali*, season one, episode two). Men are seen as the protectors of traditional values, while women are expected to be the boundaries in which these values are marked.

For many first generation immigrants, their cultural collectivities remain of utmost importance as a means through which to preserve their culture and identity but also their status in society. Often shut out from mainstream society, their ethno-religious communities offer them refuge. Women's bodies, deemed the reservoirs of culture, become the site in which to regulate boundaries. We see this tension dominate Anarkali's life, as expressed through her relationship with her mother. Mucina, (435) drawing on Homi Bhabha's work on third spaces (the in-between spaces between two cultures), discusses the many parts of second generation women's lives that are lived in secret. These concealments are to avoid the social punishments that accompany transgressions of these cultural community boundaries.

Though this tension between Anarkali and her mother pervades the story, she simultaneously recognizes the struggles the first generation endures. Though Anarkali is skeptical of the arranged marriage process, the episode ends with Instapoet Rupi Kaur's poem "Broken English." The poem captures the ambiguous relationship that permeates generations of immigrants, the constant oscillation between reverence and rebellion.

"Broken English" captures the realities of immigrant families' experiences of migrating to a new country and not knowing the language. However, instead of reiterating typical themes that focus on the challenges of integration and being accepted by mainstream or white Canadians, Kaur speaks to a uniquely second generation dilemma. Her poem lambastes children who mock their immigrant parents' "broken English." She compares a mother's broken English to great works of art. An immigrant mother's accent is one of the few remnants she maintains from her home. Kaur recognizes that society at large mocks an immigrant mother's speech and this should not be reproduced by her children in their desire for whiteness. Instead Kaur encourages them to pay homage and respect the sacrifices and the barriers their parents negotiate as the second generation continues to navigate their own lives.

> So how dare you mock your mother
> when she opens her mouth
> and broken English spills out.
> Her accent is thick like honey,
> hold it with your life,
> it's the only thing she has left from home.
> Don't stomp on that richness,
> instead hang it up on the walls
> of museums next to Dali and Van Gogh
> Her life is brilliant and tragic.
> Kiss the side of her tender cheek.
> She already knows what it sounds like
> to have an entire nation laugh when she speaks.
> She's more than our punctuation and language.
> We might be able to take pictures and write stories,
> but she made an entire world for herself.
> How's that for art.
> (Rupi Kaur qtd. in *Anarkali*, season one, episode two)

Rupi Kaur's works are integrated into the web series, typically at the end of episodes, where she is often seen reading her poems. Similarly, the web series highlights young Punjabi Canadian fashion designers, boutique owners, and musicians and their works. Rupi Kaur began sharing her work on Instagram, which led to the publication of two books. She began by self-publishing, only to later be courted by a publishing house. Her first book, *Milk and Honey*, received critical acclaim and sold more than 2.5 million copies (Mzezewa). Rupi Kaur's work has been aptly described as "performances of celebration, reclamation, resistance, and ultimately, acts of (de)colonial self-love" (Kruger). She tackles issues of gender inequality, navigating race as a second generation Canadian Punjabi-Sikh woman within a racialized society. Her writing is subversive both in content and form, sharing her work on Instagram as a self-publisher. The subversiveness of her poetry allows her to be weaved effortlessly into the web series and its storylines.

"WE WILL NOT BE OUR MOTHERS ..."

Generational differences are filtered through gendered realities. These take a particular tone when discussing life in ethnic enclaves. For example, there is one moment whereby Anarkali and her cousin go to the drug store to purchase a pregnancy test for Anarkali. The woman at the counter is Indian and the young women worry that in a tight-knit community whereby honour, or *izzat*, is contingent on sexual boundaries (Gill and Brah 73), word will spread about their purchase. These short sketches are woven into the main plot deployment, illustrating the everydayness of these realities.

In another example, in a short scene outside the main plot of the episode, Navi, Anarkali's cousin, has her boyfriend drop her off away from her house after a date. She makes this request due to fears that her parents will see her with a young man. She also asks Anarkali to covertly bring out clothes for her to change into before entering the house. The characters do not live in constant fear of these cultural dualities or allow them to paralyze their existence; the characters simply negotiate them as something inescapable that they must navigate alongside other realities of negotiating love, life, and career as they chart their own existence in these third spaces.

The women of the story are unapologetically feminists. Their feminism recognizes the reality of gender inequality while simultaneously understanding the importance of their cultural identities. They choose their own ways of accepting and discarding pieces of their culture that they deem desirable or undesirable. They do not simply adopt a Western feminism but understand the importance of both their cultural and gender identities. At the end of season three, Anarkali's cousin Roupi's wedding takes place. Before the dol ceremony (where the bride leaves her parents' home to join the groom's house) Roupi, while they toast champagne, says, "We will not be our mothers; we will put our friendships first." Roupi's comments capture their unique feminism shaped by their second generation existence within these third spaces, whereby they assert their desire to put their own needs before that of their familial, gendered, or cultural obligations. It should not go without notice that she makes this assertion simultaneously as she participates in the dol ceremony, which can be viewed as a patriarchal tradition that reinforces the idea of daughters as property to be given away. However, for Roupi and her friends this scene demonstrates the many everyday ways they subvert and renegotiate traditions. Although Roupi asserts their lives will be different than their mothers', this of course is not without contestation. In an earlier part of the show, Anarkali's aunt asserts that the feminism of the second generation children is too extreme and in opposition to their Indian values.

"PAKI DOT OR FEATHER"

Anarkali's problematization of race deviates from discussions in the established national narrative. Anarkali tackles race not as a victim of racism but rather as an agent who is well aware of its manifestations. Anarkali and her friends tackle how race infiltrates everyday aspects of life. Race is discussed frankly, not deliberated in forms of undefinable tensions. One way this is highlighted is through the telling of Anarkali and her friends' experiences on dates or encounters with men in social settings where discussions of race become unavoidable.

In one episode there is a montage of different scenarios whereby white men approach Anarkali and her friends using racialized language. They greet them with statements like "I need curry in my life"; "You look exotic"; or "What kind of Indian are you, Paki dot or feather?"; or they make assumptions about the supposed submissiveness of Indian women, "[I]t's just something like in your culture the women treat their men like God, it's something you know, I love it!" (*Anarkali*, season one, episode three).

For second generation immigrants, this has particular implications. For example, there are several instances, including an episode where Anarkali is on a date, when potential white suitors discuss how young Indian women are different now compared to when they were younger: "You have adjusted so well to the Canadian lifestyle … the girls we grew up with, they didn't date, let alone talk to us guys" (*Anarkali*, season two, episode four). Indian women are deemed more desirable now to the white gaze because they have acculturated to "Canadianness" compared to their childhood selves.

Anarkali also tackles intra-racial constructions of racial hierarchies as reaffirmed by Western standards of beauty and femininity. Anarkali and her friends on numerous occasions discuss how they are often mistaken for Latina women. However, they also recognize that some young Indian women strive to be Latina-passing. In a racialized society, being identified as Latina allows Indian women to move up the racial hierarchy and be closer to whiteness and its afforded privileges. Anarkali and her friends highlight how some young Indian women dye their hair blond and wear coloured contacts in order to distance themselves from Indianness. Latina women's stereotypical depictions as hyper-feminine, and their presumed hyper-sensuality, places them higher in the race and gender matrix. *Anarkali* recognizes that Indian women go to these measures because they do not receive the respect they deserve from second generation Indian men and other men. The third episode of the first season ends with Anarkali and her two friends making a toast to this reality: "Cheers to Indian women that don't get the respect they deserve" (*Anarkali*, season one, episode three).

The show centres discussion of racism within Canadian society. However, it misses many opportunities to discuss in any meaningful way anti-Black racism. Though Anarkali has Black friends, and in the show they often act as a conduit to explain Indian culture, there is no meaningful interrogation of anti-Black racism within Indian communities. There is only one line where Anarkali's friend asks why her cousin fetishizes Black men, since she seems to only date Black men. Apart from this one line, there is no interrogation of anti-Black racism.

Most episodes incorporate music by Indian Canadian rappers or singers. Hip-hop culture permeates the show. For example, Anarkali, on a date with Jag (a love interest), has a conversation about which hip-hop artist is better, Drake or Biggie, to which he answers Biggie. She tells him that he should support Drake because he is from their hometown (being from Toronto, Canada). This scene underscores two important issues. Firstly, this departs from typical elements of the national narrative on South Asians in Canada, which focus on the longings for homeland. For these young women, Canada is their home; never is there a doubt.

Secondly, it underlies the eschewing of meaningful discussions of race. South Asians have been able to identify with Blackness, as we witness through the infusion of hip-hop culture throughout the show, without having to pay the price of a shared racial politics (Maira 263). For example, Maira (263) argues that Indian youth are able to associate with Black youth culture through fashion, music, and cultural vernacular. However, for Indian youth this association is chosen. They have the licence to move in and out of "Black culture" as they choose, drawing on it when it benefits them and discarding it when faced with structural violence. This gives them a privilege not extended to Black youth, who, even if they wanted to disassociate with "Black culture" could not, by virtue of their skin. This also extends to their inability to escape structural realities that render Black communities socially, culturally, and economically marginalized. The association with Black culture of second generation Indian youth can be partly attributed to shared experiences of racialized identity marked by discrimination. However, they have also benefited from the proximity to whiteness within the racial hierarchy. These benefits are reproduced to maintain their own position within the hierarchy to secure relative social and economic privileges. This is most evident in the manifestation of anti-Black racism in South Asian communities.

CONCLUSION

Audial (46) aptly described the importance of South Asian Canadian women's contribution to Canadian cultural production: "In the tension between imposed identities and those asserted by multigenerational South Asian Canadian women, spaces of resistance have formed in the anthologies and other venues in which they publish, and in the act of writing itself." YouTube has brought attention to racialized peoples and their issues, which have mainly been ignored by mainstream Canadian popular culture. This is despite Canada's espousal in rhetoric of multiculturalism. Self-representation online by groups traditionally ignored within established literary and other popular cultural spaces is in itself an act of resistance. Technological innovations are often discussed and celebrated by the technology industry as disrupters; we cannot think textual cultural productions or the Canadian national narrative can be exempt from this reality. The use of social media as a way to share narratives diverges from traditional systems and challenges conventional ways of dissemination.

This chapter aimed to examine the way young second generation immigrant women are able to use non-traditional media to disseminate their cultural productions. By using unconventional methods, they are able to circumvent major publishing houses and production companies. The circumvention of these institutions allows for storytelling that diverts from catering to the white gaze. It enables the telling of stories that are important to these women. These stories are for them, by them. They are thereby able to disrupt dominant narratives in both form and content.

However, this of course is not to romanticize new media and its potentialities. Though the use of social media enables the production of counter-hegemonic stories and the rebuking of traditional forms of dissemination, it does not operate outside the capitalistic ventures represented by technology giants like Google and YouTube. We must recognize the social context in which the use of technology is situated. For example, Instagrammers who have the highest number of followers mostly continue to be those who conform to hegemonic standards of Western beauty and femininity. Despite these realities, *Anarkali* represents the possibilities that social media provides as a way to shape what and how we constitute the Canadian national narrative.

CRITICAL REFLECTION QUESTIONS

1. In what ways do you imagine the experiences of first and second generation immigrants are similar and in what ways are they different? What are the implications of this for Canadian multiculturalism policies?
2. Most research on racialized peoples in Canada tends to focus on the relationship between racialized Others and whites. What are the potential consequences of ignoring relationships between racialized groups?
3. Although social media is a great way to disrupt traditional methods of dissemination of cultural productions, what are some of its negative implications?

WORKS CITED

"Anarkali Web Series, Season 1, Episode 1, Say It Ain't So." *YouTube*, uploaded by Ms Mutta, 30 July 2015, https://www.youtube.com/watch?v=ykj6kHSFG9o.

"Anarkali Web Series, Season 1, Episode 2, Mama's Boy." *YouTube*, uploaded by Ms Mutta, 6 Aug 2015, https://www.youtube.com/watch?v=gm1FdUJh5zQ&index=3&list=PL0KgG8-LaNrennEqXOhg62oSnTPOce9JL.

"Anarkali Web Series, Season 1, Episode 3, Indian Girls." *YouTube*, uploaded by Ms Mutta, 13 Aug. 2015, https://www.youtube.com/watch?v=SCvIr3AWFFw&index=4&list=PL0KgG8-LaNrennEqXOhg62oSnTPOce9JL.

"Anarkali Web Series, Season 2, Episode 4, Bad Date. Good Date." *YouTube*, uploaded by Ms Mutta, 17 Mar. 2016, https://www.youtube.com/watch?v=y64jD-CaIUo.

"Anarkali Web Series, Season 3, Episode 1, How Did We Get Here?" *YouTube*, uploaded by Ms Mutta, 22 Feb. 2018, https://www.youtube.com/watch?v=TtyWh7GsP0Q.

Audial, Angela. "Others in their Own Land: Second Generation South Asian Canadian Women, Racism, and the Persistence of Colonial Discourse." *Canadian Woman Studies*, vol. 20, no. 2, 2000, pp. 41–47.

Backe, Hans-Joachim. "The Literary Canon in the Age of New Media." *Poetics Today*, vol. 36, no. 1–2, 2015, pp. 1–31.

Berry, Marsha, and Omega Goodwin. "Poetry 4 U: Pinning Poems Under/Over/Through the Streets." *New Media & Society*, vol. 15, no. 6, 2012, pp. 909–929.

Caldeira, S. P., et al. "A Different Point of View: Women's Self Representation in Instagram's Participatory Artistic Movements @girlgazeproject and @arthoecollective." *Critical Arts*, vol. 32, no. 3, 2018, pp. 26–43.

Calder, A. "Hiding in Plain Sight: A New Narrative for Canadian Literary History." *Journal of Canadian Studies*, vol. 49, no. 2, pp. 87–105.

Chau, C. "YouTube as a Participatory Culture." *New Directions for Youth Development*, vol. 128, 2010, pp. 65–74.

Gill, Aisha K., and Avtar Brah. "Interrogating Cultural Narratives about 'Honour'-Based Violence." *European Journal of Women's Studies*, vol. 21, no. 1, 2014, pp. 72–86.

Iribarren, Teresa. "Subaltern Mediators in the Digital Landscape: The Case of Video Poetry." *Target*, vol. 29, no. 2, 2017, pp. 319–338.

Jenkins, Henry. *Fans, Bloggers, and Gamers: Exploring Participatory Culture.* New York UP, 2006.

Kruger, Sasha. "The Technopo(e)litics of Rupi Kaur: (de)Colonial AestheTics and Spatial Narrations in the DigiFemme Age." *A Journal of Gender and New Media & Technology*, vol. 11, 2017, https://adanewmedia.org/2017/05/issue11-kruger/. Accessed 12 Dec. 2018

Kuusela, H. "Literature and Participatory Culture Online: Literary Crowdsourcing and its Discontents." *Critical Arts*, vol. 32, no. 3, 2018, pp. 126–142.

Maira, S. "Desis Reprazent: Bhangra Remix and Hip Hop in New York City." *Postcolonial Studies*, vol. 1, no. 3, 1998, pp. 357–370.

Mucina, Mandeep Kaur. "Exploring the Role of 'Honour' in Son Preference and Daughter Deficit within the Punjabi Diaspora in Canada." *Canadian Journal of Development Studies*, vol. 39, no. 3, 2018, pp. 426-442.

Mzezewa, Tariro. "Rupi Kaur Is Kicking Down the Doors of Publishing." *New York Times*, 5 Oct. 2017, https://www.nytimes.com/2017/10/05/fashion/rupi-kaur-poetry-the-sun and-her-flowers.html.

Pirbhai, Miriam. "South Asian Canadian Literature: A Centennial Journey." *Studies in Canadian Literature*, vol. 4, no. 1, 2015, pp. 5–26.

Raby, R., et al. "Vloggin on YouTube: The Online, Political Engagement of Young Canadians Advocating for Social Change." *Journal of Youth Studies*, vol. 21, no. 4, 2018, pp. 497–514.

Vivienne, S., and J. Burgess. "The Digital Storyteller's Stage: Queer Everyday Activists Negotiating Privacy and Publicness." *Journal of Broadcasting and Electronic Media*, vol. 56, no. 3, 2012, pp. 362–377.

CHAPTER 11

The Videoludic Cyborg: Queer and Feminist Appropriations and Hybridity

Roxanne Chartrand and Pascale Thériault

INTRODUCTION

Video game culture is heavily tainted with militarized masculinity and has therefore often been described as toxic by many feminist game scholars (Condis; Consalvo; Paul; Salter and Blodgett). The state of this world, which is vastly harmful to women,[1] people of colour, and other marginalized people, could be explained by the military-industrial origins of video games. Indeed, "interactive game designers and marketers, starting from an intensely militarized institutional incubator, forged a deep connexion with their youthful core male gaming *aficionados*, but failed or ignored other audiences and gaming options" (Kline et al. 265). Thus, since their beginning, video games have had thematics of war and confrontation, while targeting mainly a male audience. What Kline and colleagues called militarized masculinity is in fact a hegemonic discourse, or a dominant theme, of a "shared semiotic nexus revolving around issues of war, conquest and combat," or "militarist subtexts of conquest and imperialism" (Kline et al. 255), which ultimately resulted in evacuating marginalized people and diversity in video games to the benefit of similar content, primarily addressing a white cishet male audience. There are many incidents of harassment, violence, racism, and sexism in video game content and in many video game communities.

Even though harassment of women in gaming has always been a part of the gaming culture, it often happened behind the scenes (Kafai et al.). The sadly famous #GamerGate movement, in 2014, became part of the public discourse and showed how video game communities are toxic for women, queer,[2] and other marginalized people.[3] "Although participants framed their efforts as critiquing ethics in gaming journalism, they came under fire for namely directing their attacks and harassment at female and feminist game designers, players and critics, labeling them 'social justice warriors' in order to vilify them" (Kafai et al. 3). However, there is an increasing feminist and queer resistance against toxic culture in both video game creation and gaming practices. Canada is one of the countries spearheading this resistance, unsurprisingly, considering the importance of the video game industry in the country. For example, many feminist initiatives, such as Pixelles and Girls on Games in Montreal, Dames Making Games in Toronto, and Women in Games in Vancouver, and even a few Canada-wide initiatives, such as ReFig and Ladies Learning Code, help people who identify as women create games by providing them tools, such as courses or networking opportunities.

One of the ways in which women are investing in the gaming scene is through hacking and feminist modding[4] of existing video games. These are obvious acts of feminist resistance, because the very structure of the game is modified for political and activist means. For example, Rachel Simone Well, in her work titled *Hello Kitty World*, presents a mod that replaces the character of our dear plumber, Mario, with the likeness of Hello Kitty in the original 1985 *Super Mario Bros* (by Nintendo). The goal of this mod is to add socially constructed feminine attributes to roles usually associated with masculinity. Even without changing the structure of the game itself, playing can be a political act: one can actively and consciously choose to endorse a feminist stance: we can choose to consciously play a lesbian relationship in *Mass Effect* or *Life Is Strange*, for example, or to refuse traditional gender roles in many JRPGs by giving female characters physical strength or by exploiting the rules of the game.

Feminist resistance is also possible in game design. Faced with homogeneity of the video game landscape, several creators and marginalized people are trying to reclaim the space by resorting to several political and technological tactics in order to set up direct social change. Many independent game companies, such as Montreal-based Kitfox Games and Epsilon, are enforcing gender-balancing and inclusivity policies, both with regards to the content of their games and in their own studios. Outside of these institutionalized spaces, however, marginalized video game communities in Canada have started reclaiming the space through the creation of radically different objects, most of them falling under the AltGames movement. AltGames developers may create very different games, but they all have in common the fact that they twist and transform video game conventions in order to defy contemporary gaming expectations. This creative process and appropriation tactic can be situated within the queer game studies paradigm (Ruberg and Shaw), which proposes to understand games as a system of pleasure, power dynamics, and possibilities. Games are conceived as a space within which players are allowed to explore and subvert rules, thus shifting the focus from the content of games to their very essence. Ultimately, queerness interrogates the notion of social norms and subverts them by being voluntarily counter-cultural (Halberstam). The queering of games can also be seen as a way to perform a virtual identity, to explore the notion of the self in a disembodied form where rules are defined by a computerized entity and not by a physical one.

In this chapter, we will seek to highlight the ways in which the AltGames movement is in line with posthumanist theories, including Donna Haraway's concept of the cyborg, which poses the idea of a feminist and queer resistance within the space between the individual and the machine, as well as Donald Morton's idea of the cyberqueer and Nina Wakeford's theorization of the cyberqueer identity. This multifaceted phenomenon offers a unique opportunity for the conceptualization of the self, aiming to imagine a posthuman identity that transcends the physical norms and space, to the benefit of individuals and groups who subvert the norms of cisgendered masculine heterosexuality (Wakeford). In this sense, the Canadian AltGames community could be seen as part of a posthumanist movement that aims to recrystallize identity within a virtual space, thus getting rid of physical imperatives of identity performativity. We will argue that some games pertaining to the AltGames movement constitute a radically subversive form, approaching the ideal of Haraway's cyborg and Morton and Wakeford's cyberqueer identity.

CYBORG, CYBERQUEER, AND POSTHUMANISM

In 1984, Haraway published "A Cyborg Manifesto," where she first theorized the idea of the cyborg as a feminist utopia. She writes:

> A cyborg is a cybernetic organism, a hybrid of machine and organism, a creature of social reality as well as a creature of fiction.… The cyborg is a matter of fiction and lived experience that changes what counts as women's experience in the late twentieth century. This is a struggle over life and death, but the boundary between science fiction and social reality is an optical illusion. (Haraway 149)

In this short paragraph, the author highlights three critical aspects of her idea of the cyborg: (1) it is constituted of both organic and technological components; (2) it blurs the boundaries between fiction and social reality (distinguished here from biological reality); and (3) it defies both biological and social binary oppositions with regards to identity construction (Wolmark). Most importantly, Haraway's cyborg challenges the idea of "white feminism," which focuses primarily

on white, heterosexual biological women: the cyborg as a utopian concept transcends sex, gender, and race, but also questions biological imperatives limiting
identity construction. Similarly, Wolmark argues that Haraway's cyborg also "disrupts the gendered power relations of technology" (Wolmark 232), which have
also reinforced the patriarchal order. Springer, drawing on Hyussen's work, notes
that starting in the nineteenth century, after the industrial revolution, technology is often associated with femininity and feminine sexuality in the collective
imagination. Although men produce, own, and control technological artifacts,
technology itself is associated with femininity and "threatening entities capable of
vast, uncontrollable destruction" (Wolmark 36). Mostly realized in popular culture and science fiction works, this idea of an uncontrollable feminine strength
incarnated in a technological form is incredibly common: from *Her*'s Samantha to
Ex Machina's Ava, examples of dangerously powerful technological beings presented as feminine entities are plentiful. Although interesting, this idea reinforces
binary gendered power dynamics and fails to account for a variety of queer experiences, thus proving the importance of situating the concept of the cyborg in a
transcending space.

Although Haraway's cyborg seems to offer a promising avenue to think about
the intersections of sex, gender, and race at the crossroads of technological and
biological functions, her work remains to this day—almost 30 years later—mostly
conceptual. Indeed, Elise Paradis argues that "disembodied performance has faded
in the face of the inescapably raced, sexed, and gendered body" (Paradis 447),
thus preventing Haraway's cyborg utopia from materializing. Faced with both the
lingering technological difficulties associated with cyberware integration with the
human body as well as the inevitable reminders of heteronormativity in what cyberpunk literature calls "meatspace"—that is, the physical world—the idea of the
cyberqueer emerged. Matilda Tudor states that the cyberqueer is "the ultimate
manifestation of queer theory, as it was seen to transcend the physical world in a
parallel space, where [one] freely and flexibly could pick and choose who to be"
(Tudor 6). The cyberqueer identity refers to individuals and groups who subvert
heteronormativity by performing their identity as fluid, thus subverting binary
social norms, and do so using the many possibilities brought by the democrati-
zation of the Internet and virtual worlds. Although the cyberqueer movement
is a very loose one, mainly characterized by the idea of queerness in a virtual
space, Wakeford identifies four main themes associated with cyberqueer research:
(1) identity and self-presentation of queer folks; (2) the creation of a queer space;
(3) the electronic facilitation of a queer virtual community; and (4) new technology
and erotic practices. Although alternative game creation practices are extremely

diverse, as we aim to show in the next section with the example of the AltGames movement, all of these crucial aspects of the cyberqueer movement are also key to understanding how games can be part of a hybrid virtual identity.

Thus, drawing from Haraway's cyborg utopia as well as from the cyberqueer movement, we propose that subversive games and autobiographical games could constitute a form of posthuman being, a sort of mind-uploaded state of cyber-being. This chapter does not aim at offering a definition of what posthumanism is, nor does it claim to propose a model of the posthuman being; rather, it draws from a variety of definitions—those of Foucault, Wolfe, Hayles, and Bostrom—in order to think of videoludic[5] creation as a means of recrystallizing identity in the cyberspace, nearing a form of posthumanist utopia. More importantly, we work from Wolfe's idea that "'the human' is achieved … by transcending the bonds of materiality and embodiment altogether" (Wolfe xv). In order to distinguish between transhumanist and posthumanist thoughts, the author adds that "post-humanism is the opposite of transhumanism, and in this light, transhumanism should be seen as an *intensification* of humanism" (Wolfe xiv, xv).

ALTGAMES

AltGames, especially subversive and autobiographical games, which we argue can be seen as a form of posthumanism being, is a quite recent video game movement within the feminist and queer gaming communities. Even though the first tweets tagged with the #AltGames hashtag can be traced back to around 2009, AltGames as part of a movement seem to have emerged in 2014, at around the same time as the toxic #GamerGate saga. Rather than being distributed in conventional ways, such as through the digital distribution platform Steam or video game consoles such as Xbox or PlayStation, most AltGames can be found on alternative platforms such as itch.io. Few academic researchers have studied AltGames, mainly because of the elusive nature of the recent movement. Our own definition is based on an analysis of social media discourse, mainly from Twitter, where the movement first originated. When AltGames players and developers were asked to define what AltGames meant to them, many recurring keywords, themes, and associated hashtags emerged (see table 11.1).

This overview of AltGames discourse—alongside formal analyses of self-proclaimed AltGames and past subversive practices described in gaming manifestos—will help us to broadly define the AltGames movement. Although the label itself can and is used by many non-marginalized designers aiming to create radically different games, the AltGames community mostly unites marginalized

Table 11.1: Recurring Keywords, Hashtags, and Themes of AltGames

Associated Keywords	Associated Hashtags	Recurring Themes
• Punk games • Vignettes • Zines • Queer games • Twine revolution • NotGames • HardGames	• #gamedev • #punkgames • #indiedev • #madewithunity	• Anti-capitalism • Anti-commercialism • Liberty/freedom • Personal experience/emotions • Counterculture • Marginalized groups

people, which strongly links them to the idea of the cyberqueer. Prior to discussing the current alternative gaming scene, we must trace the diverse and multiple origins of previous movements and subversive practices in video game communities emerging in the early twenty-first century: the Scratchware, the Realtime Art, and the NotGames movements all share similarities with the AltGames movement.

Written in the early 2000s, the Scratchware Manifesto states the importance for games to move away from the conventions of the AAA[6] industry. The anonymous authors of the manifesto, all of them AAA game developers, were inspired by the Cyberpunk Manifesto (Kirtchev) and kept in mind the spirit of protest to advocate for generic diversity in video games. When they wrote, "Death to the gaming industry! Long live games," the authors of the manifesto were arguing for smaller production teams or even individual creators who create more personal experiences using "scratchware," that is, quality computer games created by micro-teams were to be celebrated and encouraged. Scratchware games, they argue, can be played by everyone, are short (from 15 minutes to 1 hour), can be replayed, and are entertaining and satisfying. They are also created with reduced budgets, using cheap or rudimentary softwares—hence the idea of "scratch," or "trash," as symbolic to the authors. However, the Scratchware Manifesto could also be seen as a genesis of independent game companies, considering the fact that they do not seek to deconstruct the very notions of what we consider as "good games" but rather take a stance against the mainstream industry.

The Realtime Art Manifesto, on the other hand, defends a more radical position and puts forward an artistic vision of video games. Written in 2006 by Belgian game developers Harvey and Samyn, the manifesto essentially echoes the Scratchware Manifesto's challenge to the traditional idea of AAA video games, even if the authors do not directly refer to it. The idea of a videogame "author" emerges in the manifesto, and it rejects consumerism by saying "stop making games, be an author" (Harvey and Samyn). That sentence could even be interpreted as "stop being a worker; be an artist." Inspired by poetry, the authors of the manifesto also say, "Make short and intense games: think haiku, not epic. Think poetry, not prose" (Harvey and Samyn). The manifesto, detailed in 10 points, proposes to recognize video games as an art form. The authors suggest operating according to what they call a "punk economy," that is, that video game creators should use alternative distribution methods such as self-publishing instead of trying to adhere to the capitalist publishing model. Even the distribution system is designed according to an alternative economy where authors are asked to make their games accessible to all types of audiences.

Finally, the NotGames manifesto, signed by Michaël Samyn (who is also one of the authors of the Realtime Art Manifesto), gets closer to the ideal of AltGames. Samyn suggests that, rather than being a genre, NotGames are both a design challenge and an artistic challenge. The question isn't whether games are an artistic object, but rather how creators might aim to produce "an experience that consists only of … beautiful moments" (Samyn) that exploits the potential of the medium by rejecting traditional ways of making games.

From these historical predecessors, we can offer a global definition of AltGames, based on the social networking discourse as well as the content of some of the games themselves, by proposing that they exist at the intersection of four main components: artistic, economic, political, and ludic. Practices regrouped under the AltGames label may be illustrated in one or all of these components; a game does not need to be representative of all four components to be an AltGame.

Artistic Component

AltGames can often be seen as aesthetically distinct from mainstream, indie, or AAA games—ideals of photorealism are often neglected or even completely rejected. In this respect, designers concerned with the artistic aspect of alternative games aim to create works of art, and many will stray from established convention in the video game world. In this section, we will concentrate on some key games that are in line with feminist and queer ideals, but it is nonetheless important to note that aesthetic choices are numerous and personal to each creator. Some openly feminist or subversive AltGames—but not all of them—put forward an aesthetic that is radically distinct from militarized masculinity. Games such as *Morning Makeup Madness* and *Unipug* by Jenny Jiao Hsia put forward a "cute aesthetic," almost cartoonesquely bubbly and stereotypically feminine, which aims to contrast with established standards in the AAA industry. The "radical softness" aesthetic, a feminist idea that takes feminine stereotypes that are often regarded as weak and uses them in a subversive way to show strength, is also often put forward in queer AltGames. Aside from the visual aspects of aesthetic considerations, the idea of communicating a personal experience or an emotional sensation is often central to the experience of AltGames. The reflexive process is an integral part of some creators' artistic approach. The artist and her experiences are an essential part of the game.

Ludic Component

Most AltGames also question traditional game mechanics, and the ideas of play/game[7] themselves. Artists try to "break" game mechanics and videoludic norms by refusing to reproduce genre conventions or popular mechanics (shooting, competition, racing, confrontation, etc.) and even by subverting expectations. A lot of AltGames propose very short experiences instead of the traditional multi-hour gaming experience offered by AAA games. The hypertextual game *Queers in Love at the End of the World*, where the player must click on hyperlinks that will give her different stories, is one of those especially short games: it only lasts 10 seconds, and the player must replay it many times if she wants to explore the whole work. Similarly, Kara Stone's *Ritual of the Moon* is a game played for a few minutes over the course of 28 days, constituting, as its name indicates, a small daily ritual of sorts instead of a continuous experience. Other AltGames present limited ludic possibilities or mechanics, such as in *Freshman Year*. In this game, we play as Nina, who is partying in a bar when she is sexually harassed. The actions the player can take within the gameworld are very limited: she can only make insignificant choices, such as deciding what to wear, for instance. When Nina is harassed, the player's agency is removed and she has to watch, powerless, a cutscene where her character gets assaulted. The idea of games having to be fun, pleasant, or fulfilling experiences for the player is often questioned within the AltGames movement. Quinn, in her article "Punk Games," writes, "So fucking what if it isn't fun?" asking if a game *must* be ludic or even fun to play.

The game mechanics themselves are often more accessible than traditional video games: AltGames have simplified mechanics that require few previous gaming experiences to master, and the learning curve is thus reduced for very casual or new players, or players with motricity disabilities. Considering the fact that most AltGames are computer games, oftentimes published on the Internet or even on mobile platforms, they can be played only with a mouse, or with one's finger (on a touch screen), making the required motor skills very basic compared with the traditional console controller, which has more than 10 buttons and triggers with different functions. Hypertextual games, for example, require few resources or skills to be played and have been increasingly popular in the past years, with platforms such as Twine being readily accessible to creators. Overall, AltGames create new videoludic experiences using the specificities of the medium, while also playing with the complexity of traditional game mechanics in order to subvert expectations.

Economic Component

Similar to the ludic component, the economic aspect of AltGames mainly consists of the rejection of traditional means of production and commercialization, distinguishing AltGames from AAA and indie games. Game creation, in that sense, doesn't depend on financial imperatives and profitability of the game, even though, as Lana Polansky, a game developer, notes on Twitter, AltGames artists should ideally be able to make a living from their work. Instead of selling individual games on traditional platforms such as Steam, some marginalized AltGames creators prefer setting up crowdfunding platforms like Patreon and Ko-Fi, adopting a strategy more akin to artist patronage than commercial capitalist practices. Thus, instead of buying individual ludic experiences, the AltGames player participates within a wider social ludic system. Other artists choose to sell their individual games on alternative platforms such as itch.io for lower prices, or offer a pay-what-you-can program, which allows players to compensate the artist before or after their experience, according to their financial means.

Another important aspect that was briefly mentioned in the last section is the crucial notion of accessibility of the means of production. For the aforementioned patronage system to be sustainable, the financial investment on the part of creators must also be reasonable—hence the importance of free creation platforms such as Twine, Construct2, and Renpy for the AltGames movement. These few examples are either free or affordable and do not necessarily require high-level programming or computer science skills to be used.

Political Component

Finally, the political aspect is probably the most crucial to a sound definition of AltGames, since one could arguably state that all AltGames are essentially political: through artistic, ludic, and economic means, artists and creators question the established social and political order. AltGames are an act of resistance, whether or not the content of the games themselves is political.

When observing the work of marginalized folks specifically within the game design community, the idea of reclaiming the videoludic medium is also important—myriad creators of AltGames are marginalized, by both the video game industry and society at large. As such, the content of a lot of these artists' games is explicitly political or aims at exploring a political issue. Most queer and feminist creators use their own personal experiences and struggles to convey political messages. For example, Nina Freeman represents her personal experiences through games that use the vignette format, a concept borrowed from literature, which consists of a brief and evocative episode that plunges directly into the heart of the experience in order to generate a strong reaction in the player (Blyth qtd. in Priestman). The power of this format lies in its ability to evoke, to incite the reader or player to imagine a story that leads to the moment described in the vignette.

ALTGAMES AND THE QUEER CYBORG

We argue that AltGames are part of the cyberqueer movement because they subvert social norms, mainly heteronormativity, through virtual means of expression and distribution that transcend physical space—they create communities where marginalized people can think and discuss their experiences. Some practices of the AltGames movement can be seen as a continuation of the posthumanist idea of mind uploading, the actual uploading of consciousness, which sees identity as a construction that is not necessarily linked to the body. Zoe Quinn's creations, such as *Depression Quest*, or Freeman's vignettes could very well be part of this posthumanist idea, in that they allow not only a virtualization of an experience but also a blurring of boundaries between binary concepts such as gender identity, reality and fiction, or the idea of self-realization.

In Nina Freeman's game *Cibele*, for example, the player plays as Nina's younger self, who is also playing a MMORPG (massively multiplayer online role-playing game). The player has access to Nina's computer and personal files, such as emails and photos—and although most of the game is spent recreating the protagonist's choices in the fictional MMORPG while performing actions that are typical of this genre's conventions, the player is encouraged to go through these files and explore 19-year-old Nina's memories when she is offline. The game is an exploration of a fragment of the author's memories that deal with her young adult years, her virtual relationships, as well as intimacy and eroticism in a virtual world. The boundaries between reality and fiction are doubly blurred: the game explores the creator's memories via a virtual world that is a representation of the one in which she herself has lived these experiences. Freeman has reproduced a virtual relational space within a gaming world as virtual as the one in which the player will experience her memories. The link between posthumanist philosophy and the idea of mind uploading in a video game is even clearer when Freeman openly plays with her own memories by adding old selfies in the game world. These can be akin to the idea of "self-downloading," and we could also see this as a form of inverted cyborg: whereas Haraway's cyborg aims for the inclusion of cyberware within the human body, Freeman includes an organic component within a technological body. The author recreates a fragment of her identity within a completely virtual space and goes beyond the bounds of organic corporeality by using the cybernetic components to re-form herself as a virtual/real hybrid identity.

On the other hand, Canadian researcher and game designer Kara Stone's 2018 game *the earth is a better person than me* is a journey of self-exploration rather than a literal mind-uploading experience. Stone's game deals with exploring one's identity, desires, and affordances in an abstract and ludic way. In the game, the player embodies Delphine, a young woman struggling with depressive symptoms who decides to go on a journey in the forest. The player can choose between and play a total of six paths, all leading to conversations with elements of wilds that she stumbles onto—a river, the moon, the sun, a tree, a flower, the dirt. The author has claimed that the game is partly autobiographical but also explores her friends' stories and larger issues—it's an expression of feelings, desires, and thoughts through a fictional dialogue with nature.

Although the game mechanics themselves are fairly simple, more akin to visual novels than to AAA games, the subjects Kara Stone chooses to explore are substantial—on Twitter, Stone writes that her game deals with "being a woman, queerness, psycho-social disability, and having sex with the world." Some paths discuss eating disorders, self-harm, the discovering of one's sexuality and desires, as well as suicidal thoughts. But mostly, the game represents the hardships of self-exploration. In that sense, the game isn't a fixed cyber-identity, it is an exploration of the eternal quest for purpose, meaning, and understanding of one's self inside a virtual world.

These two examples, although they explore the questions of queerness and identity construction in radically different ways, could both be considered as part of a posthumanist movement that aims to recrystallize identity within a virtual space in the sense that they are a way for queer creators to perform identity in a virtual world without the imperatives of physical constraints and social norms. If we use Wakeford's themes, which we have discussed in the first section of this chapter, and apply them to AltGames, we can highlight four main points in which AltGames can represent the cyberqueer identity. First, the notion of identity and self-presentation of queer folks is central to most of the games mentioned—they aim to explore personal or existential experiences, memories, sensations, and states. Second, the idea of the creation of a queer space, here, is double—the AltGames movement in itself could represent a form of a queer world (as in a spatiotemporal space within which queer and other marginalized people can interact without fear), and the many games themselves are a space of freedom where their creators can express their identity, their queerness, openly. Third, the electronic facilitation of a queer virtual community is central to the existence of AltGames—indeed, as the movement itself was born out of a Twitter hashtag, the place of the cyberspace is central to the existence of this queer community. Finally, with regards to new technology and erotic practices, although this theme isn't pervasive to all AltGames, the community has nevertheless made it possible for creators and players to explore virtual eroticism and non-normative sexual practices through a safe technological space, as is the case in *the earth is a better person than me*.

CONCLUSION

In this chapter, we have argued that AltGames are a feminist and queer resistance that takes a stand against a toxic gamer culture that excludes women and marginalized people. Not only do AltGames redefine gaming conventions, but they can be seen as a way to subvert gender norms. We propose that AltGames may be defined through four main components, namely their artistic, economic, ludic, and political aspects. AltGames, in their current and ever-evolving form, engage—or at least have the potential to engage—in a significant way with Haraway's ideal of the cyborg, as well as with Wakeford's notion of the cyberqueer identity. They seek to blur the gender boundaries, erase binarity by performing fluid identities, and subvert heteronormativity through the Internet by taking advantage of accessible means of distribution. They even thrive in forming communities of marginalized people who interact with each other, gaining a visibility never obtained before, which is in line with Wakeford's theorization of the cyberqueer. The link between posthumanist philosophy and the idea of mind uploading in a video game is even clearer when Freeman openly plays with her own memories by adding old selfies in the game world, in the case of her game *Cibele*. Virtualized self-expression succeeds in transcending physical space, thus recrystallizing identity, which could ultimately eliminate physical imperatives of gender and identity performativity.

CRITICAL REFLECTION QUESTIONS

1. Because of their elusive nature, is it really possible to define AltGames as a means of resistance against the toxic gamer culture?
2. Would feminist gaming tactics, such as modding and hacking, be considered forms of posthumanism or cyberqueer identity?
3. What are other ways to fight toxic gamer culture and help to diversify both video games and the video game community?

NOTES

1. Throughout the chapter, the term *women* will be used to include both cisgender and trans women equally.
2. The term *queer* will be used in two main ways in this chapter. First, it may refer to a queer individual, that is, a person identifying as a member of the LGBTQIA+ community. Second, it may refer to Harper and colleagues' definition, which states that queer is "deconstruction and liminality, a point of view that questions existing structures and binaries … a critique of how heteronormative power structures serve to limit and compress our understanding of the world." In other words, a queer person would also be someone whose identity (by their sexuality, gender, race, for example) challenges social norms.
3. The #GamerGate movement started when Zoe Quinn, a video game developer, became the target of harassment. Her ex-boyfriend falsely and publicly accused her of having an affair with a gaming journalist for the benefit of her career. Many gamers took to defending the supposed honour of this man by sending Quinn hateful messages and death threats. When other women defended her, they underwent the same treatment. However, this hateful movement had the beneficial effect of bringing to light the toxicity that women and marginalized people had endured for decades in gaming spaces, and thus sparked many rich discussions about diversity and inclusion in the gaming community.
4. Modding is a practice that consists of modifying the software of a game to add or change some of its components. While some mods are essentially illegal, in the sense that they modify a game's code without the author's consent, some game producers include within their games the possibility for their players to modify the game within specific parameters and encourage them to share their work with other players, creating strong modding communities.
5. *Videoludic* is an adjective describing the property of being or pertaining to a video (video) game (ludic).
6. The term *AAA* is used to describe games from a major publisher with a high production budget. These "blockbuster" games are generally in opposition to games from independent studios, where the teams and the budget are smaller.

7. This distinction is a vastly discussed topic within games studies (Juul; Salen and Zimmerman; Sutton-Smith; Walther). The idea of play is essentially the action of playing a game, whereas the game is the object itself.

WORKS CITED

Games

Cibele. Nina Freeman, PC, Mac, 2015.

Depression Quest. Zoe Quinn, PC, Mac, 2013.

the earth is a better person than me. Kara Stone, PC, Mac, 2018.

Freshman Year. Nina Freeman, PC, Mac, 2015

Hello Kitty World. Rachel Simone Weil, HACKING/MODDING/REMIXING as *Feminist Protest Expo*, Carnegie Mellon University, 2016.

Life Is Strange. Dontnod Entertainment, PC, Mac, Linux, PlayStation, Xbox, 2015.

Mass Effect. BioWare, PC, PlayStation, Xbox, Wii, 2007–2012.

Morning Makeup Madness. Jenny Jiao Hsia, PC, Mac, Linux, 2016.

Queers in Love at the End of the World. Anna Anthropy, PC, Mac, 2013.

Ritual of the Moon. Kara Stone, PC, Mac, Android, Apple, 2019.

Unipug. Jenny Jiao Hsia, PC, Mac, Linux, 2016.

Movies

Ex Machina. Directed by Alex Garland, 2014.

Her. Directed by Spike Jonze, 2013.

Secondary Sources

Condis, Megan. *Gaming Masculinity: Trolls, Fake Geeks, and the Gendered Battle for Online Culture*. University of Iowa Press, 2018.

Consalvo, Mia. "Confronting Toxic Gamer Culture: A Challenge for Feminist Game Studies Scholars." *Ada: A Journal of Gender, New Media, and Technology*, vol. 1, 2012.

Halberstam, J. *The Queer Art of Failure*. Duke UP, 2011.

Haraway, Donna. *Simians, Cyborgs and Women: The Reinvention of Nature*. Free Association Books, 1991.

Harvey, Auriea, and Michaël Samyn. "Realtime Art Manifesto." *Tale of Tales*, 2006, http://www.tale-of-tales.com/tales/RAM.html.

Hyussen, Andrea. *After the Great Divide: Modernism, Mass Culture and Post-Modernism*. Indiana University Press, 1986.

Juul, Jesper. *A Casual Revolution. Reinventing Video Games and Their Players*. MIT Press, 2010.

———. "The Repeatedly Lost Art of Studying Games." *Game Studies*, vol. 1, 2001, http://www.gamestudies.org/0101/juul-review/.

Kafai, Yasmin, et al. "The Need for Intersectional Perspectives and Inclusive Designs in Gaming." *Diversifying Barbie and Mortal Kombat: Intersectional Perspectives and Inclusive Designs in Gaming*, edited by Yasmin Kafai et al., ETC Press, 2016, pp. 1–20.

Kirtchev, Christian. "Le Manifeste Cyberpunk—A Cyberpunk Manifesto." *La revue des ressources*, 2012, http://www.larevuedesressources.org/un-manifeste-cyberpunk-le-cyberpunk-manifesto,2317.html.

Kline, Stephen, et al. *Digital Play: The Interaction of Technology, Culture, and Marketing*. McGill-Queen's UP, 2003.

Morton, Donald. "Birth of the Cyberqueer." *PMLA. The Journal of the Modern Language Association of America*, vol. 110, no. 3, 1995, pp. 369–381.

Paradis, Elise. "Bodies, Boxes and Belonging: A Review of Queer Online." *Journal of LGBT Youth*, vol. 6, 2009, pp. 446–451.

Paul, Christopher. *The Toxic Meritocracy of Video Games*. University of Minnesota Press, 2018.

Priestman, Chris. "The Experimental Narrative Vignettes of André Blyth." *Kill Screen*, 2014, https://killscreen.com/articles/andre-blyth/.

Quinn, Zoe. "Punk Games." BoingBoing.net, 2015, https://boingboing.net/2015/03/16/punk-games.html.

Ruberg, Bonnie, and Adrienne Shaw. *Queer Game Studies*. University of Minnesota Press, 2017.

Salen, Katie, and Eric Zimmerman. *Rules of Play: Game Design Fundamentals*. MIT Press, 2004.

Salter, Anastasia, and Bridgett Blodgett. *Toxic Geek Masculinity in Media: Sexism, Trolling, and Identity Policing*. Palgrave Macmillan, 2017.

Samyn, Michaël. "Not a Manifesto." *Notgames Blog*, 2010, http://notgames.org/blog/2010/03/19/not-a-manifesto/.

"Scratchware Manifesto." *Home of the Underdog*, 2000, http://www.homeoftheunderdogs.net/scratch.php.

Sutton-Smith, Brian. *The Ambiguity of Play*. Harvard UP, 1997.

Tudor, Matilda. *Cyberqueer Techno-Practices. Digital Space-Making and Networking among Swedish Gay Men*. The Department of Journalism, Media and Communication (JMK), Stockholm University, 2012, http://www.diva-portal.org/smash/get/diva2:532984/FULLTEXT01.pdf.

Wakeford, Nina. "Cyberqueer." *Lesbian and Gay Studies: A Critical Introduction*, edited by A. Medhurst and S. R. Munt, Cassell, 1997, pp. 20–38.

———. "Cyberqueer." *The Cybercultures Reader*, edited by D. Bell and B. M. Kennedy, Routledge, 2000, pp. 403–415.

———. "New technologies and cyber-queer research." *Handbook of Lesbian and Gay Studies*, edited by D. Richardson and S. Seidman, Sage, 2012, pp. 115–144.

Walther, Bo Kampmann. "Playing and Gaming: Reflections and Classifications." *Game Studies*, vol. 3, no. 1, 2003, http://gamestudies.org/0301/walther/.

Wolfe, Cary. *What Is Posthumanism?* University of Minnesota Press, 2010.

Wolmark, Jenny. *Cybersexualities: A Reader on Feminist Theory, Cyborgs and Cyberspace.* Edinburgh UP, 1999.

CHAPTER 12

Playing with Identity: Exploring the Role of Gender, Death Positivity, and Queer Representation in *A Mortician's Tale*

Victoria Kannen and Aaron Langille

INTRODUCTION

We decided to start this chapter the way that we would tell this story to our students, so, as we would say to them—stay with us. We think you'll like this story.

> Victoria is not a video game person, per se. She plays video games, but she wouldn't identify as a gamer. Aaron is definitely a video games person, a video game scholar, and would identify as a gamer. One day, Aaron came upon a game he thought Victoria would like. He knows she likes lead characters who are women, queer positive representations, and discussions of death, so he asked her to play *A Mortician's Tale* with him. The soothing music compelled her, the narrative was unusual, and she was playing a game where she got to embalm people (in a purple, cartoony, beautiful sort of way). She loved it.

We are both educators who consider the role of representation within popular culture to be pedagogically foundational. In other words, we see the power of popular culture as resting in its ability to distort, shape, and produce reality while it impacts the ways in which we think, feel, and operate in the social world. In Victoria's communications and sociology classrooms, she approaches teaching with playfulness. Her lectures and seminars are filled with as many creative examples and exercises as possible, both to keep the attention of her students and to engage them in joy (even while learning about difficult subjects, such as sexism and racism). In Aaron's video game design classrooms, he often begins by encouraging students to play or watch other students play video games that are then used as points of reference for discussing the importance of play, cultural impact, violence, representation, and more. Whenever appropriate, he connects with students through humour, analogy, and contemporary cultural references.

Thinking about the role of play in our lives can conjure up many ideas. As adults, we often play in many ways that are not even seemingly obvious. We entertain ourselves throughout our daily life—with sports, video games, board games, social media, films, literature, sex, food, and so on. We can also play with our identities—our appearance, gender, sexuality, the language we use, and how we carry ourselves. As student-focused educators, we aim to use this chapter to explore how a Canadian video game—*A Mortician's Tale*—can function as a site for non-normative gendered representations, feminist ethics, death positivity, and a reimagining of the possibilities of pedagogy, identity, and play.

In *A Mortician's Tale*, a Canadian, independently published, narrative-driven video game, players are exposed to a death-positive, queer-positive, and female-led experience. This chapter will explore the role of identity and play, and their overall connection to representations of death. Following this, we will consider the ways in which video games are pedagogical—meaning that they can teach us about identities, culture, power, pleasure, and resistance. Lastly, we will discuss how this game engages with the concepts of the feminist ethics of care and death positivity to explore morality and the neoliberal critique that the game provides of the commodification of death.

IDENTITY AND PLAY

We all have identities—gender, race, class, age, ability, sexuality, religion, education level, family structures, and so on. Identity, like representation, is a relational concept. To say that identity is relational means that the concept of identity comes from the process that we use to understand ourselves, others, and groups at any given time, in any given place (Kannen). We can refer to identity as a process for two reasons:

1. Identity is relational. The ways that we understand identities are always related to social power.
2. Identity is impermanent. Identities are not unitary, nor do they have consistent meanings.

When considering our identities, they must be also discussed in terms of intersectionality, or the ways that our identities are never disconnected from each other.

Intersectional analyses suggest that biological, social, and cultural categories such as gender, race, class, ability, sexual orientation, and other axes of identity interact and intersect on multiple and often simultaneous levels. These intersections lead to how we all experience social privilege *and* systemic inequality every day of our lives and this is all intimately connected to the popular culture that we experience, create, and participate in.

Gameplay, whether through video games or otherwise, is important to consider in relation to identity because "to play a game is to experience the game: to see, touch, hear, smell, and taste the game; to move the body during play, to feel emotions about the unfolding outcome, to communicate with other players, to alter normal patterns of thinking" (Salen and Zimmerman 314). Video games offer us a medium where identities can be presented liminally. Liminality is "an abstract term that describes the threshold in-between or on the margins of more well-defined time and space. It is a space that is ambiguous, disorienting, and often transitional. In more concrete terms, it describes the places and people who exist outside of normative, structured society" (Marchessau 218). It is in these liminal spaces where gender non-conformity can be articulated and *played* with. To be gender non-conforming refers to people who do not adhere to social rules about appearance, behaviours, and activities that are based on their biological sex and gender assignment. A gender non-conforming person may choose to present as neither clearly masculine nor clearly feminine, or as gender-free (Friedrichs).

We believe that video games, as a uniquely interactive medium, can encourage and inform inclusive and gender non-conforming worldviews. Games such as *Towerfall: Ascension, Ikenfell, Celeste, dys4ia,* and more provide evidence of the possibilities of intersectional representations within video games. While these examples can act as evidence of change in both gender and race representation in recent video games, particularly in "indie" titles (Langille), formal studies suggest there is still a long way to go. In 2011, Donghee Yvette Wohn (201) surveyed 200 casual video games, a category to which one could argue *A Mortician's Tale* likely belongs, and of the 130 video games with human primary characters, only 8 games, or 6 percent, featured non-white primary characters.

IDENTITY, PLAY, AND DEATH

A Mortician's Tale takes us through Charlotte's (Charlie's) growth as a young funeral director, including both the technical aspects of dealing with the deceased and the more personal details that permeate her life, such as her friendships, work hierarchies, and neoliberal expectations of conformity.

The game takes place almost entirely within Rose & Daughters Funeral Home—either in Charlie's office, which also serves as the preparation room and crematorium (see figure 12.1), or in the visitation room. Gameplay alternates between a first-person view when Charlie is interacting with her office computer or preparing a deceased person for funeral or cremation and a third-person view when she is walking around her office or attending a funeral. The change in perspective during different activities may help reinforce the players' sense of projection, or sense of oneness with Charlie, and the players' sense of empathy for Charlie in first-person and third-person respectively (Schell 348).

The core mechanic, or repeated action, of the game is a series of point-and-clicks that players use to control Charlie's activities and push the narrative forward. In the visitation room, players can, through Charlie's movements and actions, listen to conversations between non-player characters and pay their final respects to the deceased. It is worth noting that the player cannot return to the office area until final respects are completed. In the office, key activities include reading emails that provide information about Charlie's life outside of the funeral home as well as the politics within.

Death and dying are subjective experiences that each of us must grapple with. Questions such as "What images of death do people carry in their heads?" (Riley Jr. 195)

Figure 12.1: Charlie Standing in Her Office, Which Also Functions as the Prep-Room and Crematorium Inside of Rose & Daughters Funeral Home
Source: Laundry Bear Games Press Kit, available at http://laundrybear.com/presskit-laundry-bear-games/

are what we each need to consider as we explore representations of death in popular culture. In society at large, death is often considered a taboo topic that entices, intrigues, and horrifies us. Silence around death is still extremely common in Western culture—except with our fetishization of imagined death in major Hollywood blockbusters and video games (Tocci)—and *A Mortician's Tale* embodies this duality.

> No matter how it is framed by dialogue or narrative, in the visual world what you see is what you get. In other words, Hollywood's narrative fictions are visual fantasies; the question is, why these fantasies? Violence, it seems, is now more and more not being presented as a choice that may define our relationship to the social order or to ethical life. Instead, it is rather aestheticised—fetishised—as nothing more than a source of visceral pleasure; what we "see" is the subordination of all other content to the fascination with sumptuous violence. (Green 137)

The game takes a less obviously fetishized approach to death as it connects with death in a *quiet* way while also making death the foundational element of the entire game. With one exception (described below), there are no dialogue options or ways for Charlie to respond to either emails or to mourners in the visitation room. In our interview with Gabby DaRienzo, the creative director and designer of *A Mortician's Tale*, she discussed the ways in which Charlie would serve better as a "silent protagonist":

> Death and grief are so so so unique from person-to-person, and it was much more effective to have Charlie act as a vessel for players to insert their own feelings into. That being said, Charlie still has her own personality that we see come out through the actions taken over the narrative arc of the game, but also how she's visually designed (tattooed arms and her refusal to cover them up even after the new owner of the funeral home asks her to). (DaRienzo, Email Interview)

Emails are the mechanism through which the player learns the details of a deceased person's history and final wishes, which in turn leads to the activity of embalming or cremation. While the narrative is primarily linear, there is an email exchange between Charlie and Amy Rose, the owner of the funeral home. In the exchange, Amy describes a scenario where a young man who has died by suicide has no valid will and his family is given the right to override his wishes for cremation by requesting an open-casket visitation. In this exchange, Amy asks Charlie, or rather the player, if they are comfortable preparing the body despite the deceased's wishes not being respected. If the player answers yes, the game proceeds accordingly. However, if the player answers no, a deceased person with no backstory is prepared by the player instead. This meaningful choice that the player is offered empowers the player to form an ethical relationship to the game and to their own moral engagement with death customs and dilemmas.

The creators of the game wanted to demonstrate what death positivity looks like in action: "I wanted to honestly depict western funeral traditions. That meant the challenges, the ways the industry is innovating in an ecological sense, and how the industry needs to respond to ways queer people—especially trans people—are mistreated" (Tremblay, Email Interview). DaRienzo discussed the influence of Caitlin Doughty's *Smoke Gets in Your Eyes: And Other Lessons from the Crematory* on the creation of the game. Doughty's book, in turn, was heavily influenced by the death positivity movement and the death acceptance organization that she founded, called the Order of the Good Death. The following are some of the major tenets of death positivity:

- I believe that talking about and engaging with my inevitable death is not morbid, but displays a natural curiosity about the human condition.
- I believe that the laws that govern death, dying and end-of-life care should ensure that a person's wishes are honored, regardless of sexual, gender, racial or religious identity.
- I believe that my death should be handled in a way that does not do great harm to the environment.
- I believe that my open, honest advocacy around death *can* make a difference, and *can* change culture. (Order of the Good Death)

These principles are foundational to *A Mortician's Tale* and enable the player to see the ways in which video games can teach us about new ideologies (video games as pedagogical) and provide us with ethical frameworks through which to play with identity and socio-cultural ideas (feminist ethics of care and death positivity). It is to these two sections that our discussion now turns.

VIDEO GAMES AS PEDAGOGICAL

Popular culture is pedagogical, meaning that it teaches us about the possibilities of creativity, relationships, and citizenship, and in so doing, it represents how we are supposed to relate to one another. Our understanding of popular culture simply suggests that what is popular are those things that are a part of our everyday life—not necessarily the most popular elements that are "cool" or trending at this cultural moment. This definition doesn't simply encompass entertainment or art, but anything from the food that we eat to the design of our streets. We understand popular culture in its most inclusive sense, because we see that the representations that surround us are always already teaching all of the things we need to know about our culture and, subsequently, ourselves.

While pop culture can be considered educational, it is also supposed to be that which gives us joy and entertainment. We argue that it does both— it teaches us while it stimulates and/or pleases us. In relation to video games, we can think about the role of pleasure in a variety of ways, one of which is to consider how pleasure evolves through our playing of the game. As Katie Salen and Eric Zimmerman argue, "all the possible states and experiences of a game are contained within the theoretical construct called the space of possibility.… Every play of the game will be unique, even though the rules of the game, its formal structure remain fixed.… We refer to this concept by the shorthand term *same-but-different*" (340). While Salen and Zimmerman are referring to the specifics of pleasure within gameplay, we can extend their ideas to consider how—even though the core mechanics of gameplay remain the same for all players—the representations within a game can speak different conceptual languages to the diverse audiences that are engaging with it. For those who have not been exposed to queer representations or death-positive ideas, playing through *A Mortician's Tale* will offer a unique learning and representational experience. Similarly, for those who might not see themselves represented in the game—as the game features predominantly light-skinned characters—moving through the game could offer an alienating experience.

DaRienzo stated the following:

> The *Mortician's Tale* team is primarily made up of women, genderqueer, and queer folk (myself included) so I think very naturally we wanted to include characters that represented us as well as our partners, friends, and family who are also part of the LGBTQ+ community. Speaking personally, one of the most important things I wanted to make sure we talked about in the game was about how often LGBTQ+ folk—especially trans folk—can be mistreated after death, and give some practical advice to the player on how they can better protect themselves and their loved ones from this mistreatment. (Email Interview)

In one of the most important pedagogical moments of the game, Charlie receives an email in the form of a newsletter (see figure 12.2). It is from "Funerals Monthly" and the subject is "LGBTQ Funerals: Respect." This newsletter outlines the best practices that funeral directors should follow in order to honour trans people who have died. The email is lengthy and provides the player with valuable information regarding queer bodies and the ethics of care that are fundamental to proper funeral practice.

The newsletter states, "we care a lot about this because we believe in treating every person with the same level of compassion, respect, and care. And this absolutely extends to pronouns, and respecting the deceased's wishes as per their lived experience."

The importance of discussing respect as it relates to trans pronouns (and everyone's chosen pronouns) is extremely important to note here. Pop culture representations of genderqueer and non-binary pronouns help to normalize the practice of announcing pronouns in general. In the press kit for *A Mortician's Tale*, the inclusivity that the game creators desire is evidenced in their own pronouns being listed next to each of their names. It is within actions like these that we see how it is not only the responsibility of gender non-conforming folks to teach society that pronouns matter—naming pronouns is a practice that should be undertaken

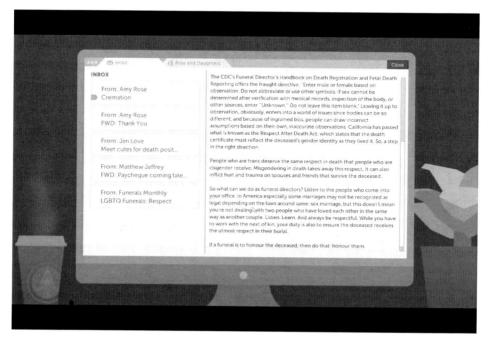

Figure 12.2: In-Game Newsletter, "LGBTQ Funerals: Respect"
Source: A Mortician's Tale screen capture

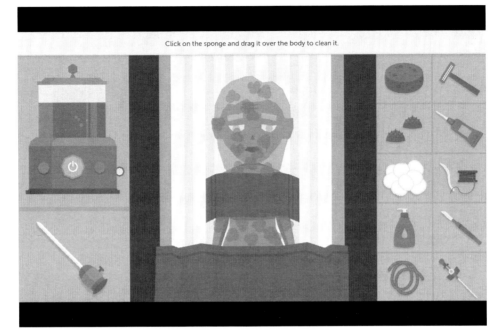

Figure 12.3: Players Clean and Prepare the Deceased for Funeral
Source: A Mortician's Tale screen capture

by everyone. In progressive spaces, it has become a more common practice to include our "preferred gender pronoun" or "personal gender pronoun" in ice breakers, name tags, email signatures, and Twitter bios (to name a few), but this practice still needs to be more widespread.

FEMINIST ETHICS OF CARE AND DEATH POSITIVITY

In *A Mortician's Tale*, we, acting through Charlie, need to practise ethical engagements with the deceased. In so doing, we clean, shave, and massage the bodies prior to preparing them for their funeral wishes. We also have to ensure that Charlie always pays her respects to the deceased during their funeral service, prior to moving forward in the game. The repetition of play in these practices seems connected to their overall pedagogical intentions in the game, but it is also addressing a core ethical intention as well.

In particular, within care ethics, moral courage is defined as "the determination to speak truthfully, with integrity, to tell a story that has not been welcomed by the world" (Rogers 273). Hence, as with conventional research on moral courage, care-based definitions reflect a focus on speaking with authenticity and

integrity, despite pressure to do otherwise or the possibility of censure. The existence of *A Mortician's Tale*—a game that intends to position death positivity as a
natural state, queer representations as integral (not token), and feminist politics as
foundational—is, itself, an act of moral courage. While a focus on moral courage is
demonstrated by the game, an argument can be made that players' actions within
the game demonstrate a feminist ethics of care. As Rosemarie Tong has argued,
"care-focused feminists regard women's capacity for care as a human strength" (162).
This is not to say, however, that women are somehow best at caring, but it is to
point to the ways that hegemonic gender constructions have positioned women's
caring as somehow a feminine weakness, when care-focused feminists would argue that it is an inherent strength that all genders should strive to espouse.

This feminist ethics of care is demonstrated in DaRienzo's discussion of the
feminist intentionality of the game: "Speaking personally—I've always, always,
always intended for *A Mortician's Tale* to have a feminist feel. Not to be too corny,
but I think death in and of itself is inherently a very feminist thing—we are all
equal in death, and as creatives it was important for us to showcase this in the
narratives and characters we created for our little game about death" (DaRienzo,
Email Interview). Kaitlin Tremblay, lead writer for *A Mortician's Tale*, agrees that
death is "inherently feminist." Tremblay goes on to say, "I also think it's a space
that involves a lot of vulnerability. Not just in talking about death, but also in
dying (e.g., we trust our wishes to be followed for our burial). Queerness and feminism to me was so much about beginning to accept and nurture my own vulnerability, that they feel so inextricably linked for me. Talking about death is allowing
ourselves to be vulnerable" (Tremblay, Email Interview).

When Rose & Daughters is absorbed into a larger funeral conglomerate called
Hillside Hills, the feminist ethics of care is made clear through the resistance
offered by Charlie's co-workers and friends as they are critical of the depersonal-
ization and corporatization of Rose & Daughters. In emails to Charlie, we see the
insistence from the new owner on what is most cost-effective—to the detriment of
the deceased's wishes—and he criticizes Charlie for her refusal to upsell mourning
families. As Sara Ahmed says, "Feminism often begins with intensity: you are
aroused by what you come up against.... Feminism can begin with a body, a body
in touch with a world, a body that is not at ease in a world; a body that fidgets and
moves around. Things don't seem right" (22). While Ahmed is speaking of corporeal beings, we can apply her ideas to the *dis*-ease that Charlie and her friends
experience with the neoliberal attitudes that they are coming up against. At the
conclusion of the game, we see Charlie in a different office, where she is offering
natural burials through her own new business, Magnolia Forest: Funeral Home

and Natural Burial Park. The positioning of Charlie as a woman who also resists corporatization not only reasserts her commitment to death positivity but also reifies for the players her feminist resistance to the neoliberal power structures that she was previously existing within.

CONCLUSION

At the start of this chapter, we described how we both use playfulness, exercises, humour, analogy, and popular culture references to tackle difficult themes including violence, sexism, and racism in our classrooms. In a similar vein, it is not uncommon for video games to tackle dark themes, such as those found within *A Mortician's Tale*, but with the overarching goal of shedding light and positivity. For example, *That Dragon Cancer* uses a point-and-click narrative to guide players through a family's suffering and experiences caring for a one-year-old child who, at the end of the narrative, dies from cancer. According to Gareth Schott, the game "explicitly addresses the subject of death, using the medium for personal expression and communication, translating the developers' personal experience and story" (6). In a 2013 essay published on Kotaku, Jenn Frank wrote "We will all meet this thing, or have already met it. Maybe that should be scary, but *That Dragon Cancer* is about sustaining the hope and joy of life for just as long as we can." Similarly, *Papo & Yo* is a puzzle-platforming game often described as an allegory of Vander Caballero's (the game's developer's) childhood and relationship with his alcoholic father. Despite this dark theme, Caballero describes *Papo & Yo* as an "empathy game" and in a 2014 Gamasutra interview says, "I want to take someone on an emotional journey.... Then the question is 'what can I bring to someone's life that's going to be important and meaningful for them, a lesson that will help people in their life?'"

We believe that video games, as all spaces and places of popular culture, are sites rife for gendered resistance and pedagogical exploration. We're glad that you stayed with us. While Victoria would still not identify as a gamer, this "little game" has opened her eyes to the spaces of possibility that video games can offer. She played it once and she wanted to play it again. As Tremblay said, "Everything about [*A Mortician's Tale*] was written around respect, honesty, vulnerability, and those are main pillars of my own feminism and queerness" (Email Interview). This is meaningful because there are many of you who may be reading this who also would not identify as gamers, but keeping an open mind to video games or branching out to smaller Canadian games could speak to you, your identities, and your politics in ways that you may not expect.

In relation to their "same-but-different" principle, Salen and Zimmerman go on to say that this idea also relates to when a player plays a game more than one time. When playing a game again, "the rules remain the same, but the play is different. It doesn't always happen, but if the play is meaningful enough, if the pleasure is rich and flowing, then a player will want to play a game again.... This same-but-different mechanism makes for an extremely powerful engine of desire" (Salen and Zimmerman 340). In wanting to play the game again, Victoria now wants to play more games that challenge her perceptions, as well as educate and entertain her. These feelings seem to coincide with the intentions that Tremblay had for the game:

> I hope players will walk away with at least a sense of feeling understood, or accepted, or validated in their own experiences of grief. A major part of the writing for me was to show all the various ways grief manifests as valid. Learning more about the western funeral industry is important to me as well, but my main hope is that people take away a greater ability to talk about death in their own daily lives, to be more kind to themselves about how they experience grief, and to find more understanding and community for their own unique vulnerabilities. (Tremblay, Email Interview)

CRITICAL REFLECTION QUESTIONS

1. What video games have you played or heard of that have enabled you to question normative understandings of identity and/or social structures?
2. How might you apply an intersectional feminist analysis to other social customs that incorporate, but also move beyond, gender as a category of analysis?
3. How does the interactivity of video games affect the importance of representation compared to passive media such as movies, music, or television?

WORKS CITED

Ahmed, Sara. *Living a Feminist Life*. Duke UP, 2017.

Anthropy, Anna. *Dys4ia*. 2012. [Online, Flash]

DaRienzo, Gabby. "Re: A Mortician's Tale—Book Chapter." Message to Aaron Langille, email interview, 29 Jan. 2019.

Frank, Jenn. "Cancer, The Video Game." *Kotaku*, 4 Sept. 2013, https://kotaku.com/cancer-the-video-game-471333034. Accessed 3 Feb. 2019.

Friedrichs, Ellen. "What It Means to Be Gender Non-Conforming." 1 April 2018, https://www.liveabout.com/what-does-it-mean-to-be-gender-non-conforming-1415327. Accessed 10 Jan. 2019.

Graft, Kris. "Designing for empathy, with Papo & Yo dev Minority Media." *Gamasutra: The Art and Business of Making Games*, 17 April 2014, http://www.gamasutra.com/view/news/215340/Designing_for_empathy_with_Papo__Yo_dev_Minority_Media.php. Accessed 3 Feb. 2019.

Green, Philip. *American Democracy*. Palgrave Macmillan, 2014.

Happy Ray Games. *Ikenfell*. 2019. [Various]

Kannen, Victoria. "Pregnant, Privileged and PhDing: Exploring Embodiments in Qualitative Research." *Journal of Gender Studies*, vol. 22, no. 2, 2013, pp. 178–191.

Langille, Aaron. "Canadian Indie Video Games: More Than Locations, Landmarks, and Loonies." *The Spaces and Places of Canadian Popular Culture*, edited by Victoria Kannen and Neil Shyminsky, Canadian Scholars, 2019.

Marchessau, Nicole. "Red, White and Grey: Un-defining Canadian Popular Culture." *The Spaces and Places of Canadian Popular Culture*, edited by Victoria Kannen and Neil Shyminsky, Canadian Scholars, 2019.

Matt Makes Games. *Towerfall: Ascension*. 2013. [Various]

———. *Celeste*. 2018. [Various]

Minority Media. *Papo & Yo*. 2012. [Various]

Numinous Games. *That Dragon Cancer*. 2016. [Various]

The Order of the Good Death. "Death Positive." 2019, http://www.orderofthegooddeath.com/death-positive. Accessed 20 Jan. 2019.

Riley Jr, John W. "Dying and the Meanings of Death: Sociological Inquiries." *Annual Review of Sociology*, vol. 9, 1983, pp. 191–216.

Rogers, Annie. "Voice, Play, and a Practice of Ordinary Courage in Girls' and Women's Lives." *Harvard Educational Review*, vol. 63, no. 3, 1993, pp. 265–295.

Salen, Katie, and Eric Zimmerman. *Rules of Play: Game Design Fundamentals*. MIT Press, 2004.

Schell, Jesse. *The Art of Game Design: A Book of Lenses*. AK Peters/CRC Press, 2014.

Schott, Gareth Richard. "That Dragon, Cancer: Contemplating Life and Death in a Medium that has Frequently Trivialized Both." *Digital Games Research Association Conference (DiGRA)*, vol. 14, no. 1, 2017.

Tocci, Jason. "'You Are Dead. Continue?' Conflicts and Complements in Game Rules and Fiction." *Eludamos. Journal for Computer Game Culture*, vol. 2, no. 2, 2008, pp. 187–201.

Tong, Rosmarie. *Feminist Thought: A More Comprehensive Introduction*. Westview Press, 2009.

Tremblay, Kaitlin. "Re: A Mortician's Tale—Book Chapter," Message to Aaron Langille, email interview, 1 Feb. 2019.

Wohn, Donghee Yvette. "Gender and Race Representation in Casual Games." *Sex Roles*, vol. 65, no. 3–4, 2011, pp. 198–207.

PART V

NECESSARY, NOT RADICAL: GENDER INCLUSIVITY
IN PERFORMANCE, PODCASTS, AND MUSIC

CHAPTER 13

Indigenous Rage Incarnate: Irreconcilable Spaces and Indigestible Bodies

Jill Carter

It's gotta stop. Our women are leaders in our culture, and if our leaders are murdered and missing, then we will never have stability as a people.

    —Candy Blair

ON THE ART OF BEING SEEN

I am sitting at the Queen Mother Café in Tkaronto with Cree-Mohawk performer Candy Blair (Otsikehta). As we discuss their recent foray into performance art, their eyes begin to smolder, while their face, belying the rage-fuelled energy that crackles around them, maintains its measured serenity. As Candy recounts a series of uncomfortable (and, at times, dangerous) encounters with white males who seem to have aggressively targeted them because they present as an Indigenous woman, the air around us becomes heavier. Time conflates. History becomes immediate, reverberating down through the generations of Indigenous femininity. Before me, I see a girl who could be my daughter. And they are telling an old story—my mother's story, my story, their story …

    I am compelled to think back to the attempted (perhaps, accomplished?) gang rape of the sister of Michi Saagiig Chief Wabakinine[1] and the murder of this Chief and his wife. I ask what became of Wabakinine's sister? How does her story end? Would we, a century later, have ever learned about the assault on her person and the murder of her family members if those family members had not been a Chief and the daughter of a Chief? In the absence of such high-ranking family members, would even the sparse, currently accessible exposition of the insults offered her by British military personnel and the violence enacted upon her person have survived erasure? Wabakinine's sister is barely visible to us today, despite the indisputable fact that her Michi Saagiig female body was targeted as a receptacle for a growing swell of disgust, resentment, prurience, and violence that directed the attitudes and behaviours of settlers toward their Indigenous hosts and neighbours. I regard her history, buried as it is in the lands occupied by Toronto's St. Lawrence Market (now frequented religiously by tourists and local "foodies"), as an origin story, an opening chapter in the traumatic saga of the Missing and Murdered—a story of slippage in which each protagonist has lived and ultimately disappeared into an interstice between the hyper-visibility of exotic prey and the invisibility of the unremarkable, uncounted, and valueless.

> I was wondering if they sold Indian costumes for Halloween in sex stores. Because that would be really outrageous, right? They wouldn't do that, right? So, then when I did actually look into it [...] I found [...] this sex shop that sells five different kinds of Indian costumes. And they all have really disturbing quotes. One of them was like "get your pow wow on." That was the one I had [in performance]. I had "Get Your Pow Wow On." And they're really perverted costumes. Such cultural appropriation. So, I decided [...] I was very conflicted by this because I didn't want to buy their stupid costumes. But [...] I wanted to get one of those Indian costumes, put myself in it and then lay down on the ground, and have blood all over myself—especially around my crotch area—and just lay there. And see if people would actually care and make the connection—that these costumes are sexualizing our women, which is leading a big part to the murdered and missing Indigenous women. Because if we didn't have the sexualization, at least like I feel like we'd have a bit more respect. (Blair, Interview)

Candy Blair is discussing *I'm Not Your Pocahontas*, a project they began developing for a performance art workshop, hosted by Toronto's Centre for Indigenous Theatre and facilitated by mentors Lori Blondeau and Adrian Stimson (September–October 2018). Donning a blood-soaked bra and loincloth and accessorizing these with requisite headband and feather, Blair laid their bloodied, semi-nude body down on Shaw Street, outside the Centre for Indigenous Theatre, to briefly interrupt the journeys of pedestrians and drivers and engage them as allies in our struggle to end a historic, state-sanctioned campaign of violence against Indigenous womanhood. With this early iteration of *I'm Not Your Pocahontas*, Blair lay raw and exposed on a well-travelled thoroughfare outside a public building for 10 to 15 minutes. To be sure, the duration of their first performance of this work was relatively short. Still, the fact that only one passerby stopped to express concern (first for the performer and then—realizing that the performer was not in actual distress—for the story their prone body communicated) is a disturbingly familiar story.

The very presence of the performing Other who refuses to be consumed by what Monique Mojica terms "the pornographic gaze" (Mojica, Conversation, January 20, 2017) presents an embodiment of resistance to and potential destabilization of the hegemonic structures that contain it. And yet a question remains for those who place their bodies in the fray ("hands up; don't shoot"): "How am I [as a body performing resistance] in service to this time and place?" (Mojica, Conversation, January 20, 2017).

This question rests at the centre of the several tables at which I have sat with friends and colleagues (Indigenous sisters, all) to collaboratively reflect upon Indigenous resistance as a performance that is inseparable from the Indigenous body. This question anchors our ruminations over the Indigenous body that wears its nation's teachings and performs as human shield, protecting a multitude of bodies—bodies of land, bodies of water, bodies of the Missing and Murdered—from the capricious depredations of the restless spirit of the West. Are the narratives raging in the blood and nesting in our cells rendered visible through our performance? Do they call upon our audiences to bear witness, or are we read merely as "hypervisible text[s] against which the viewer's indistinguishable body fades into a seemingly neutral, tractable, and invulnerable instrument of the autonomous will, suitable to the uniform abstract citizenry [White Paper Liberalism] institutes" (Thomson 10)?

Where the voyeur consumes what is outside of and apart from herself for her own edification (or titillation), the Indigenous witness has been charged (traditionally) with the responsibility of carrying the entire bundle of what has been given, of stewarding that bundle, and of delivering it (or any part thereof) intact at any time back to the community for its edification and empowerment (see Qwul'sih'yah'maht 185). The witness embodies communal (hi)story in that her body becomes the vessel upon which that history is written, her mind becomes the surface upon which its details are imprinted, and her voice becomes the vehicle through which that history is transmitted, passed back to those who may have forgotten, and passed forward to those who will have to remember. The voyeur, by contrast, stands apart and remains disembodied—disengaged and disconnected from the spectacle, from the *monstrous*. This monstrous other—a carrier of signs and portents[2]—is seen to exist in every age "to be exploited for someone else's purposes" (Thomson 2).

AN EDIFYING ENCOUNTER WITH MONSTERS AND MEAT HOOKS

Take, for instance, settler playwright Colleen Murphy's 2013 treatment of the Murdered and Missing phenomenon—an ongoing serial event with which Canada is now being forced into a reckoning. *Pig Girl* speaks to the global phenomena of misogyny and femicide; it is inarguably specific, inviting Murphy's audience onto the pig farm of serial murderer Robert Pickton to observe the gruesome mechanics of his violation and disposal of the female bodies he lured or forcibly conveyed into his improvised abattoir. Murphy's play reads like a "peep show" of the final, tortured hours remaining to a young missing woman as she is sexually violated and methodically murdered. As Canada's Missing and Murdered (collectively represented in the person of Murphy's "Dying Woman") physically and verbally struggle against their/her attacker, their/her impotent struggles are mirrored in a parallel encounter that plays itself out alongside the murder. Here, Dying Woman's sister wrestles the systemic racism and the violence of apathy in the Canadian justice system, as she spars with an RCMP Officer, demanding—to no avail—his aid in locating the missing woman before she becomes one of the murdered.

In her preface to the published play, Murphy tells us that she has no wish to "exploit" the Missing and Murdered "or to feed off the pain" of those who mourn their loss (n.p.). Her stated aim is to inspire Canadians to "care enough for a woman they never knew and *perhaps would not want to know*"[3] (n.p., emphasis added), to care also about her murderer, and to care about an indifferent system that colludes with the perpetrators by refusing to act on the behalf of those in whom it sees no value. And *caring*, Murphy tells us, "means to witness the horror, and in the case of the Dying Woman, to witness her heroic refusal to submit to the horror visited upon her" (n.p.). Masquerading as a project that raises awareness within and rouses the sympathy of the Canadian populace, Murphy's play, it seems, realizes itself as a twenty-first-century iteration of a Barnum Side Show in which displays of the *monstrous* were dramaturged to arouse and titillate, even as the publicity that surrounded such displays was dramaturged to highlight their educative aspects (see Odell qtd. in Thomson 5).

While *Pig Girl* indicts the negligence of the systems that have been put in place to protect the populace, its critique is seasoned with a *moral* lesson that is hard to ignore: *certain women*, by virtue of their lifestyle and profession, come to a bad end. Further, while Murphy's indictment of victim-blaming finds its voice within the unfolding encounter between frantic Sister and indifferent RCMP Officer, ultimately, the visual lesson that assaults its audience is one contained within the spectacle of a *failed*, aberrant (?) female body suspended from a meat hook as it is degraded, defiled, and finally murdered. As with Charles Perrault's 1697 version of *Little Red Riding Hood*,[4] the eye of the spectator is fixed upon the miscreant female (who has flouted popular wisdom by taking "candy" from a stranger), *not* upon the two-legged wolf who savages her.[5] And all the while, the critique of the larger (institutional) monster is sidelined by the more spectacular scenes of degradation and torture.

My intent here is not to enumerate or to discuss the merits of any one of the arguments that erupted in the wake of *Pig Girl*'s November 2013 premiere. Calls for boycotts and pleas for a change in title were counterbalanced by expressions of support by those who believe that this play "bring[s] a voice to a silenced demographic" (Arluk qtd. in Wohlberg n.p.). My intent here is to ask what is required in this historic moment: Is settler-sympathy desired? Is settler-intervention required for Indigenous voices to be heard?

> Anyway the only reason they went to that show was Gloria got some free tickets through work. Said once the show got going she felt like such an asshole, 'cause she didn't know there'd be a fucking meat hook display! She took a bunch of the women who were staying at the fucking halfway house! They were cool about it, though. They just left at halftime and went for Chinese. Gloria says when they were leaving she heard all these people saying "this is so powerful" and "this work is so important" while they were like, twittering about it. And she yells *"Enjoy your pain porno!"* and out she went. (laughs.) And that is Gloria. (Beat.) I really love her." (Beagan 5, emphasis added)

With *Deer Woman*,[6] Ntlaka'pamux-Irish playwright Tara Beagan calls upon her Blackfoot protagonist to respond to these queries through an obstreperous jibe that calls out *Pig Girl* and unsettles its audiences for their ongoing complicity in the violence that continues to be visited upon Indigenous mothers, sisters, aunties, and daughters. What did all the Twitter-buzz generated by the 2013 premiere of Murphy's play actually *affect*? One year after *Pig Girl*'s premiere, (then Prime Minister) Stephen Harper told journalist Peter Mansbridge that a national inquiry into the Missing and Murdered wasn't "really high on [his government's] radar" (Kappo n.p.). Two years after that, in 2016, an Angus Reid poll showed that while most Canadians voiced their support for a national inquiry into the Missing and Murdered, most of these Canadians also believed that such an inquiry would change nothing (Global News). Five years after its premiere (in February 2018), a Canadian jury delivered a "not guilty" verdict in the case of a Saskatchewan farmer who shot and killed a Cree youth, Colten Boushie. And not two weeks after that, a second jury vindicated the man accused of fifteen-year-old Tina Fontaine's murder.

Did the 2013 production of an award-winning Canadian play mobilize a community of witnesses who, fuelled by acute awareness, planned and performed intentional actions designed to intervene in an unacceptable situation? Or did it, rather, sate voyeuristic cravings born of privilege and ennui?

"You think we're not at war here?" (Beagan 6).

Think again.

"YOU THINK WE'RE NOT AT WAR HERE?"

The phenomenon of dual reception—that is, the frontier that separates the witness from the voyeur—is a central [technical] question, which Indigenous artists are only just now beginning to investigate (Mojica, Conversation). "How do we dislodge the pornographic gaze?" Mojica asks (March 18, 2017), or how might we reverse it?

The larger conversation from which this chapter emerges works through these questions, considering current strategies that refuse the voyeuristic gaze through reflection or deflection. Here, I invite readers to consider the *indigestible* Indigenous body that refuses to disappear, as it forcefully pushes back against its enfreakment, against the consumption of its suffering, and against the dismissal of its resistance. As Indigenous bodies and/or discarnates perform their successful *refusal* to be consumed, they offer themselves as palpable articulations of Indigenous rage. In their engagement with the monstrous, they give form to our rage. And in so doing, they answer David Garneau's call for "irreconcilable spaces of Aboriginality" (28), carving out, for the Indigenous witness, an interior antechamber in which to commune with angry spirits and release them—engineering a singular (and necessary) experience of catharsis. To those outside such spaces, nothing is (unapologetically) offered up for consumption or for comfort. Indigenous flesh—made rage—is indigestible.

"CAN YOU SEE MY ANTLERS?"[7]

Canadian audiences have been long accustomed to viewing the Indigenous body perform itself as a receptacle for settler rage. On stage (as in life), the Indigenous human is verbally assaulted, threatened, sexually assaulted, tortured, and killed. Sometimes, Indigenous bodies survive the staged trauma; sometimes, they succumb to their injuries; sometimes, they *decide* to stop breathing. Regardless of the "fate" of these characters, their bodies manifest themselves as objects (that may voice objection to, but) that receive and absorb the rage of others.[8] Such performances are often deemed "important" or "powerful" when they successfully appeal to settler-sympathy for an abject Other.

With her *Deer Woman*, Beagan answers settler-sympathy with a refusal to display the Indigenous body as *tragos* (the bleeding sacrifice) on the altar of conquest.[9] Indeed, Beagan's title (which speaks to the intimate kinship between her Indigenous protagonist with the non-human world) signals *refusal* in its nod to an ancient story about relational responsibility and its violation: the Anishinaabeg had long enjoyed a treaty relationship with the non-human persons who constitute the hoof clan (e.g., Deer, Moose, and Caribou). This relationship comes with certain benefits and entails certain responsibilities. The non-human members of this clan sacrifice themselves so that their younger relatives in creation might eat and so survive. In return, the Anishinaabeg are obliged to repay this sacrifice with respect—to take only what is needed, to use all of what is taken, to treat the fleshly remains of the taken creatures with respect, and to remember and honour this sacrifice in ceremony. A time came (as these times do) when the human beings—perhaps overcome with *hubris*—forgot their debt to the hoof clan and violated the terms of this ancient agreement, taking more than they needed, wasting what was taken, failing to express gratitude for the blood sacrifice that was sustaining their lives, and failing to perform their ceremonial obligations. So the membership of the hoof clan *refused* relationship with the Anishinaabeg and disappeared, leaving the people to starve (see Simpson, *The Gift* 9–13). As Leanne Simpson demonstrates, there are two lessons to be taken from this story of "generative refusal." The first lesson requires heuristic inquiry: Are we as Anishinaabeg living up to the terms of the treaties our ancestors ratified with the non-human world? The second lesson offers us valuable instruction in light of our human-to-human relationships in this historical moment: "Refusal is an appropriate response to oppression, and within this context it is always generative; that is, it is always the living alternative" (Simpson, *As We Have* 33).

Refusing to countenance settler-assumptions or to gratify settler-expectations, Beagan re-*presents* the living (and intact) Indigenous body through which she "gives form to our [Indigenous] rage" (Mojica, Personal communication, November 25, 2017), intentionally engineering a cathartic affect in Indigenous witnesses while contextually withholding the pity and terror that would be necessary to generate the same affect in settler audiences. Here, Beagan wields her poetics like a blade, carving out a performative space of refusal—a space that is unapologetically "irreconcilable" and *unsettlingly* Indigenous.

In the pre-show gloom, shadows dance while a doe glides silently into view, foraging through the dense, digital foliage that covers an upstage scrim. Into this tranquil scene of pastoral majesty bursts the irrepressible Lila—"Lyle" to her friends. Lyle sets up her smart phone, activates the appropriate app, and begins to record herself. She has dressed specially for this occasion; she is leaving a digital record of her truth; she asserts her sanity; she acknowledges the illegality of her actions (intended or completed?); and she apologizes to her lover. Through the taping, we meet Lyle's family; we learn that she is a survivor of childhood sexual abuse and parental desertion. We learn, too, that she is grieving the murder of her younger sister and that this sister was taken and murdered on Canadian soil while Lyle was serving abroad in Kandahar (Beagan 25). Mesmerized as we are by Lyle's story, we are left, at this point, without any surety about where Lyle may be taking us.

Hence, some might be excused, here, for assuming that this "proud Blackfoot woman" (Beagan 3), overwhelmed with grief and survivor's guilt, has made the decision to end her life in this isolated setting. But Beagan's work asserts its place within a fresh, insurgent *oeuvre* that is being collectively crafted by Indigenous artists across Canada in the wake of this nation's showy but insubstantive response to the Final Report of the Truth and Reconciliation Commission and its 94 calls to action. Like so many Indigenous works coming out of this historical moment, Beagan's play neatly "unsettle[s] the surface of expectation and perception. There are no crying Indians here for you, no screaming children, no horror to consume" (The New BC 65). They have absented themselves in this space of refusal. What horrors there are to come will prove as indigestible to the settler-viewers as they are unanticipated at this moment in the play.

"One thing I am concerned about is how people [take notice and] gather when Indigenous bodies are dying," Cree scholar Karyn Recollet commented during a meeting of our University of Toronto working group Native Performance Culture and The Rhythm of Re Conciliation: Re-membering Ourselves in Deep Time on April 7, 2017. The living Indigenous body, with its immediate concerns, is too often rendered invisible: entire communities living for generations without potable water in one of the most water-rich land bases on this earth. Our young men spirited away in the night in police vehicles, stripped of their boots and winter jackets, and left to die on the frozen outskirts of some city or town. Our girls and women taken, consumed, and discarded without ceremony, without leave-taking, in ditches, over highways, under farmers' fields, in water. Our children spirited from their families to be murdered (in body or spirit) by the agents of the state who have been entrusted with their care. *Who sees? Who listens? What changes?*

As Monique Mojica asks, "What is it we have to do to be seen?" (February 18, 2017). How does the Indigenous body, disrobing to reveal the violence perpetrated upon it, reconfigure colonial sites of viewing—our contemporary *theatrons*? How do we reflect back to our viewers their own *visibility*; their own *complicity* within a system of oppression that, by turns, punishes, spectacularizes, and disappears Indigenous bodies; their *accountability* to the living Indigenous body; and their *responsibility* to respond to that body as witness, not consumer? *What do we have to do to be seen and not eaten?*

Beagan's protagonist models a potent response: *Become the predator and begin to "feed."* By chance, at a vigil for the Missing and Murdered, Lyle recognizes a predator. This white man who dresses in leathers and feathers and self-consciously assumes a watery-eyed sympathetic expression (Beagan 22) has not joined these women as fellow mourner, ally, or witness. Taking photos and "measuring everyone," (Beagan 23) he has come to this gathering of the wounded and the vulnerable to "feed" (Beagan 24). Alert to his hunger (Beagan 24) and taking it upon herself to use her skills to protect her Indigenous sisters, Lyle begins to investigate by first stealing his wallet.[10] A quick scan of its contents reveals a suspected (random) predator to be, in fact, the murderer of her younger sister.

We have not been invited into these woods to hear the story of Lyle and her murdered sister. Indeed, we are told from the very beginning that her story is "not for [us]." It is for the digital archive, and it is to those for whom that archive is intended that Lyle speaks (Beagan 3). We have not been invited here to "care" for Lyle, for her murdered sister, for all the murdered sisters, or for the predatory monster now turned prey. If we are Indigenous, we already care. We have already borne witness to and carry in our marked bodies countless stories of pain and loss. If we are non-Indigenous, perhaps, we have yet to discover and accept the monumental weight that comes with true witnessing.

From behind the pastoral woodland scrim, Lyle drags her mangled prey. And in that instant, Beagan has neatly flipped the script, casting the consumable Indigenous body as the predatory avenger. Yet despite the horror of the scene, despite its seeming madness, there is nothing of the maddened monster in this predator.

This "Deer Woman" is not a grotesque to arouse terror and titillation. She is eminently human, and in this historical moment, she offers an appropriately human, rational, and honest response to an ongoing and undeclared war against Indigenous people. To those who would condemn Lyle's actions, dismissing her as inhuman, Beagan holds up a mirror, confronting them with the specter of their own monstrosity: "You trained me! Not you, you, but the government. I mean, I had natural talent, and hunting experience, but it was the armed forces that really honed that, you know what I mean? Fuck! And as good as you train us, you don't untrain us" (Beagan 5).

"Deer Woman" (despite urban legend and popular distortion) is no monster.[11] In this too—in her very title—Beagan subverts expectations. As Lyle recounts a fateful road trip, during which her Uncle Gary hits a fawn, we come to understand that Lyle carries a rare gift—a gift she has earned in the exercise of her humanity. Paralyzed by guilt and shock, Uncle Gary (who has "trained" Lila/Lyle in kindness) is unable to face the damage s/he has inadvertently wrought. So, in a supremely authentic act of *witnessing*, the child Lila becomes the corporeal bridge between species (deer and human / predator and prey) and between the realms of flesh and spirit, cradling the wounded creature and singing her into the darkness (Beagan 20). The fawn breathes her last into her human comforter's belly, and Lila is forever changed: "*Lila and Deer. Both*" (Beagan 20, emphasis added). Invested with the energies of doe and buck, of predator and prey, Lyle carries two spirits.

The monster whose execution we are invited to witness, by contrast, is spirit-*less*: he is voiceless (Lyle has slit his windpipe), and he is nameless—even in the program where his participation in the drama is unacknowledged. There is nothing in this indistinguishable carcass to astound—nothing to edify. And just as Beagan offers no lessons to be gleaned from this monster, so she refuses to satisfy the North American appetite for stories of Indigenous victimization and embodied expressions of Indigenous grief. What is it then that the settler is supposed to understand?

Throughout the play, we have understood that Lyle is speaking to posterity through the digital archive that she is recording. It seems during her direct addresses to "you" that Lyle speaks to the audience. She knows we are there. She accepts our presence, and she sets her boundaries: we don't "deserve" to know what she has to tell. "It's for the video, not [us]" (Beagan 3). But when Lyle's prey is revealed, and she speaks directly to him, she communicates the same message: "Even though *you* don't deserve it, *you're* gonna learn what I know.… But it's for the video, not *you*" (Beagan 31, emphasis added). She then goes on to emphasize the irreconcilability of the space they (we?) share: "*So don't go thinking I'm trying to make up or anything*" (Beagan 31, emphasis added).

The broken monster whom Lyle addresses is not the monster Beagan is *showing us*. This broken, unnamable thing is merely a proxy for the colonial monster who, as ever, is driven by its craving for a "little taste of empire" (Sy 52). Within these woods, playwright Tara Beagan, director Andy Moro, and performer Cherish Violet Blood have curated a space in which to reconcile with the irreconcilable. *The monstrous Other, which commands the fascinated gaze of its audiences, looks back in horror, communicating in its visage a reflection only of the monstrosity it sees.* Within these woods, a ceremony[12] of bloodletting becomes a bitter cathartic that answers Indigenous rage, activating ease through its controlled release by the Indigenous woman (whom I receive as a trusted proxy). The bundle of savage cravings on whom this rage will be unleashed exists on stage as the corporeal container and activating agent of the collective that is Canada, its genocidal policies, and its crimes against Indigenous humanity. While pity and terror may be kindled in the hearts of Canadian spectators, their release (which would constitute catharsis) is withheld. In these woods, the *monstra* of Canadian monstrosity and the heretofore consumable Indigenous body have been rendered indigestible.

CRITICAL REFLECTION QUESTIONS

1. How might artists and educators effectively curate "irreconcilable spaces of Aboriginality" (see Garneau 28) in the lecture hall, in the classroom, and in the rehearsal hall, so as to ameliorate relations between Indigenous and non-Indigenous students and/or fellow artists and foster between them a deeper understanding, an increased trust, and a greater willingness to communicate? When/where might such spaces be necessary?

2. Consider Tara Beagan's strategy here—specifically, her rejection of audience sympathy. In light of a long history of settler-authored/settler-sponsored plays, films, and/or books that focus the gaze on the victimized Indigenous body and in light of the recently released Final Report on the Missing and Murdered Indigenous Women, how effectively does Beagan's strategy confront Canada's refusal to honestly address the continuing systemic racism and genocidal campaign against Indigenous peoples?

3. How might we transform (either through education or through the affect generated by our productions) our audiences from passive spectators (or voyeurs) into active witnesses? What alterations in our own praxis (as theatre-workers or as educators) might we enact to facilitate such a transformation?

NOTES

1. In 1796, Chief Wabakinine, his wife, and his sister travelled to the site of what is today Toronto's St. Lawrence Market to sell the salmon they had harvested from the Credit River. At some point during their visit, a Queen's Ranger (Charles McCuen) offered Wabakinine's sister a bottle of rum and one dollar to sexually service him (Smith n.p.). When she failed to accede to his wishes, he and two comrades followed the family to where they were sleeping under their canoes, dragged her out from her resting place, and began to assault her. Her screams roused her brother and sister-in-law, who rushed to her aid. The rapists turned their energies on Wabakinine and his wife, beating them mercilessly. Wabakinine succumbed to his injuries within hours of the assault; his wife, within days (Smith n.p.).

2. Rosemarie Garland Thomson reminds us that the Latin word *monstra*, from whence the contemporary *monster* derives, means to show, to warn, or to sign; hence, the monstrous body in Western antiquity was received as a revelation of "divine will" (3).

3. Murphy's assertion that *caring is witnessing* is disingenuous in this context. Witnessing traditionally carries high stakes (of which the witness is acutely sensible) and engenders a profound relationship (based in knowing and being known to one another). Further, the implication that Dying Woman may be so unregenerate and unlikeable that other human beings would not want to know her is deeply troubling.

4. Charles Perrault committed this folktale to writing for a seventeenth-century French audience. Prior versions highlight the cleverness of the tale's protagonist, or her *good fortune* in being saved. Perrault's version, however, communicates an explicitly cautionary message. The disobedient child is eaten, and there is no reprieve. In the event that either moral or metaphor escapes his reader, Perrault concludes the story by delivering the lesson "never talk to strangers" and by explaining that there are two kinds of "wolves" in the world, and the clean-shaven "smooth"-talker is often the most dangerous wolf of all (27). Perrault also adds a prurient twist to the story: His little heroine is dressed in a *red* riding cap. Is there, here, a hint of sexual precocity that must be smothered or else destroyed? (See Hallett and Karasek 21.)

5. "The truth is, when people come to the play, they're going to see me [as Dying Woman] on stage. And they're going to start focusing on me" (Arluk qtd. in Wohlberg n.p). Renalta Arluk played Dying Woman in a second iteration of *Pig Girl* in 2016.

6. Performed by Blackfoot actor Cherish Violet Blood and directed by Andy Moro (Article 11), *Deer Woman* was first brought to the public in November 2017 at Native Earth Performing Arts' Weesageechak Begins to Dance 30. It has been created with active and embodied input from several Indigenous performers, including Cheri Maracle, Sophia Moussa, Lacey Hill, and Sarain Carson-Fox (Beagan 1). Cherish Violet Blood—who was also instrumental in the play's development—has continued to perform Lila/Lyle, the play's protagonist, for its June 2018

premiere at the Kia Mau Festival in Wellington, New Zealand, and for its January 2019 run at the Sydney Festival.

7. See Tara Beagan's *Deer Woman*. I borrow these lines (uttered separately in performance) from Beagan's protagonist.

8. Dying Woman's articulation of refusal—"I got a life an' I'm gonna keep it" (Loc. 874)—may be "heroic," but it is no match for *Manifest Destiny*. Her resistance, her rage, and her love are, in the final analysis, bodiless—borne on words that die into whispers as her breath ceases.

9. This play is a companion piece to Beagan's 2013 production of *In Spirit*, a piece that presents a corporeal manifestation of a child who has long been counted among the Missing and Murdered. Beagan's play features an exuberant girl-child on the eve of her thirteenth birthday. As *In Spirit* progresses, we and she come to the awful realization that this birthday will never come. Like us, she must come to first discover and then accept the fact that she has been dead for more than three decades. And to do this, she must piece together both the shattering story of a terrible night and the shattered bicycle she was riding when she was abducted. Like *Deer Woman*, *In Spirit* is a story told by one young woman and, like *Deer Woman*, it subverts all expectation, carrying us into the chaos where monsters lurk.

10. Lyle is no thief; she is not interested in this strange man's money. After lifting his wallet, she returns his money to his pocket. This action, no doubt, arises out of Lyle's scrupulous ethics. But this action also constitutes a brilliant psychological maneuver, which would, no doubt, unsettle and unbalance the enemy. It is an act of war.

11. John Landis's 2005 film, for instance, distorts traditional understandings of "Deer Woman," casting her as a feral, thrill-seeking female who seduces and murders random strangers for fun.

12. "Dressing" the taken deer is a ceremonial act. The removal of the hide and antlers, the removal of the offal, the preparation of the carcass for transport, and the ceremonies that are performed to honour (in that moment) the gift of sustenance that carries so dear a price are all necessary protocols that reflect, in action, the principles binding human and deer in an ancient treaty. These are acts performed in a careful and loving way to honour a treasured relationship.

In Beagan's irreconcilable space, however, this ceremony is subverted, becoming a spectacle of gore and desecration to mark a murderer's *wilful forfeiture of any relational position* within creation's web. Guts are tossed; genitals are mocked; pain is inflicted deliberately and painstakingly intensified. We are taken through each step of the process verbally (in clinical detail) and then visually as Lyle demonstrates her technique. These final acts are not acts intended to garner sympathy or to facilitate understanding from audiences who have come to "care."

Has Canada also irrevocably forfeited its right to relationship with those it has wilfully and systematically sought to destroy? Lyle tells her prey, "I will be crushing your skull" (Beagan 33). And Lyle will crush this skull not in a futile attempt to inflict pain on a corpse but to erase the identity of this creature that once outwardly resembled a human being—kin to Lyle, kin to a murdered sister, kin to all that lives in the creation. This, she tells us, is "not something you'd ever do" with a fallen deer (Beagan 33). But when we discard kinship obligations and forfeit relationship, this is perhaps the only fitting end to our story—utter obliteration. To become as if we had never been.

WORKS CITED

Beagan, Tara. *Deer Woman*. Unpublished script in development, 24 Nov. 2017. (Provided—with permission to cite—by Tara Beagan.)

Black, Jaime. *REDress*. University of Toronto, St. George Campus, March 2016. [Outdoor Installation]

Blair, Candy. Interview. Queen Mother Café, Toronto, 27 Oct. 2018.

Garneau, David. "Imaginary Spaces of Conciliation and Reconciliation: Art, Curation, and Healing." *Arts of Engagement: Taking Aesthetic Action In and Beyond the Truth and Reconciliation Commission of Canada*, edited by Dylan Robinson and Keavy Martin, Wilfred Laurier UP, 2016, pp. 21–42.

Global News. "Most Canadians Support Inquiry into Missing and Murdered Indigenous Women: Poll." *Global News*, 2 March 2016, https://globalnews.ca/news/2552548/majority-of-canadians-support-mmiw-inquiry-poll/. Accessed 7 May 2018.

Hallett, Martin, and Barbara Karasek, eds. *Folk and Fairy Tales*, 2nd edition. Broadview Press, 1998.

Kappo, Tanya. "Stephen Harper's Comments on Missing, Murdered Aboriginal Women Show 'Lack of Respect.'" *CBC News* (Opinion), 19 Dec. 2014, http://www.cbc.ca/news/indigenous/stephen-harper-s-comments-on-missing-murdered-aboriginal-women-show-lack-of-respect-1.2879154. Accessed 7 May 2018.

Mojica, Monique. Conversation. L'Espresso Café, Toronto, 20 Jan. 2017.

———. Conversation. University of Toronto, 18 Feb. 2017.

———. Conversation. University of Toronto, 18 March 2017.

———. Personal Communication. Native Earth Performing Arts, Toronto, 25 Nov. 2017.

Murphy, Colleen. *Pig Girl*. Kindle ed., Playwrights Canada Press, 2015.

The New BC Indian Art and Welfare Society Collective. "Unreconciling Public Art." *The Land We Are: Artists and Writers Unsettle the Politics of Reconciliation*, edited by Gabrielle L'Hirondelle Hill and Sophie McCall, Arbeiter Ring, 2015, pp. 52–65.

Perrault, Charles. "Little Red Riding Hood." *Folk and Fairy Tales*, 2nd edition, edited by Martin Hallett and Barbara Karasek, Broadview Press, 1998, pp. 25–27.

Qwul'sih'yah'maht (Robina Anne Thomas). "Honoring the Oral Traditions of the Ta't Mustimuxw (Ancestors) through Storytelling." *Research as Resistance: Revisiting*

Critical, Indigenous, and Anti-Oppressive Approaches, edited by Susan Strega and Leslie Brown, Canadian Scholars' Press, 2015, pp. 177–198.

Simpson, Leanne Betasamosake. *As We Have Always Done: Indigenous Freedom Through Radical Resistance*. University of Minnesota Press, 2017.

———. *The Gift Is in the Making: Anishinaabeg Stories*. Highwater Press, 2013.

Smith, Donald B. *Sacred Feathers: The Reverend Peter Jones (Kahkewaquonaby) and the Mississauga Indians*, 2nd edition. Kindle ed., University of Toronto Press, 2013.

Sy, Jovanni. *A Taste of Empire*. Talon Books, 2017.

Thomson, Rosemarie Garland. "Introduction: From Wonder to Error—A Genealogy of Freak Discourse in Modernity." *Freakery: Cultural Spectacles of the Extraordinary Body*, edited by Rosemarie Garland Thomson, New York UP, 1995, pp. 1–19.

Wohlberg, Meagan. "Playing Dead in Pig Girl: Reneltta Arluk on Taking a Lead Role in a Controversial, Disturbing Play about the Pickton Murders." *Edge*, 26 Jan. 2016, https://edgenorth.ca/article/playing-dead-in-pig-girl. Accessed 7 May 2018.

CHAPTER 14

"If I Disappear … Come Find Me": Seeking Trans Feminine Music in Canada

Valley WeeDick[1]

INTRODUCTION

In early 2018, Black soul singer Jackie Shane's *Any Other Way*, a compilation of 45s and a Toronto live performance from 1967, was nominated for a Grammy in the category of Best Historical Album. Shane became a prominent figure in the 1960s music scene in Toronto (and Montreal and Boston) but abruptly retired and seemingly disappeared in 1971. Elaine Banks's 2010 radio documentary *I Got Mine: The Story of Jackie Shane* sparked new interest in Shane, and she was discovered alive and well and living in Nashville, openly transgender. Following Shane's Grammy nomination, many news reports declared her "back from the dead" (Dunn). Equally prominent in the articles about Shane was a recurring question: "Why would she disappear?"—from music, from Toronto, from Canada—often embellishing the magnitude of her success and, more importantly, her acceptance as a Black, visibly gender non-conforming, out-but-not-*precisely*-out trans woman in Toronto. Shane's story here serves as a jumping-off point, framing a discussion on how trans musicians, especially trans feminine BIPOC (Black, Indigenous, and People of Colour), are subject to multiple literal and figurative disappearances, erasures, absences, and deaths. These figurative deaths echo the real systemic and physical violences faced by marginalized trans folx in everyday life.

That the "Best Historical Album" Grammy category *technically* honours the producers and engineers who (re)discovered and reissued the music, and not Jackie Shane herself, is one repetition of the kinds of erasures that confront trans musicians in (and out of) Canada. Some of the musicians discussed in this chapter have abandoned music for extended periods of time or permanently, often at the moment of "coming out" or "transition." Shane herself made few formal declarations of identity during her performing career, only "coming out" decades after she had stopped performing. Late in her life, Shane acknowledged that she understood herself as trans from an early age, but she strategically avoided articulating herself in those labels during her time as a performer. Because trans artists often abandon public transition in order to transition safely or privately, there are few genealogies of trans/feminine music, both in Canada and elsewhere. In this chapter there is a historical abyss in between Shane's recordings and performances in the late sixties and early seventies and the more contemporary artists of the past fifteen years.

When reading Jackie's story, I could come up with a laundry list of intertwined reasons why she would vanish from music performance because I had performed a similar, though less magnificent, disappearing act in 2018. Shane's narrative, engraved decades before I was born, punctuated by racial and historical straits more dire than my own, deeply resonates with my own relationship to and experience in non-trans, non-queer, socio-musical spaces. This project began not only as a means to discuss why trans musicians disappear, but also to consider how to approach trans art and artists after they have disappeared. Both disappearance and "discovery," thinking with the colonial resonance of that word, operate along the familiar and violent fault lines of colonization, racism, misogyny, and transphobia. As such, I also interrogate what it means to "come find" or seek out "trans" (recognizing the complicated resonances of this colonizer/settler identity category) musicians if and when they disappear. Erasure structures trans lives and creativity and their relationship to space and place, performance and audience, but contemporary trans artists also use their creativity to critique and combat that erasure. Trans musicians' "disappearances" are a self-directed strategy of survival as much as an imposed exile that preempts and prevents any continued or prolonged emergence. So although we may "want to be found so badly" (Mason, "if i disappear ...") it requires consideration for trans lives and livelihood to provide a context in which we actually want to (re)appear. Without these considerations, visibility and appearance places trans lives at risk.

In the sections that follow, I first discuss Jackie Shane's career as one of the earliest and most well-known trans performers situated in Canada, attending to how gender non-conformity both enabled her success and likely contributed to her eventual disappearance. I then shift to the contemporary moment to consider reasons why trans artists continue to disappear, using my perspective as a (former) musician, including the lack of trans-inclusive music spaces and the effort involved in navigating transness in public social spheres like music. I then conclude by discussing how trans artists take up space, forge their own, and use their voices and their anger to critique both cis sociality and trans erasure, returning back briefly to discuss Shane's performance style in contrast to contemporary trans artists.

"IT'S FATIGUING BEING A JACKIE SHANE"[2]

In Elaine Banks's aforementioned documentary, Jackie Shane is referred to at different moments, by different people, as being gay, a crossdresser, a transvestite, a drag queen, a female impersonator, or just an "unusual" person (*I Got Mine*). Steven Maynard similarly compiles a number of news articles from Shane's performing years that highlight various confused and derogatory readings of her gender. Shane's gender was read and misread based on the context, as trans and gender non-conforming folx are mis/gendered differently depending on the context. Audiences' perplexity at Shane's gender (identity) allowed for her performances to be read in multiple, often contradictory, ways. Interpretation of Shane's innuendoes and sly turns of phrase depends both on how spectators interpret Shane's identity and how well they know her slang. Many folx have described how Jackie Shane "bent" the lyrics of "Any Other Way" to imply homosexuality (either gay male or lesbian) when she sang "Tell her that I'm happy / Tell her that I'm gay / Tell her I wouldn't have it / Any other way." Her use of the slang "chicken" for young(er) gay male partners has been similarly highlighted. While this may well have been recognized by gay spectators who were in the know, assuming that all of Shane's spectators picked up on her slang might be giving too much credit for their ability to read queer and Black performance. Instead, we might consider some of Shane's success in light of audiences' (mis)readings of her performances as cisgender, as straight, or within a racist economy where chicken is just chicken and never registers as slang. In her live performance of "Money (That's What I Want) [Live]," Shane asserts how she will "enjoy the chicken, the women, and everything else that I wanna enjoy," but these bi/pansexual utterances are wilfully obscured in favour of strictly homosexual interpretations.

Treva Ellison describes how Sir Lady Java, a female impersonator and contemporary of Jackie Shane, "challenged viewers' trust in gender as a visually verifiable trait" in her stage act (8). While Shane would occasionally perform as a female impersonator when context and compensation encouraged it, she engaged in slightly different tactics than Java. Like Java, Shane engaged "her hyper-visibility as a gender-nonconforming woman as a source of livelihood" (Ellison 15) with her androgynous voice, name, and attire. While Java's performance visualized a male-to-female transition on-stage, beginning by "portraying a debonair gentleman ... and ending her shows in a sequined bikini" (Ellison 7–8), Shane instead walked the thin line of gender ambiguity, that, like Java, left audiences, critics, and listeners guessing as to her "true" sex. Part of both her performance and survival strategy involved leaving that ambiguity unresolved, refusing to offer up the "facts" of her identity or embodiment to inquisitive, invasive strangers. Shane's later anecdotes suggest that her practice of *not* naming identity was deliberate. Although Shane never hid her gender non-conformity, she refused to speak to it in identitarian terms, taking a pragmatic approach to outness, which was "maintained agentically and allowed [her] considerable control over the circumstances of" her life (Masoumi 197). While her gender non-conformity made her hyper-visible, her avoidance of naming identity meant that she was never visible *as* "transgender." Shane's story coheres with Masoumi's assertion that "taking and making space necessarily rely on some form of coming out; and in the landscape we inhabit, coming out has become a compulsory step in the production of 'proper' queer and trans subjecthood" (189). Naming or claiming identity, though, would undoubtedly alter the reception of Shane's music and reactions to Shane herself in ways that she would not be able to control, especially at a moment when understanding of and familiarity with trans identities was fairly minimal.

Jackie Shane's rediscovery has been put in the service of a history of Toronto's gay progress and Canada's racial inclusivity. That she was Black and queer/trans and loved Toronto and the people of Canada has become a talking point. At the same time, any discussion of how being Black and trans and in Toronto may have negatively affected her career has been circumvented. Put another way, while her presence is located within Toronto's progressive history, her disappearance is described in entirely personal terms. As a result, the forces that prevented Shane from being out, successful, and permanent remain unexamined. When an artist disappears, as Shane did, as so many trans performers do, can we really count their temporary, conditional presence as evidence of the benevolent tolerance and welcoming openness of Toronto/Canada, or of "How Toronto Got Queer" (*Any Other Way*)?

"SHAPE-SHIFTER AM I": WHY WE DISAPPEAR[3]

With her hidden transness and possible transition after leaving music, Jackie Shane prefigured a gambit taken by many trans feminine musicians. With its social costs, ongoing labours, and multiple forms of precarity that follow, social transition often takes a huge toll on trans folx, even when it provides certain benefits or the hope for livability. For some artists, it forecloses careers, as Elena Rose describes: "I was a classically trained singer before transition. It's very hard to be a lady basso profundo, so I let that go" (39). For many, coming out as trans jeopardizes access to work and a stable wage, housing, and health care, all of which can depend upon identification documents, which may not match lived names or gender and are expensive to change (Tang 368). Transition destabilizes support systems. Kortney Ryan Ziegler describes both the creative and financial losses succinctly:

> Before I transitioned, I had spent so long doing so many incredible things. After I transitioned, I spent two-and-a-half-plus years with nothing. I was depressed. I lost so many things that I need. I lost my filmmaking equipment. I almost lost my home. All the skills and creativity—I almost lost those because I almost lost my mind. (64)

Transition upends life, finances, and creativity, and consequently impacts access to institutional forms of artistic support like grants, as well as money for supplies and venues that often require pay-to-play booking fees. When creative practice only drains your money, at a certain point you begin to question whether it is really worth the time and labour, particularly when performing in environments that are not supportive or that invalidate trans identities.

For folx who change names and/or pronouns, there is constant effort involved in informing and repeatedly correcting everyone you have met on your "new" name and pronouns, even after they are hardly new. This is amplified for those who change their names or pronouns multiple times. Negotiating these changes in highly public settings is complex, fraught, and exhausting; a process that is frequently disheartening rather than gratifying. Shaughnessy describes it as suddenly feeling "as if my gender issues were visible to the entire room" (25). Music spaces are often highly social and require constant negotiation with others: booking agents, promoters, producers, engineers, sound techs, security guards, bartenders, other bands, managers, labels, friends, and audiences. All this negotiation occurs before even taking the stage, literally making your gender visible to the entire room.

While transition and changing names and appearances can be an act of self-care or self-actualization, it is also agonizing, as the trans Brown songwriter Carolina Brown sings, "I almost killed myself on Sunday / And here I was with my new looks and my new name" ("Sunday"). The consequences of *trans visibility* are more acute for racialized and non-passing trans women. Vivek Shraya describes how being constantly confronted with descriptions of violence against trans women of colour can be "a reminder that I need to be afraid and try to be as invisible as possible" (3) as a means of avoiding potential harassment and violence herself. Similarly, trans and two-spirit poet Amir Rabiyah describes how "as someone who is Two-Spirit and mixed and has a lot of different complicated identities and chronic health issues—*just existing is a risk*" (67, emphasis added). Viviane Namaste argues that being trans is often "about the banality of buying some bread, of making photocopies, of getting your shoe fixed," (*Sex Change* 20) and in the context of musicians, walking the labyrinthine hallway to your rehearsal studio, getting to and from a gig *safely*, and showing up as trans in an unfamiliar city or venue.

When trans folx do name and claim their identity alongside their performance, it often becomes the primary lens through which their work is received, consumed, and understood.[4] Discussing criticism of Wu Tsang's film *Wildness*, Jeanine Tang describes how "writers have fixated on Tsang's voice, biography, dress, and gender identity in sensationalizing and judgmental ways" rather than on elements of the film itself (371). For trans artists, these gendered and bodily criticisms reflect the various judgments, harassment, and dismissals that face trans folx when they enter public spaces, and can be encouragement to disappear from publicly exhibiting or performing their work. The criticisms of Tsang demonstrate how trans artists (or queer artists, or artists of colour) are critiqued along the lines of identity, setting up a dichotomy between "identity art" and art proper. In this economy, good art is made by (and for) white, straight, cis men who do not "politicize" their identity or artistic practice. But for trans artists, without concrete recognition or naming of trans identity, there is frequent "misgendering of artists, confusing of persona with identity, and use of given rather than chosen names" (Tang 371).

Even when performers are clear and public about their transition, name(s), and trans identity, writers may situate trans performers in relation to deadnames or identities that the performers do not claim, use the wrong pronouns, or rely upon binary language to describe non-binary individuals. In a roundtable discussion, trans musician Geo Wyeth asks, "Do I have to name myself to be visible?" (qtd. in Adsit et al. 193). Naming transness holds the simultaneous possibility of visibility and erasure, as artists can be forced to (re)call upon deadnames as a means of preventing their past work from disappearing. A 2014 *Vice* article that names Cassia Hardy of Wares as "Edmonton's first transgender musician" begins by using Hardy's deadname: "When I first saw Cassia Hardy on stage, I knew her as [_____]" (Lamourex).[5] Using deadnames can emphasize legitimacy and longevity through a longer history of writing, recording, and performing, a necessary strategy for acquiring shows, for grants, and for festival applications. Jia Qing Wilson-Yang, for example, refers to all of the names that she has recorded under on her Bandcamp page, while also addressing her past work through her trans identity. However, many artists do "not want to have their transness [or deadnames] mentioned, outed, or emphasized" (Tang 372) except in certain safe contexts or when a performer knows how their work will be displayed or received. DJ and visual and performance artist Juliana Huxtable asks more pointedly, "Are they ... tapping into a derivative pornographic obsession with transgender bodies? Are they putting me on display as a circus freak show, in a 'We're all secretly laughing at you' sort of way?" (Gossett and Huxtable 42). Audience reception can be near-impossible to gauge, especially if "safe" spaces are few and far between. This begs a question of how (and *if*) we approach and document trans creators within an ethics of care, for the safety and creativity of individual artists who approach both transness and identity in diverse ways.

"IF I DISAPPEAR ... COME FIND ME": VANISHING SPACES[6]

In late 2016, I played a show with my band, Family Secrets, at the Holy Oak Café, an extraordinarily cramped café venue that had queer music nights. The show was special for me because our band of four was all-queer and half-trans, and the band we shared the night with also had queer/trans members. Everyone I knew in the audience was queer or trans or both. It was our only show. Many trans bands come together temporarily and then fracture because we move, because music is expensive, and because maintaining long-term creative groups/friendships is difficult (especially through transition), or sometimes your bandmates are fucking or they break-up and can't stand the sight of each other anymore! And there are no photos or recordings or documentation, or the laptop dies, or accounts expire and the files vanish. There will be no encore, no second show, no mini tour. In an anti-trans climate, trans performances, like trans people, identities, bodies, and lives, are ephemeral. "Transgender art is vulnerable," subject to, and "also symbolic of[,] the precarity of trans practices and the imminent loss of its histories" (Gregory and Vaccaro 353). Family Secrets will only be a group that is recalled by the band members and perhaps a few close friends. Often the traces of trans music exist only in the minds and memory of a few folx who were involved or present for that one specific, disappearing moment. Those traces exist largely in undocumented small-h histories that are not considered for preservation or remembrance.

With their "counter-archiving" Marvellous Grounds project, Haritaworn and colleagues question "Who is worthy of archiving and thus remembering?" ("Marvellous" 220). The Marvellous Grounds project calls attention to how "the colonial definition of the archive ... is invested with permanence, stability, and legitimacy defined by authority" (Haritaworn et al., "Marvellous" 221) and critiques queer archives, spaces, and histories for centring whiteness while obscuring the presence and contributions of QTBIPOC (Queer and Trans Black, Indigenous, and People of Colour). Archives rely upon stable artifacts, while marginalized folx frequently "engage in traditions or productions that are resistant to archival pres-ervation, like oral tradition, embodied practices, cultural productions without a tactile, preservable product" (Haritaworn et al., "Introduction" 4). Creating music that *can* be archived, in digital or physical recordings, requires money, access to gear, or recording space, or an engineer, and so on. In short: documentation is ex-pensive. Writing in 1996, José Esteban Muñoz similarly emphasizes how, for mar-ginalized folx, "ephemeral evidence grants entrance and access to those who have been locked out of official histories" (9). The restlessness and mutability of trans embodiment and identity means that much trans art and many trans artists do not fit within the "factual" and static preservation that archives demand. When teas-ing out histories of trans music amidst constant disappearance, memory and rem-iniscence is often the only trace of presence that remains. These reminiscences are sometimes stitched together through scattered, piecemeal conversations: "What was the name of that Saskatoon band that we played with in like … 2009?" / "At Amigo's?" / "Yeah, and they had a really androgynous bass player!"

Holy Oak would close within a year of the Family Secrets show. By February 2018, three younger inclusive performance spaces along the same stretch of Bloor Street between Lansdowne and Ossington would close: D-Beatstro, The Steady, and Less Bar, which stayed open just a few months. These closures also occurred during a year where numerous Toronto venues were shuttered. A *Now Magazine* headline summed up the situation succinctly: "Vanishing music venues: three months into 2017 and we've already lost seven" (Gillis). In the Bloor/Lansdowne area, the gen-trification that ushered in spaces like Holy Oak also inevitably forced their closure. But more importantly, the gentrification of this neighbourhood began by actively forcing out marginalized and poor folx, QTBIPOC, and sex workers, thus govern-ing who gets to live and create, perform and exhibit their work in these gentrified "queer" areas (Haritaworn et al., "Marvellous Grounds"). Or as Haritaworn and col-leagues put it, "Queer space on Turtle Island is formed within a racial and colonial logic of space that systematically displaces and erases racialized and colonized com-munities to reinscribe the grounds thus cleared for white and middle-class owner-ship and governance, including gendered governance, both middle-class and queer" ("Introduction" 8). Within this colonial logic, queer space is created exclusively for "respectable" white, queer citizen-subjects, at the expense of most trans folx and QTBIPOC, and then repurposed for subjects who are not queer.

Beyond a few inclusive venues or festivals, trans folx are forced to navigate predominantly cis white musical spaces and to negotiate how their transness will be (re)presented and received there. If you are queer and stuck in a small place without much going on, the "music scene" can be one of the few things that keep you going. But it also requires musicians, even in large "queer" cities, to constantly negotiate misogyny, homo- and transphobia, and racism in varying degrees, depending on the venues, the band, their fans, or the night. Being involved in local "indie" music scenes in Canada often means only ever seeing white boys take the stage, and witnessing "community" routinely celebrate and coalesce around performances of whiteness and masculinity. Lindsay Nixon captures the mix of elation, frustration, and despair in their recollections of the Regina punk scene in the 2000s. On the one hand, "the small-town punk scenes of these little prairie towns existed in what felt like a frozen empty tundra, connecting us where it seemed connections weren't possible" (Nixon 76). And yet on the other hand, "it's always the same sea of yt faces, conveniently glossing over the fact that Queen City Punk was largely made up of folx who were openly skinhead punks" (Nixon 77–78). The kinds of violence that take place in music spaces—typically directed at women, people of colour, queers, and trans folx—are often glossed over, dismissed, or outright denied, and there is rarely recourse for marginalized folx to address or resolve this violence. With little accountability, the folx who experience that violence are never welcome and are made to disappear. While Roy Pérez suggests that "identity does not walk into a room fully made, but takes shape in the refraction and refashioning of social relations as they shoot through bodies in a space" (287), from another angle, bodies or identities can be unmade and undone by sociality that reflects only certain modes of being. In order to get on stage in predominantly cis straight spaces, trans artists may have to compartmentalize or disguise parts of ourselves or engage in certain acts of self-preservation to be perceived in the least damaging ways that are possible. However, we may choose not to slough off parts of ourselves and instead decide to stop taking the stage, stop going into spaces that harm us, especially when those harms outweigh the benefits we might receive. Much like Nixon, "I felt beaten down like there was no place for women and queers" by my experience in "the scene" (79). But many indomitable trans artists continue to take space and critique tokenizing inclusion and hegemonic structures of belonging that play out in musical spaces.

"IT'S EITHER FIRE OR BEING ERASED": TAKING SPACE AND VOICING ANGER[7]

Trans musicians use the voice to diverse effect: for education, to reject and confuse stereotypes, to exaggerate (if you want disgust I *will* disgust you), for joy and hope, and for anger. Within space and spaces of violence, denial, exclusion, and dismissal, our songs are protection spells, love letters, odes to self-preservation, self-sufficiency, and survival. So many songs articulate a defiant stance, trans folx singing that "we don't need to be you" or belong (Brown, "Really High"). Jia Qing Wilson-Yang sings, "I want no part in making sure we who don't fit fit in" ("god forbid!"). Similarly, Jordaan Mason sings, "Why do we still want to fit when the world just just just just just just rejects us?" ("why fit?"). Rather than conform to the politics, behaviours, and modes of being that cis spaces and society demand, trans singers take their anger at those power structures and hierarchies and dream elsewhere, dream of an elsewhere, and, often, disappear into it. While Masoumi argues that "taking space … involves costs, negotiations, and compromises" (188), many trans artists refuse to make those compromises for the sake of non-trans audiences, instead engaging in confrontational call-out performances, which thus limit spaces in which they can appear. In many cases, trans women of colour are talking back to the forces and people who would do violence against them, as well as the stereotypes of hyper-sexuality that follow both women of colour and trans women.

Trans artists who control their own recordings and creativity rarely speak of transness in ways they are "supposed" to, and thus experience an explicit and implicit "refusal to disseminate the artistic work they produce" (Namaste, *Sex Change* 42). Instead, in music, we are far more familiar with songs about trans folx (often, though not always, in belittling ways) or other "gender bending" artists who employ gender non-conformity as a part of their performance styles but not always their everyday lives. Trans musicians use their songs and voices to critique mainstream narratives and desires for trans bodies and people. In their song "Bare Minimum," Too Attached impersonate the mix of self-congratulation and fragility that accompanies performative allyship. As a method of critique, Vivek Shraya sings indignantly, "I have a gay son / I have a black friend / I'm sure a good mom / I'm such a great friend / … I want a pat on the back for doin' the bare, bare minimum" ("Bare Minimum"). From a different angle, in their song "BPD," Carolina Brown talks back to the autobiographical imperative and also subverts the expectations of how trans folx are "supposed" to talk about their bodies and genitalia. After singing about how much "your mom" is "so quick to lick" their "Big Puta Dick," Brown sings "Haha! Because I'm trans you thought I wouldn't go there?/ Jaja! I'm a she-demon, I go anywhere that I please!" Similarly, Backxwash flips hip-hop scripts to insert transness, asking "how many cis [n****s] do I gotta dismember or disfigure with my quick temper? My dick's bigger I'm fixing to get a lick or a rise outta these whack bitch [n****s]" ("JANE DRO"). Both artists manipulate cis fascination with trans genitalia while muddling a "trapped in the wrong body" narrative of trans embodiment and sexuality. They impersonate tropes of juvenile, competitive masculinity—"your mom" insults and pissing contests—while euphemistically nodding toward cisgender desire for trans bodies.

Discussing the late artist Mark Aguhar's *Casting a Glamour: Peony Piece* and how it forced audiences to engage affectively with trans embodiment, Pérez states, "Among the mediums here are … the audience's affective transformations as [they entered into] the space of Aguhar's gender drift for prolonged reckoning, in contrast to the chance and fleeting encounters of everyday life" (282). Pérez focuses on the function of gaze, particularly the twin gazes of the spectator on Aguhar and of Aguhar's glances toward the audience. For Pérez, Aguhar's gaze, "alternatingly demure, beseeching, and hostile … invited the audience to take inventory of its own feelings about her transition and her body" (282). Similar to Aguhar's practice, live trans musical performance engages a push-and-pull of gazes exchanged, invited, challenged, seductive and combative. From a performance perspective it can be a game of enthralling, captivating, or winning over an unfamiliar or disinterested audience. One of Jackie Shane's raison d'êtres was to make the audience love her in spite of whatever initial reactions—bemusement, desire, or disgust— they may have had to her gender, daring the audience *not* to love her in her glamour, graciousness, and talent. Performers may also challenge without love, like Aguhar with her gaze of hostility.

Like Aguhar, some trans musicians foreground their transness both lyrically and performatively to challenge the perceptions of a (presumably non-trans) audience. Taking the stage can be a defiant act of taking up space when trans folx are encouraged to take up as little public space as possible; to shrink down, quiet or deny our voices, make ourselves more palatable, more passable, less unfamiliar and strange, thus more worthy of tolerance and love and less "deserving" of violence and harassment. Taking the mic and turning an amp up **LOUD** can be simultaneously reparative and hostile, demanding that folx look up, shut up, witness us in our transness, and listen to our fucking voices or leave. Elena Rose argues that in a context where "people are supposed to respond to [trans folx] being in public with disgust and violence.… Listening to me is a political act and me speaking is a political act" (39). Simultaneously, trans voices are ignored and dismissed amidst a preoccupation with trans bodies, genitalia, and sexuality (Namaste, *Sex Change*). In this context, taking the stage and amplifying our voices becomes a mode of talking back to power and hierarchical structures that fundamentally burden trans people and routinely deny our voices. As Leah Lakshmi Piepzna-Samarasinha says about QTBIPOC, "We don't control a lot of things. But we can sometimes control a stage" (xii). Sometimes controlling that stage is not about casting a glamour over a crowd, but about making deafening noise, screaming your guts out, and filling a room with your voice, so that, if only for a few moments, that space belongs to you.[8] Even if, once you step off the stage and back into the audience, that space and the relative safety of the performance are over.

CONCLUSION: "SO CROSS THE STARS AND GALAXIES IF YOU CAN'T FIND ME!"[9]

In the summer of 2018 I quit playing music. I sold or packed away all my gear, stopped playing, stopped writing, and stopped singing. I had been sick of performing and playing shows for a long time, but they became unbearable as my relationship to my gender shifted. Getting constantly misgendered was exhausting, especially alongside the polite platitudes of performance etiquette: "Great show, dude!" When performing, I stopped drinking fluids and made constant calculations of which bathroom was safer, less busy, and how quickly I could get in and out without being seen or harassed. I was dealing with chronic physical pain that was exacerbated by the physical demands of performance, to say nothing of the emotional frustration and exhaustion I felt being in those spaces. These matters weighed on me while the people around me seemed to be having a fine time. Before transition, music performance, rehearsal, and ritual was one of the few ways of *feeling* and *feeling in* my body that was not fraught or dissociative. Music and its spaces began to feel fraught and dissociative as I found new, less debilitating ways to inhabit my body.

In comments to Elaine Banks on CBC *Q*, Jackie Shane was deeply ambivalent about her rediscovery: "I thought I was well hidden, and I wasn't. *You found me ...* I wasn't comfortable with that, but I can adjust.... I don't get too close to other people, and it was a bit much at first." Whether this reluctance toward public visibility began only after "transition" or becoming open about transness will likely remain unclear now that Jackie has passed. Shane seemed perfectly content to continue leading her solitary life without the spotlight, without ever being celebrated or reappearing. She was deeply enamoured with the idea of performing and giving the people what they want, and toyed with the idea of returning to the stage when she spoke with others. She never seemed to kick that desire, but tellingly never made that return to the stage (three weeks after her interview on *Q* in February 2019, Shane passed away). To seek out trans folx in light of our impelled, compelled, and self-imposed disappearances means actively engaging with trans folx on an individual basis, to "ask us who we are, how we want our histories to be honoured, and what respect looks like to us" (Shaughnessy 29).

This project started from a place of despair. While I had carved out niche places in music, I began to feel like those "worlds weren't enough to help us stay above the weight of what the world really was" (Mason, "it does not get better"). Instead, music was a constant reminder of the weight of what the world really is. But when I turn to trans musicians I find love letters to trans bodies, to trans girls, and to the grey and ambiguous area between and outside of gender; songs to hold on to. There are dreams for potential "future queers" and also dreaming of possibility, for ourselves, for trans futurity. In "Can't Tell (Confusing not Confused)" Lonely Boa works through serpentine melodies and lyrics that themselves transform as they negotiate the ambiguous and confusing space of transition, before ending with the definitive "We are real / I am real." It is a song that beautifully encapsulates a trans struggle for self-determination. These are love letters for our own survival; a means of connection and a lifeline. Hearing Carolina Brown's powerful refrain of "I'm in love with my body" ("My Body"), Too Attached's anthemic "Come into your power!" ("Grateful"), and Backxwash's declarative, "I'm strong, I'm powerful: Black fucking Sailor Moon" ("I GOT A PENTAGRAM TATTOO") keeps me hanging on. I come back to these and other trans performers because I need to know that other trans folx have found the will to sing and dance and scream and survive, because I need the hope that someday soon I will want to sing and survive. If I disappear ...

CRITICAL REFLECTION QUESTIONS

1. How do the experiences of trans artists outlined here differ from or mirror the experiences that cis women have had in creative or theatrical spaces?
2. How can communities cultivate spaces where trans artists are supported beyond mere lip service, so that we can move toward more appearances and fewer disappearances? What might modes of inclusion or fandom that are not tokenizing, exoticizing, or appropriative look like?
3. What are safe spaces?

NOTES

1. With thanks to Carly Boyce, Kat Burns, Matty Davey, Anne Day, Brendan Howlett, Alison Lang, Cee Lavery, Jordaan Mason, Morgan M. Page, and Liz Schieck.
2. Jackie Shane, "Money (That's What I Want) [Live]"
3. Jia Qing Wilson-Yang, "colour changer"
4. One possible reason why Shane never relied upon identity-based labels.

5. Writing that claims certain trans musicians as the "first" either in a particular place or genre dovetails with conceptions of musical (and other kinds of) history that have written out trans people and other actors, as Viviane Namaste argues about early punk ("A Gang"). Arguing that punk history was fundamentally rewritten as masculinist, Namaste notes how "the mainstream media ignored the experience and contributions of women, transsexuals, and prostitutes within punk cultures" ("A Gang" 86). These reinscriptions contribute not only to the invisibility of trans folx in past musical history but also to the conditions of misunderstanding, misnaming, and misgendering that encourage trans folx to disappear in the present moment.

6. Too Attached, "Love Is Not Love"

7. Too Attached, "Angry"

8. In this regard I can think of no more exemplary artist than Montreal's "trans girl death industrial" artist Girl Circles, whose music is beautiful, guttural, and absolutely deafening ("Girl Circles").

9. Mason, "if i disappear …"

WORKS CITED

Adsit, Lexi. "Interview by Nia King." *Queer and Trans Artists of Color Volume Two: Interviews with Nia King*, edited by Elena Rose, n.p. 2016, pp. 91–100.

Adsit, Lexi, et al. "Representation and Its Limits." *Trap Door: Trans Cultural Production and the Politics of Visibility*, edited by [Tourmaline] et al., MIT Press, 2017, pp. 191–200.

Backxwash. "I GOT A PENTAGRAM TATTOO." *Black Sailor Moon*, 2018.

———. "JANE DRO." *Black Sailor Moon*, 2018.

Brown, Carolina. "BPD." *Divas have no friends, they always cut their own throat last*, 2018.

———. "My Body." *Divas have no friends, they always cut their own throat last*, 2018.

———. "Really High." *Carolina Brown*, 2017.

———. "Sunday." *Carolina Brown*, 2017.

Dunn, Lindsay. "Back from the Dead: Transgender Pioneer Jackie Shane Nominated for Grammy." *CityNews*, 22 Jan. 2019, https://toronto.citynews.ca/2019/01/22/jackie-shane-grammy-nominee/. Accessed 19 March 2019.

Ellison, Treva. "The Labor of Werqing It: The Performance and Protest Struggles of Sir Lady Java." *Trap Door: Trans Cultural Production and the Politics of Visibility*, edited by [Tourmaline] et al., MIT Press, 2017, pp. 1–22.

Gillis, Carla. "Vanishing Music Venues: Three Months into 2017 and We've Already Lost Seven." *Now Magazine*, 1 March 2017, https://nowtoronto.com/music/torontos-vanishing-music-venues/. Accessed 1 April 2019.

"Girl Circles." *Bandcamp*, https://girlcircles.bandcamp.com/. Accessed 15 July 2019.

Gossett, Che, and Juliana Huxtable. "Existing in the World: Blackness at the Edge of Trans Visibility." *Trap Door: Trans Cultural Production and the Politics of Visibility*, edited by [Tourmaline] et al., MIT Press, 2017, pp. 39–56.

Gregory, Stamatina, and Jeanne Vaccaro. "Canonical Undoings: Notes on Trans Art and Archives." *Trap Door: Trans Cultural Production and the Politics of Visibility*, edited by [Tourmaline] et al., MIT Press, 2017, pp. 349–362.

Lamourex, Mack. "Cassia Hardy Found a New Perspective With Her New Identity." *Vice*, 6 Nov. 2014, https://www.vice.com/en_ca/article/rp79z6/cassia-hardy-new-voice-new-perspective. Accessed 15 April 2019.

Lorinc, John, et al., eds. *Any Other Way: How Toronto Got Queer*. Coach House Books, 2017.

Haritaworn, Jin, et al. "Introduction: Queering Urban Justice." *Queering Urban Justice: Queer of Colour Formations in Toronto*, edited by Jin Haritaworn et al., University of Toronto Press, 2018, pp. 3–26.

Haritaworn, Jin, et al. "Marvellous Grounds: QTBIPOC Counter-Archiving against Imperfect Erasures." *Any Other Way: How Toronto Got Queer*, edited by John Lorinc et al., Coach House Books, 2017, pp. 219–223.

I Got Mine: The Story of Jackie Shane. Inside the Music, CBC, 28 Feb. 2010, http://www.cbc.ca/player/play/1573021090/.

"The Late Jackie Shane in Her Own Words: A Rare Interview with the Pioneering Musician." *Q*, CBC, 8 Feb. 2019, https://www.cbc.ca/radio/q/friday-feb-8-2019-david-foster-jackie-shane-and-more-1.5009904/the-late-jackie-shane-in-her-own-words-a-rare-interview-with-the-pioneering-musician-1.5010217.

"Jia Qing Wilson-Yang." *Bandcamp*, https://jiaqingwilsonyang.bandcamp.com/. Accessed 15 July 2019.

Lonely Boa. "Can't Tell (Confusing Not Confused)." *Something Other Than*, 2016.

Mance, Ajuan. "Interview by Nia King." *Queer and Trans Artists of Color Volume Two: Interviews with Nia King*, edited by Elena Rose, n.p., 2016, pp. 113–128.

Mason, Jordaan. "if i disappear ..." *Earth to Ursa Major*, 2018.

———. "it does not get better." *Earth to Ursa Major*, 2018.

———. "why fit?" *Earth to Ursa Major*, 2018.

Masoumi, Azar. "Compulsory Coming Out and Agentic Negotiations: Toronto QTPOC Narratives." *Queering Urban Justice: Queer of Colour Formations in Toronto*, edited by Jin Haritaworn et al., University of Toronto Press, 2018, pp. 187–201.

Maynard, Steven. "A New Way of Lovin': Queer Toronto Gets Schooled by Jackie Shane." *Any Other Way: How Toronto Got Queer*, edited by John Lorinc et al., Coach House Books, 2017, pp. 11–20.

Muñoz, José Esteban. "Ephemera as Evidence: Introductory Notes to Queer Acts." *Women & Performance: A Journal of Feminist Theory*, vol. 8, no. 2, 1996, pp. 5–16.

Namaste, Viviane. "A Gang of Trannies: Gendered Discourse in Punk Culture." *Invisible Lives: The Erasure of Transsexual and Transgendered People.* University of Chicago Press, 2000, pp. 73–92.

———. *Sex Change, Social Change: Reflections on Identity, Institutions, and Imperialism.* Women's Press, 2005.

Nixon, Lindsay. "Queen City Punk." *Nitisânak*, Metonymy Press, 2018, pp. 75–80.

Pérez, Roy. "Proximity: On the Work of Mark Aguhar." *Trap Door: Trans Cultural Production and the Politics of Visibility.* Edited by [Tourmaline] et al., MIT Press, 2017, pp. 281–292.

Piepzna-Samarasinha, Leah Lakshmi. "Foreword." *Queer and Trans Artists of Color Volume Two: Interviews with Nia King*, edited by Elena Rose, n.p., 2016, pp. xi–xiv.

Rabiyah, Amir. "Interview by Nia King." *Queer and Trans Artists of Color Volume Two: Interviews with Nia King*, edited by Elena Rose, n.p., 2016, pp. 67–78.

Rose, Elena. "Interview by Nia King." *Queer and Trans Artists of Color Volume Two: Interviews with Nia King*, edited by Elena Rose, n.p., 2016, pp. 37–54.

Scott, Toi. "Foreword." *Queer & Trans Artists of Color: Stories of Some of our Lives*, edited by Jessica Glennon-Zukoff and Terra Mikalson, n.p., 2014, pp. i–iv.

Shane, Jackie. "Any Other Way." *Jackie Shane: Any Other Way*, Numero Group, 2017.

———. "Money (That's What I Want) [Live]." *Jackie Shane: Any Other Way*, Numero Group, 2017.

Shaughnessy, Kyle. "Name Game: Being Seen in My Entirety." *The Remedy: Queer and Trans Voices on Health and Health Care*, edited by Zena Sharman, Arsenal Pulp, 2017, pp. 25–30.

Shraya, Vivek. *I'm Afraid of Men.* Penguin, 2018.

Tang, Jeanine. "Contemporary Art and Critical Transgender Infrastructures." *Trap Door: Trans Cultural Production and the Politics of Visibility*, edited by [Tourmaline] et al., MIT Press, 2017, pp. 363–392.

Too Attached. "Angry." *Angry*, 2018.

———. "Bare Minimum." *Angry*, 2018.

———. "Grateful." *Angry*, 2018.

———. "Love Is Not Love." *Angry*, 2018.

Wilson-Yang, Jia Qing. "colour changer." *eight steps in the recent moves of,* 2013.

———. "god forbid!" *eight steps in the recent moves of,* 2013.

Ziegler, Kortney Ryan. "Interview by Nia King." *Queer & Trans Artists of Color: Stories of Some of our Lives*, edited by Jessica Glennon-Zukoff and Terra Mikalson, n.p., 2014, pp. 61–68.

CHAPTER 15

Inviting Women to Speak: The Boundaries of Gendered Access Intimacy within the Context of Podcasts with Sick and Disabled Guests

Jessica Watkin

Feminism often begins with intensity: you are aroused by what you come up against. You register something in the sharpness of an impression. Something can be sharp without it being clear what the point is. Over time, with experience, you sense that something is wrong, or you have a feeling of being wronged. You sense an injustice. You might not have used that word for it; you might not have the words for it; you might not be able to put your finger on it. Feminism can begin with a body, a body in touch with a world, a body that is not at ease in a world; a body that fidgets and moves around. Things don't seem right.

—*Sara Ahmed*, Living a Feminist Life

INTRODUCTION: HAVING A DISABLED FEMALE VOICE IN CANADA

This chapter is rooted in the lived experience of my disability and is framed by a personal method of intersectional disability, feminist, and performance studies. To follow the path of Carrie Sandahl, Audre Lorde, Christine Kelly, and Mia Mingus, my experience of the world informs my analysis. My lived experience of disability shapes my experience of feminism. To position my analysis amongst the personal also emphasizes a listener's relationship to any podcast—intimate listening, through headphones or speakers, in public or in private—and instills a relational engagement with the material. This chapter asks readers to dance with the idea of a personal disclosure and analysis as critical practice. This chapter is an offering of experience for meaningful engagement and learning.

When I listen to podcasts, I tend to do so intentionally. I use it for learning as I walk, while on long car journeys with my partner, while resting my eyes before bed, and ultimately as an accessible entryway into media that works for me as a Blind Canadian woman. I am a cis white settler who experiences the world with very low vision and have found the land of podcasts to be a reprieve from the world of constant beratement of visual culture and propaganda. Podcasts are more informative and mentally active than binge-watching *Grey's Anatomy* on Netflix. Podcasts, particularly the ones that I listen to anyway, are one (or both) of two things: social justice shaded or funky, offbeat, and informative.

In 2014, I was asked to be a part of the Canadian Broadcasting Corporation's (CBC) first original podcast series, called *Campus*, where I was interviewed by one man, Albert Leung, and supported by two other male producers. As of September 2015, the episode was launched and my voice was a part of the Canadian media as a Blind female contrasted with the male interviewer. I felt in control of my story, despite having to repeat certain moments over and over to get the right performative aesthetic that they wanted, and continue to, as it is repeated and uploaded onto iTunes. Friends, past acquaintances, and strangers alike send me Facebook messages saying how inspirational I sound on the podcast, and it has led to other personal interventions on the airwaves for me as well as other speaking and written opportunities.

I did feel like the only woman in the room, though. The room being a small recording studio in Toronto's CBC building, dimly lit, with strange albeit CBC employees whom I'd only briefly met previous to the interviews. I never felt quite uncomfortable and always felt safe, but with the awareness of being in a nice dress and wedged heels, on Canada Day in 2015, when I first heard the entire interview, I felt myself clam up.

Maybe some women will understand and recognize the feeling when you are the only woman in a group of men in a small space. Imagine an elevator, meeting room, or even a crowded subway car, if you are the only woman holding on to a pole when the rest of the sweaty hands around yours are men's hands. There's an awareness, even as a Blind woman, that I am surrounded by that male energy.

It isn't quite discomfort, but it isn't quite comfort either. It doesn't shade my experience as bad per se, but it does *feel* different than being in a room of female or nonbinary people.

I believe my sense of awareness of this kind was heightened when I entered graduate school, as I was spending hours in classrooms dominated by male voices, despite the classes having an uneven number, slanted higher in the direction of female. A professor of mine, when I asked her if there was anything I could improve on in her introduction to performance theory seminar in my master's, responded with, "You're doing great work, just talk more!"

As a Blind woman involved in both artistic and academic circles, my voice is part of my "brand," but socializing is difficult when I cannot see faces. I am unsure of when the gaps are in conversation, who is speaking at any time, and if my voice will even be heard. In Canadian disability art culture we have developed an inclusive discussion technique where we say our name every time we speak, and when we are done speaking we say "That is the end of my current thought." I consider this a disabled and feminist practice that dissuades interruptions, encourages active listening, and makes space for voices otherwise unheard. But this practice is new, and so participation in "normal" conversation and discussions, which would otherwise be easy for my colleagues, is a barrier for me. In a master's seminar I cannot see my colleagues' hands in the air waiting for their turn, so I tend not to speak at all. Interacting with others, engaging in academia, and using my voice as a disabled woman in Canada is different and more complex than anyone might assume. Therefore, the ways in which we invite sick and disabled women to speak is important and takes more complex thought than just making space for them.

PODCASTS WORTH LISTENING TO

I want to listen to podcasts that use feminist and radical methods to create care-full and healing spaces to share and witness. I desire shows that have dominant female and feminist voices that amplify other female and feminist voices. *Call Your Girlfriend* was the first podcast show for which I ever listened to the entire back log. *The Guilty Feminist* is the next, followed by *Feminist Killjoy, PhD*, and I am a huge fan of the Canadian *Witch, Please* and *Secret Feminist Agenda*, which take on Harry Potter culture and feminism in our current world climate, respectively. All of these regular rotations on my headphones have strong, brilliant, intersectional feminist women and non-binary humans speaking about radically taking care of each other and our communities through gentleness, softness, and rage. Aminatou Sow, Deborah Frances-White, and Hannah McGregor are three voices that regularly dominate my thoughts. Their intersectional and honest views on being a female today has impressed upon me a duty to pay more attention to what I'm listening to.

The other podcasts that I listen to are for my learning needs. As a PhD candidate who is Blind, reading anything educational outside of my own thesis work is out of the question—my eye just cannot handle it—so podcasts have saved me the eye fatigue and have also brought me handfuls of beautiful work. CBC's *Un-Reserved* with Rosanna Deerchild is my favourite Indigenous pop culture show, *She's All Fat* addresses fatphobia and the malaise of the body positivity movement in social media and pop culture. There is a theme of my favourite and most listened to podcasts: women's voices.

The final genre of podcasts that I love but have a hard time listening to regularly is podcasts hosted by or interviewing disabled people. Andrew Gurza, the host of *Disability After Dark*, talks about his experiences of having a disability and being unapologetically sexually active. Gurza has also been a guest on *Sickboy*, the podcast this chapter will focus on, which interviews people with different illnesses and conditions that deserve to be stripped of the negative and medicinal stigma that plagues sick and disabled people and their stories. I have been searching for a disability- or sickness-run podcast by women that I could listen to and identify with, but to no end. I would wager that by the time this is published many more podcasts will have popped up already. What does it say about my own ingrained misogyny and ableism that I prefer disability podcasts with male hosts, and even within those have a hard time regularly listening? I, too, have a hard time unlearning the processes of respecting disabled women's experiences, and I am one.

EXPERIENCING *SICKBOY*

In early January 2018, I had put my headphones in before donning the rest of my Canadian winter garb: large mittens over small gloves, coat, scarf, boots, long johns, bus pass and keys already in hand, and was listening to a podcast that had been suggested to me by a friend: *Sickboy*. I had never listened to an entire episode, but the first one of the year was an interview with a woman, Nadia, who had been dealing with a new diagnosis of cervical cancer, and so I pressed play and was on my way to my partner's house. In my ears I heard three distinctly vibrant male voices introducing the podcast, and one female voice, a little quieter. The story was intense and beautiful, and there was a moment when Nadia explained how she had been hoping to have children but, from her illness, was left unable to conceive. At this point she was quite emotional; her husband was also in the recording studio and was providing words and anecdotes of comfort in lieu of her own words, and I found myself also feeling teary-eyed, waiting at the bus stop, hopping from foot to foot so my feet wouldn't freeze. The moment was broken not by an offer of concern or comfort from the three podcast hosts, however, but by confusion and ignorance. The emotional moment was almost drawn out to be a joke, which became my first hint of the possibility of what the male voice provides in the context of podcasts: just as physical space can be coded and monopolized by men, so too the voice gendered as male can monopolize a soundscape. Even without physical presence, the podcast hosts still dominated a narrative that was intimately personal for Nadia. I was furious and turned off the episode immediately.

In the months following this instance I tried to listen again but found myself annoyed by the male voices of the podcast. Jeremie, the main host, has cystic fibrosis, and I *should* like him, shouldn't I? He's gone through so much, and the hosts are all nice-sounding gentlemen with good intentions. They all teach at the same yoga studio and talk openly about their relationships with their female partners and their sex lives. Considering this awkward moment with Nadia that I experienced, I went back to find other moments throughout the podcast's history to hear how the female guests were treated.

On October 5, 2015, *Sickboy*'s episode "Bipolar II" begins with Jeremie saying "Thank god that there's now a female on the show cause I feel like the amount of like … dick talk that's happened on the show," and apologizes to Nadine, the first female guest on the show (1:56). On February 22, 2016, at the beginning of the episode "Endometriosis," following the three male hosts making jokes about masturbation and sex, referring to their guest, Lesley, Jeremie asks, "How are you? Are you good? You feel safe, right?" and she responds, "Yes, I've heard your show, so I was expecting this" (2:11). Later in 2016, Donald Trump would excuse his lewd pussy-grabbing behaviour and language by citing "locker room talk," which sparked ripples of implications: social media erupted in feminist debates over the acceptability in contemporary culture for such remarks. As a feminist listening to the *Sickboy* podcast in the aftermath of Bill Cosby, Donald Trump, and Harvey Weinstein inspiring public debate over sexual assault and the complicated #MeToo movement, the ways in which the female guests are introduced and taken care of is obvious and important to me. As Sara Ahmed explains the texture of being a feminist, "You are aroused by what you come up against. You register something in the sharpness of an impression. Something can be sharp without it being clear what the point is" (22). I can hear and *feel* that the construction of the female narratives within the podcast are strange, off, but I cannot clearly pinpoint the discomfort. The hosts are well-meaning, but the misogynistic tone of the podcast and how the hosts contextualize, question, and interrupt the sick and disabled female voices confirm a feeling of strangeness. As contributors to a movement of change for the de-stigmatization of illness and disability, the *Sickboy* podcast fails to intersectionally engage, which is integral to making change at all.

NARRATIVES OF SICKNESS

While thinking through cultural conventions of the experience of sickness, I was drawn to Patrick Anderson's book *Autobiography of a Disease* wherein he describes it as

> [an understanding of] illness not as a patient's monologue or biography, but as a profoundly social, richly durational, and multiply perspectival encounter. It seeks to describe how illness makes meaning of the world even as it threatens to dissemble the world in which it occurs. (ix)

Save the foreword and concluding paragraphs, the book reads as a nearly fictional story of Anderson's illness told from the third-person perspective as well as from the perspective of the illness itself. Anderson suggests that by taking control of his own narrative, much of the world around him can be revealed, particularly when it comes to the ways in which society considers *care* (health *care*, family and friends, and living and independent/interdependent life).[1] *Sickboy* falls under this umbrella for me as it isn't just one voice giving an inspirational talk about their experience overcoming illness, or even a monologic auto-ethnographic/biographic explanation of the lived experience of an illness. The inherent dialogic nature and multiple perspectives available in *Sickboy* offer a less cringe-y version of stories of sickness and disability in a culture that is dominated by people in wheelchairs overcoming their obstacles, people with chronic illnesses living a happy life despite their diagnosis, and inspiring Blind PhD candidates in the humanities having only used their ears to absorb their research.

The tone of the *Sickboy* podcast is that of exciting, cool, and interesting stories of the lifestyles and struggles of disabled and sick people with total acceptance and understanding that everyone experiences their diagnosis and body differently.

The *Sickboy* podcast is a kind of ethnographical exploration of being sick, ill, and disabled in the mid 2010s. Beginning from the auto-ethnographical perspective of one of the hosts, Jeremie, who has cystic fibrosis, the first interview episode explores Jeremie's experience of his illness, rejecting it, getting married young, and starting a podcast to explore different experiences from different people with different diagnoses. The *Sickboy* website self-identifies the podcast as:

> More than just a podcast. It's a movement. A community built on the foundations of compassion, vulnerability, and humour. Join the tens of thousands of people across the world in changing the conversation surrounding illness, and dying with laughter in the process.

This mandate resonates deeply with Mia Mingus's articulation of access intimacy:

> The intimacy [one feels] with many other disabled and sick people who have an automatic understanding of access needs out of our shared similar lived experience of the many different ways ableism manifests in our lives. Together, we share a kind of access intimacy that is ground-level, with no need for explanations. Together we can hold the weight, emotion, logistics, isolation, trauma, fear, anxiety and pain of access. [We] don't have to justify and we are able to start from a place of steel vulnerability. (Mingus)[2]

Sickboy episodes embody the tone of acceptance and vulnerability despite the line of interview questions being driven from the three male hosts' gaps in knowledge. The laughter that dominates most episodes of *Sickboy* is emblematic of the intimacy created within each interview, but as the episodes delve into topics of female biology (transitioning to female, abortions, pregnancy, and menstruation), the self-identified goal of "compassion, vulnerability, and humour" is compromised as the boys shift from mutual understanding of access to the depths of the unknown.

Particularly in their episode on pregnancy and miscarriages, as well as sexual assault, the hosts express their disbelief and lack of knowledge of the female and people with wombs—having experiences that they do not have. The entire podcast is dominated by discovering and sharing the experiences that the hosts do not have, but in episodes with their male guests the method of inquiry seems to be driven by the unknown and possibly strange. In an episode with the experience of endometriosis, however, the interview moves into a direction driven by disbelief. Does anything change when the intention and direction of an interview shifts from interest to disbelief? Does it matter? It *feels* different for me. The shift of intention in the episodes changes the way I want to listen to the female guests. The access intimacy responds differently when it is gendered. As a disabled female it is easier for me to engage in intimate recognition of a shared experience when coming from a woman or non-binary person. Further, I also believe that access intimacy is not as simple as familiarity or recognition based on understanding, but is entangled in a network of vulnerability and care that comes with hearing someone's story and feeling it within yourself. This feeling comes from active engagement and witness to another's experience, full respect, and willingness to share.

INVITING WOMEN TO SPEAK AND THEN LISTENING

When listening to women and non-binary folks I find my ears wrapping up their voices in comfort and desire to hold the space. While listening to Jeremie's first episode on his own cystic fibrosis, I laughed and felt tender feelings for his experiences and felt the access intimacy Mingus hopes that we as disabled and sick folk can find in this hard world. But while listening to their interviews with women, the user experience of someone who is used to well-edited feminist podcasts that normally dominate in political and social justice is unsatisfying. That is not even the word I need, I need something stronger: disappointing? The tone and energy of holding space and bearing witness feels like a texture beyond vulnerable: unsafe. When we listen and, further, when we choose to listen, we actually engage in a culture of holding space and witnessing. As a cis female podcast listener I sometimes feel uncomfortable listening to *Sickboy*'s episodes with women. Are the hosts not listening as well? Do they not feel the discomfort, or is that part of the curiosity experience? Just because the podcast aims to improve understanding of disability and sickness in North American society does not mean they can ignore the ways in which they are reproducing the patriarchy in their interviews with women. Improving our society for sick and disabled people will not occur without an intersectional and feminist approach. What I mean is that we cannot effect social change for sick and disabled people until we consider all of those people as having valuable perspectives and give them the respect they deserve. Humour can be a useful and powerful tool for creating respect; listen to any episode of *Secret Feminist Agenda* and Hannah McGregor will fiercely invite humour into her social justice, but there is no room for perpetuating uncomfortable locker room talk.

In my first-year university English seminar I would answer any question from my instructor with "This might be wrong, but …" and had to be explicitly told that I was cutting myself short before speaking. As a young woman, I did not notice when men interrupted me or spoke without waiting their turn. I did not notice until my first seminar during graduate school, where a classroom of seven women/non-binary folks and four men was dominated by the male voices, because they either took up a lot of discussion time, vocally working through their own understanding of a theory, or would not put their hand up before speaking but interrupt whenever a thought occurred. It was from that moment that I realized how impactful the silence of women's voices—despite women dominating the room in terms of head count and having an open invitation to speak during a discussion—can be, and how harmful it is to ignore when women's voices are oppressed. Now every time I watch a film, listen to the news, or listen to a podcast, I am aware of the amount of sound and space the women present take up, and when women are not present how and why that might be. Call me a polite Canadian lady, but I have some questions about the way in which we should be expected to conduct a respectful interview:

Why would you invite someone to be a guest on your program and then speak more than they do? Why would you have a podcast that is for increasing awareness of the experiences of your guests, but then interrupt them while they are speaking? If you were inviting someone over for dinner to talk about a traumatic thing that has affected their life, would you want them to feel comfortable? Would you dominate the introduction of your discussion by expressing how uncomfortable you are made by the topic or how little you know about it?

These are all methods that are used throughout the *Sickboy* podcast's episodes. The podcast feels as though we have been invited into the hosts' basements, living rooms, kitchens, and sometimes bedrooms, and are experiencing an informal discussion between them and their guests. I believe that *Sickboy* uses humour to bridge the gap between knowing and unknowing, discomfort and comfort, and possibly male and female. I dislike endorsing the binary here, especially since the show has had experience of transgender women who speak to the non-binary nature of their experiences. But the three male hosts continually reinforce this binary by pointing out that, despite each of them having female girlfriends, they have little knowledge in the experiences of having a uterus. The constant vocalization that the guys do not understand these experiences or, after the endometriosis episode, repeating that they are "experts" in everything menstruation creates an *us and them* energy that perpetuates some of the othering stereotypes that their podcast is aiming to derail. *Sickboy* invites listeners to submit or apply to have an episode and tell their own story. But having an episode about pregnancy in a podcast dominated by illness does not sit well with me. Claiming that pregnancy is a condition that is misunderstood does not do it justice: people with uteruses who choose to become pregnant do understand that experience. What the hosts and production team are saying by having episodes about pregnancy and sexual assault is that because it is not normally experienced by men, it requires further understanding in a context of a "condition" or "diagnosis." This is an extremely important distinction for me: the beginnings of these episodes should be handled with context and instead are handled by acknowledging that it will be a different episode than usual. To further other the guests who speak about pregnancy, Jeremie also talks about how disgusted he feels by the mere idea of pregnancy, relating the disgust to his experience of watching *Alien* and seeing a gross being erupt from a human's stomach. This began the episode about pregnancy with one of the most disrespectful openings I've experienced in their backlog. By not focusing on the ways in which they construct the narratives of their female guests with care and intentional respect for their voices, the podcast fails to make meaningful change in an intersectional way. These are a group of well-meaning dudes, but that is part of the problem: they haven't spent enough time ensuring the compassion aspect of their mandate.

Another podcast that explores the stories of sick and disabled people is *Terrible, Thanks for Asking*, which follows host Nora McInerny and her experience with sickness, death, and grieving in her life, which brings her to other people's stories. In episode "5: Help Me Remember" McInerny interviews Dawn Pereda and her family as they are living with the aftermath of a head injury and memory loss. The interview is well edited and begins with McInerny contextualizing the opening moment of the interview as a technique her podcast team uses to ease into the topic of trauma. Pereda's family includes her two young daughters, and the interview begins with McInerny and her co-interviewer asking everyone present what they had for breakfast. This question infuses the discussion with humour, and the context that memory is subjective, as Dawn may not remember what she has had for breakfast. This tool is almost radically simple but a beautiful introduction to a hard and transparent discussion with a family navigating a new trauma. McInerny and Pereda share the narrative responsibility of telling Pereda's story both in the room of the interview and afterwards in an edited voiceover.

The care present in this simply contextualized but heavily edited episode differs from *Sickboy*'s nearly unedited, unfiltered episodes because it prioritizes the narrative of the guest and emphasizes that the knowledge-making is led by the guest, by Pereda's responses to the questions. *Sickboy* can potentially sacrifice the ease of narrative or understanding of the precise details of a guest's story to prioritize feelings. The hosts would rather understand how certain moments of their guests' experiences made them feel. While feelings and visceral experiences of our lives are important, a lot of the stories in both of these podcasts are traumatic in nature and possibly triggering. In *Sickboy*'s episode from May 8, 2017, called "Sexual Assault," their guest Lauren says near the beginning that she feels uncomfortable sharing her experience and is concerned of backlash from listeners. The episode's description even says that "it's a conversation that three privilege[d] males have little skin in the game aside from feelings of empathy and frustration at how some people can be so horrendous." I actually could not finish listening to the episode because it was mildly triggering for me, as Lauren's assault occurred on a university campus, which brings up visceral memories. The intimacy I feel from her story was almost too much for me to share in. That is what I want to listen to. That is the audio culture I want to participate in. But what I want is for all of the voices telling their stories to feel respected, comfortable, and empowered to tell those stories in a relatively safe and supported way. What I am trying to get at here is that I am unsure if that is being achieved by *Sickboy*, intentionally or not, especially from a female listener's perspective.

CONCLUSION

There isn't a way to conclude my thoughts. There isn't a way to conclude a feeling of strangeness. I began by contextualizing my experience being a disabled female guest on a podcast, being invited to tell my story and having the result be an edited, charming, and affective piece of audio culture. Even in a space where I was given support and appropriate context for telling my story I still felt a bit strange. When sharing stories of trauma and life-changing events or illnesses, we deserve care-full-ness. We deserve to laugh after it hurts and feel comfortable to share or stay silent when we decide it is right for us. The problem with the patriarchy, misogyny, racism, and ableism in this context is that they are all so learned and entrenched in our culture and understanding of ourselves and the world that it is so hard to feel the difference between what is right and what is strange or off or just not right. It has been so difficult for me to articulate these feelings because I do think the work that the *Sickboy* podcast does is important, but the way they are doing it hurts me. It hurts me to listen to other women and non-binary people be interrupted regularly when they speak because I have felt those interruptions. I have felt the awkwardness during conversations when men continually talk about masturbation or make sexual innuendos about what I have said. I have shared an intimate and traumatic experience and have had listeners respond with disbelief. The access intimacy that I experience while listening to this podcast is not with the experience of diagnosis and disability, but with the negotiation of discussing my experiences with men who self-identify as ignorant and oblivious or are outright disgusted by what I have to go through. I am calling for change, for accountability, and for people to remember the responsibility of the work that they create: people are actually going to listen to these podcasts. People who are different than the hosts, different than the guests, and people who may feel uncomfortable, as I have. Podcasts are relatively public and free if you have access to a computer and wireless Internet (and a pair of headphones, to be polite), and so the podcast hosts should be held accountable to be part of a solution, and not part of the problem of perpetuating the issues that they aim to dismantle.

CRITICAL REFLECTION QUESTIONS

1. What does it mean to actively listen in a feminist context?
2. How could podcasts provoke, invite, and engage with lived experiences of trauma, disability, and intersectionality in a respectful and mindful way?
3. Why is it important for digital movements to de-stigmatize sick and disabled people to include voices from women, non-binary people, Indigenous people, and people of colour? How can this be accomplished long-term without tokenization or invitation?

NOTES

1. Access intimacy is political and normally a practice in disability or crip solidarity. I am suggesting here that access intimacy is a feminist practice, that it is active and aims to move past solidarity and push further toward alliances and allyships that band together non-disabled folks to create an intimacy of growth.

2. Interdependence is defined in many texts (Clare; Kafer; Kuppers) as being a practice of care that usurps the binary of a giver and receiver—a network of caring that flows between all those who are involved. The best way I can describe this is to contrast it with a collaboration, which I conceptualize as a number of individuals bringing their own thoughts/work to a project, and if one left the project, the project would still exist. In an interdependent practice, the project is only the project with all individuals present and working together.

WORKS CITED

"5: Help Me Remember." *Terrible, Thanks for Asking*, 26 Dec. 2016.

Ahmed, Sarah. *Living a Feminist Life*. Duke UP, 2017.

Anderson, Patrick. *Autobiography of a Disease*. Routeledge, 2017.

"Bipolar II." *Sickboy*, 5 Oct. 2015.

Chicago Tribune Staff and Hawbaker, K. T. "#MeToo A Timeline of Events." *Chicago Tribune*, 23 Jan. 2019, https://www.chicagotribune.com/lifestyles/ct-me-too-timeline20171208-htmlstory.html. Accessed 30 Jan. 2019.

Clare, Eli. *Brilliant Imperfection: Grappling with Cure*. Duke UP, 2017.

"Endometriosis." *Sickboy*, 6 Feb. 2016.

Kafer, Alison. *Feminist, Queer, Crip*. Indiana UP, 2013.

Kuppers, Petra. "Towards a Rhizomatic Model of Disability: Poetry, Performance, and Touch." *Journal of Literary & Cultural Disability Studies*, vol. 3, no. 3, 2009, pp. 221–240.

Mingus, Mia. "Access Intimacy: The Missing Link." *Leaving Evidence*, 17 April 2017, www.leavingevidence.wordpress.com. Accessed 17 Oct. 2018.

"Miscarriages Suck!" *Sickboy*, 8 Feb. 2016.

Nelson, Louis. "From 'Locker Room Talk' On, Trump Fends Off Misconduct Claims." *Politico*, 12 Dec. 2017, https://www.politico.com/story/2017/12/12/trump-timeline-sexual misconduct-allegations-defense-292146. Accessed 28 Jan. 2019.

"Pregnancy and Breastfeeding." *Sickboy*, 22 Aug. 2016.

"Sexual Assault." *Sickboy*, 8 May 2017.

Recommended Readings

Collective Resistance: Building Futures through Histories

When we read and write feminist work, we contribute to the histories and futures of feminist thought. In concluding this volume with other recommended readings, which might align with or extend the ideas presented in this book, I am attempting to pay tribute to current and past scholars and artists who continue to create more equitable artistic cultures, who seek and build spaces of feminist belonging, and who hold media accountable for the ways it perpetuates troubling norms.

The suggested reading list comprises six parts, correlating with each part of the book. But, like this volume, there are many ways readings and topics intersect. These lists could be organized in multiple configurations under many headings. While I attempt to provide an intersectional perspective, these suggestions are by no means comprehensive and it is important to emphasize that it is based primarily in a Western context to align with the focus of this collection. Ultimately the objective of this list is to support scholars, researchers, artists, and feminists in continuing to explore the diverse intersections of gender, nationhood, and media.

INTRODUCTION: MEDIATED NATION: GENDERS AND GEOGRAPHIES OF POPULAR CULTURE

The texts recommended here offer an opportunity to explore media through feminist and queer theory. They are, in many cases, what I consider to be foundational texts and very much what inspired the conception and framework of this collection.

Ahmed, Sara. *Living a Feminist Life*. Duke UP, 2017.

Bannerji, Himani. "On the Dark Side of the Nation: Politics of Multiculturalism and the State of 'Canada.'" *Journal of Canadian Studies*, vol. 31, no. 3, 1996, pp. 103–128.

Berland, Jody. "The Politics of the Exasperated: Arts and Culture in Canada." *ESC: English Studies in Canada*, vol. 33, no. 3, 2009, pp. 24–30, doi:10.1353/esc.0.0061.

Hall, Stuart. *Representation: Cultural Representations and Signifying Practices*. Sage, 2013.

hooks, bell. "Theory as Liberatory Practice." *Yale Journal of Law and Feminism*, vol. 4, no. 1, Fall 1991, pp. 1–12.

Lorde, Audre. *Sister Outsider: Essays and Speeches*. Crossing Press, 1984.

Petersen, Anne Helen. *Too Fat, Too Slutty, Too Loud: The Rise and Reign of the Unruly Woman.* CELA, 2018.

Rothe, Dawn L., and Victoria E. Collins. "The Illusion of Resistance: Commodification and Reification of Neoliberalism and the State." *Critical Criminology,* vol. 25, no. 4, June 2017, pp. 609–618, doi:10.1007/s10612-017-9374-7.

Sarkeesian, Anita, and Ebony Adams. *History vs Women: The Defiant Lives That They Don't Want You to Know.* Feiwel and Friends, 2018.

Zeisler, Andi. *We Were Feminists Once: From Riot Grrrl to CoverGirl®, the Buying and Selling of a Political Movement.* Public Affairs, 2017.

PART I: NOTEWORTHY AND NEWSWORTHY: THE POLITICAL AND THE POPULAR

When we study popular culture and media studies, we cannot assume that these are separate or supplementary to broader considerations of culture and politics in Canada. Systemic structures of power can be supported and naturalized through popular mainstream media—making stereotypes and violence seem neutral, acceptable, and expectable. At the same time, these mediums can provide an opportunity to reveal inequities and combat political norms. In keeping with the themes addressed in part I of the book, the suggested readings listed here bring together themes at the intersections of politics, race, nationhood, and media representations.

Atluri, Tara. "Black Picket Signs/White Picket Fences: Racism, Space, and Solidarity." *Queering Urban Justice,* 2018, pp. 148–168, doi:10.3138/9781487518646-010.

Diverlus, Rodney, et al., editors. *Until We Are Free: Reflections on Black Lives Matter in Canada.* University of Regina Press, 2020.

Dryden, OmiSoore H., and Suzanne Lenon. *Disrupting Queer Inclusion: Canadian Homonationalisms and the Politics of Belonging.* UBC Press, 2016

Johnston, Genevieve. "The Kids Are All White: Examining Race and Representation in News Media Coverage of Opioid Overdose Deaths in Canada." *Sociological Inquiry,* Mar. 2019, doi:10.1111/soin.12269.

Kojima, Dai, et al. "Introduction: Feeling Queer, Feeling Asian, Feeling Canadian." *TOPIA: Canadian Journal of Cultural Studies,* vol. 38, 2017, pp. 69–80, doi:10.3138/topia.38.69.

Leung, Helen Hok-Sze. "Our City of Colours: Queer/Asian Publics in Transpacific Vancouver." *Inter-Asia Cultural Studies,* vol. 18, no. 4, Feb. 2017, pp. 482–497, doi:10.1080/14649373.2017.1387091.

Nelson, Sarah E., Annette J. Browne, and Josée G. Lavoie. "Representations of Indigenous Peoples and Use of Pain Medication in Canadian News Media." *The International Indigenous Policy Journal*, vol. 7, no. 1, 2016, p. 5.

Roth, Jenny, and Chris Sanders. "'Incorrigible Slag,' the Case of Jennifer Murphy's HIV Non-Disclosure: Gender Norm Policing and the Production of Gender-Class-Race Categories in Canadian News Coverage." *Womens Studies International Forum*, vol. 68, 2018, pp. 113–120, doi:10.1016/j.wsif.2018.03.004.

Tabobondung, Rebeka, and Syrus Marcus Ware. "The Sacred Uprising: Indigenous Creative Activisms." *Queering Urban Justice*, 2018, pp. 202–211, doi:10.3138/9781487518646-013.

PART II: FEMINIST, EH? RE-READING CANADIAN TEXTS AND TV

The second part of this collection focuses on popular texts and TV series. It is, perhaps, the section that considers the most "popular" media texts in the collection. The sources listed here help to provide insight into discussion of broadcasting, Canadian literature, and race, thinking carefully about how geographies influence not only development and production of mainstream media but also consumption habits, expectations, and readings and interpretations.

Ahmed, Sara. "A Phenomenology of Whiteness." *Feminist Theory*, vol. 8, no. 2, Jan. 2007, pp. 149–168, doi:10.1177/1464700107078139.

Fahs, Breanne. "Killjoy's Kastle and the Haunting of Queer/Lesbian Feminism." *Women, Sex, and Madness: Notes from the Edge*, Routledge, 2019.

Kispal-Kovacs, Joseph, and Tanner Mirrlees. *The Television Reader: Critical Perspectives in Canadian and US Television Studies*. Oxford UP, 2013.

McGregor, Hannah, et al., editors. *REFUSE: Canlit in Ruins*. Book*hug Press, 2018.

Phoenix, Aisha. "From Text to Screen: Erasing Racialized Difference in *The Handmaid's Tale*." *Communication, Culture and Critique*, vol. 11, no. 1, Jan. 2018, pp. 206–208, doi:10.1093/ccc/tcx018.

Rintoul, Suzanne, and Quintin Zachary Hewlett. "Negotiating Canadian Culture Through Youth Television: Discourse on Degrassi." *Jeunesse: Young People, Texts, Cultures*, vol. 1, no. 1, 2010, pp. 125–147, doi:10.1353/jeu.2010.0005.

Vipond, Evan. "'100% Dude': Straightening Degrassi's Adam Torres." *Queer Cats Journal of LGBTQ Studies*, vol. 1, no. 31, 2016.

Williams, David. *Imagined Nations: Reflections on Media in Canadian Fiction*. McGill-Queens UP, 2014.

Zarranz, Libe García. "Where Is the Transgender in the TransCanadian? Kai Cheng
    Thom and Vivek Shraya's Response-Able Fictions." *Revista Canaria De Estudios
    Ingleses*, vol. 78, 2019, pp. 141–153, doi:10.25145/j.recaesin.2019.78.010.

PART III: IN SHINING ARMOUR: COPS, ROBBERS, AND SUPERHEROES

Science fiction, fantasy, and heroic detective narratives often create a guise of
fighting adversity while maintaining the status quo. The chapters in part III by
and large critique narratives in this medium, but other scholars have considered alternative possibilities. While some of the chapters listed introduce important questions regarding the relationship between representations of power,
strength, race, and gender in a range of heroic narratives, other sources listed
here continue the conversation to consider speculative fiction, disability, and
crip theory.

BedoreIf, Pamela. "A Colder Kind of Gender Politics: Intersections of Feminism and
    Detection in Gail Bowen's Joanne Kilbourn Series." *Detecting Canada*, edited by
    Jeannette Sloniowski and Marilyn Rose, Wilfrid Laurier UP, 2014.
Lavender, Isiah. *Black and Brown Planets: The Politics of Race in Science Fiction*. University
    of Mississippi, 2014.
Lempert, William. "Decolonizing Encounters of the Third Kind: Alternative Futuring
    in Native Science Fiction Film." *Visual Anthropology Review*, vol. 30, no. 2,
    pp. 164–176.
Maynard, Robyn. "Reading Black Resistance through Afrofuturism: Notes on
    Post-Apocalyptic Blackness and Black Rebel Cyborgs in Canada." *TOPIA:
    Canadian Journal of Cultural Studies*, vol. 39, 2018, pp. 29–47, doi:10.3138/
    topia.39.04.
Miller, Kathryn L., and Joshua Plencner. "Supergirl and the Corporate Articulation of
    Neoliberal Feminism." *New Political Science*, vol. 40, no. 1, Feb. 2018, pp. 51–69,
    doi:10.1080/07393148.2017.1416568.
Patterson, Natasha. "Becoming Zombie Grrrls on and off Screen." *Braaaiiinnnsss! From
    Academics to Zombies*, edited by Robert Smith, University of Ottawa Press, 2011,
    pp. 225–248.
Salvaggio, Ruth. "Octavia Butler and the Black Science-Fiction Heroine." *Black
    American Literature Forum*, vol. 18, no. 2, 1984, p. 78, doi:10.2307/2904131.
Schalk, Sami. *Bodyminds Reimagined: (Dis)Ability, Race, and Gender in Black Women's
    Speculative Fiction*. Duke UP, 2018.

Symonds, Gwen. "'Solving Problems with Sharp Objects': Female Empowerment, Sex, and Violence in *Buffy, the Vampire Slayer.*" *The Aesthetics of Violence in Contemporary Media*, 2008, doi:10.5040/9781628928341.ch-005.

Wilbanks, Rebecca. "*Orphan Black* and Race: Omissions and a New Realism." *Science Fiction Film and Television*, vol. 11 no. 3, 2018, pp. 395–400. *Project MUSE*, muse.jhu.edu/article/705228.

PART IV: TAKING CHARGE: RECASTING POP CULTURE THROUGH PARTICIPATORY MEDIA

The chapters in part IV share themes of participation, digital storytelling, and social media. The suggested readings that follow continue the conversation on participatory media and resistance, considering not only digital activism in social media and gaming in diverse communities, but also the politics of digital labour.

Baer, Hester. "Redoing Feminism: Digital Activism, Body Politics, and Neoliberalism." *Feminist Media Studies*, vol. 16, no. 1, 2015, pp. 17–34, doi:10.1080/14680777.2015.1093070.

Banner, Olivia. "Technopsyence and Afro-Surrealisms Cripistemologies." *Catalyst: Feminism, Theory, Technoscience*, vol. 5, no. 1, Jan. 2019, pp. 1–29, doi:10.28968/cftt.v5i1.29612.

Bezio, Kristin M. S. "Ctrl-Alt-Del: GamerGate as a Precursor to the Rise of the Alt-Right." *Leadership*, vol. 14, no. 5, 2018, pp. 556–566, doi:10.1177/1742715018793744.

Freelon, Deen, et al. "How Black Twitter and Other Social Media Communities Interact with Mainstream News." May 2018, doi:10.31235/osf.io/nhsd9.

Gajjala, Radhika. *Cyber Selves: Feminist Ethnographies of South Asian Women*. AltaMira Press, 2004.

Hamraie, Aimi, and Kelly Fritsch. "Crip Technoscience Manifesto." *Catalyst: Feminism, Theory, Technoscience*, vol. 5, no. 1, Jan. 2019, pp. 1–33, doi:10.28968/cftt.v5i1.29607.

Kim, Dorothy, et al. "Race, Gender, and the Technological Turn: A Roundtable on Digitizing Revolution." *Frontiers: A Journal of Women Studies*, vol. 39, no. 1, 2018, p. 149, doi:10.5250/fronjwomestud.39.1.0149.

Nakamura, Lisa. "The Unwanted Labour of Social Media: Women of Colour Call Out Culture As Venture Community Management." *New Formations*, vol. 86, no. 86, 2015, pp. 106–112, doi:10.3898/newf.86.06.2015.

Tovar, Virgie, and Hannah McGregor. "'I Needed to See the Politic Being Lived': Virgie Tovar on Fat Activism and Digital Platforms." *Digital Feminist Counter-Publics*, vol. 38, no. 2, 2017.

Willox, Ashlee Cunsolo, et al. "Storytelling in a Digital Age: Digital Storytelling as an Emerging Narrative Method for Preserving and Promoting Indigenous Oral Wisdom." *Qualitative Research*, vol. 13, no. 2, 2012, pp. 127–147, doi:10.1177/1468794112446105.

PART V: NECESSARY, NOT RADICAL: GENDER INCLUSIVITY IN PERFORMANCE, PODCASTS, AND MUSIC

Opening up the conversation beyond the screen, part V of this collection looked to other forms of media, such as music, podcasts, and performance. The suggested reading list offers further opportunities to explore these mediums both in and beyond Canada. There are endless ways media can enact resistance; by moving beyond the screen, this section offers insights into other modes and mediums of refusal.

Childs, Becky, and Gerard Van Herk. "Work that –S!: Drag Queens, Gender, Identity, and Traditional Newfoundland English." *Journal of Sociolinguistics*, vol. 18, no. 5, 2014, pp. 634–657.

Drake, Sunny. "Transitioning the Theatre Industry." *Canadian Theatre Review*, vol. 165, 2016, pp. 55–59, doi:10.3138/ctr.165.011.

Hancock, Maren. "Stereo/Types: Female DJs in Canada and the Gimmick/Token Binary." *The Spaces and Places of Canadian Popular Culture*, edited by Victoria Kannen and Neil Shyminsky, Canadian Scholars, 2019.

Kuppers, Petra. "Toward a Rhizomatic Model of Disability: Poetry, Performance, and Touch." *Journal of Literary & Cultural Disability Studies*, vol. 3, no. 3, 2009, pp. 221–240.

Magnat, Virginie. "Can Research Become Ceremony? Performance Ethnography and Indigenous Epistemologies." *Canadian Theatre Review*, vol. 151, 2012, pp. 30–36.

Piepzna-Samarasinha, Leah Lakshmi. *Care Work: Dreaming Disability Justice*. Arsenal Pulp Press, 2018.

Recollet, Karyn. "Gesturing Indigenous Futurities through the Remix." *Dance Research Journal*, vol. 48, no. 1, 2016, pp. 91–105.

Veerkamp, Honna. "Feminist Frequencies: Why Radio Needs Feminism." *Journal of Radio & Audio Media*, vol. 21, no. 2, 2014, pp. 307–315.

Author Biographies

Andrea Braithwaite is an associate professor (teaching) at Ontario Tech University (University of Ontario Institute of Technology), in Communication and Digital Media Studies. Her research examines gendered discourses of sociability and belonging in pop culture. She looks at gender, crime, and detection stories across media, especially Canadian media. She also discusses representations of and responses to feminist activism in online and gaming communities.

Syeda Nayab Bukhari is a research associate at the Simone de Beauvoir Institute at Concordia University. She earned her doctorate in Gender, Sexuality, and Women's Studies from Simon Fraser University, and a master's in Journalism and MPhil in Mass Communications from Pakistan. Interested in race, class, and gender vis-à-vis mainstream and ethnic media, she analyzes lived experiences of minority ethnic communities in Canada. Her areas of interest include race, class, and gender relations; immigration studies; settlement and integration; health communication; ethnic media; and gender and international development. She has published in her areas of interest and has extensive experience teaching in public and private universities as well as working in collaboration with grassroots level to international NGOs.

Claire Carter is an associate professor in Women's and Gender Studies at the University of Regina, Treaty 4 territory. Her current research examines the relationship between movement/exercise and the embodiment of gender within the changing dynamics of queer and trans communities in Canada. She teaches courses on feminist methodologies, queer theory, and popular culture, and some of her work has been published in *Queer Studies in Media and Popular Culture, Leisure Studies, Sexualities,* and the *Journal of Gender Studies*.

Jill Carter (Anishinaabe-Ashkenazi) is an assistant professor with the Centre for Drama, Theatre, and Performance Studies; the Transitional Year Programme; and Indigenous Studies at the University of Toronto. Jill strives to support the development of new Indigenous works and to disseminate artistic objectives, processes, and outcomes through community-driven research projects. Her scholarly research, creative projects, and activism are built upon ongoing relationships with Indigenous Elders, artists, and activists, positioning her as witness to, participant in, and disseminator of oral histories that speak to the application of Indigenous aesthetic principles and traditional knowledge systems to contemporary performance.

T. Nikki Cesare Schotzko is an associate professor of Performance Studies at the University of Toronto. Her first book, *Learning How to Fall: Art and Culture after September 11* (Routledge, 2015), investigates the changing relationship between world events and their subsequent documentation in mainstream and social media, positing contemporary art and performance as not only a stylized re-envisioning of daily life but, inversely, as viable means by which one might experience and process real-world political and social events. Her current project engages feminist theories of care, mothering studies, and ecological feminisms to explore the potential of performance to enact radical care. An occasional dramaturge, Dr. Cesare Schotzko has collaborated on musical theatre productions in Toronto, Ontario; New York, New York; Chicago, Illinois; and Morelia, Mexico.

Roxanne Chartrand is a PhD student in Film Studies and Videogame Studies at Université de Montréal, where she is affiliated with the Video Games Observation and Documentation University Lab (LUDOV). Her research focuses on the philosophy of videogames, mainly on the metaphysical and metaethical considerations of the player's (inter)actions in the gameworld. Aside from her main research interest, she has a fascination with queer and feminist alternative games. Outside of academia, she's an amateur ballerina with a *Star Trek* tattoo and too many plants.

Victoria Kannen writes and teaches on the subjects of identity, privilege, education, and popular culture. She holds a PhD in Sociology and Equity Studies in Education from the Ontario Institute for Studies in Education at the University of Toronto. She is a co-editor of *The Spaces and Places of Canadian Popular Culture* (Canadian Scholars, 2019). Further, her work has been published in such journals as the *Journal of Gender Studies*; *Culture, Theory and Critique*; and *Teaching in Higher Education*.

Chris Klassen teaches in the Religion and Culture department at Wilfrid Laurier University. Aside from her work on Nelvana, she has published analyses on Ms. Marvel, the Swamp Thing, *Avatar*, *Star Wars*, and *Battlestar Galactica*. She also works in the area of feminist analysis of nature religion, and is currently exploring the possibilities of decolonizing the university.

Aaron Langille holds a PhD in environmental science from the University of Guelph and is currently a professor of computer science and video game design at Laurentian University in Sudbury, Ontario. His interests include all things related to the development and design of video games but more specifically the demographic representation of characters, tangential learning through video games, and the gamification of post-secondary curricula.

Olga Marques is an assistant professor in the Criminology and Justice program at Ontario Tech University (University of Ontario Institute of Technology). Teaching and research interests focus on the construction, policing, and regulation of sexed, gendered, and raced bodies, and the interrelationships between gendered/sexed social norms, social control, and resistance.

Christine Mazumdar is a PhD candidate at the Centre for Drama, Theatre and Performance Studies at the University of Toronto, focusing on the athlete as performer through the language of movement in aesthetic sport. A former rhythmic gymnast and nationally certified coach, Christine considers the interrelationship between sport and art through the virtuosic body. Her coaching pedagogy emphasizes consent, agency, and the need to abolish aesthetic sport's culture of silence. An avid writer and musician, Christine also holds a teaching degree with a specialization in arts education from Queen's University and works part-time for the English Montreal School Board as she completes her doctoral thesis.

Dilyana Mincheva is an assistant professor in the Department of Communication Studies and Multimedia at McMaster University. Her most recent research is engaged with the culturological study of Islamic feminism, religious iconoclasm, the politics of image in cinematic terrorism, and utopia. She is the bearer of two international awards for research excellence (2012 and 2015) granted by the *Journal of Religion and Spirituality in Society*, and is the author of the monograph *The Politics of Western Muslim Intellectual Discourse in the West: The Emergence of a Western-Islamic Public Sphere* (Sussex Academic Press, 2016).

Anuppiriya Sriskandarajah is an assistant professor in the Children, Childhood and Youth Program at York University. She is a sociologist by training and teaches research methodology. Her research interests include youth, culture, race, and second generation youth experiences.

Pascale Thériault is a PhD candidate in Film Studies and Videogame Studies at Université de Montréal. She's also affiliated with the Video Game Observation and Documentation University Lab (LUDOV) where she works on diversity in video game journalism. Her thesis focuses on feminist play and queer practices as a way to resist toxic culture and sexism in video games. She is also a lecturer at Université de Montréal and Université du Québec en Abitibi-Témiscamingue, where she teaches screenwriting and ethics in video games.

Cheryl Thompson joined the School of Creative Industries at Ryerson University in 2018 as an assistant professor. Thompson previously held a Banting postdoctoral fellowship (2016–2018) at the University of Toronto's Centre for Theatre, Drama and Performance Studies and the University of Toronto Mississauga's Department of English and Drama. In 2015, she earned her PhD in Communication Studies from McGill University. Her first book, *Beauty in a Box: Detangling the Roots of Canada's Black Beauty Culture* (Wilfrid Laurier Press) was published in 2019. Her next book, *Uncle: Race, Nostalgia and the Politics of Loyalty* (Coach House Books) will be published in 2020.

Jessica Watkin is a Blind PhD student at the University of Toronto's Centre for Drama, Theatre, and Performace Studies. Her work focuses on accessible and innovative approaches to creating theatre for and with disabled artists. She has been published in the *Canadian Theatre Review* considering topics of cultivating accessible audiences and stages, and non-visual approaches to creation. She is a practising playwright and will be a part of Cahoots Theatre Company's Hot House Creator's Unit in their 2018–2019 Season.

Valley WeeDick is a musician, writer, and illustrator living in Toronto. In a past life, they performed across Canada with several bands. They research gender and sexuality in popular music and are working on a fanzine about trans musicians.

Laine Zisman Newman is a post-doctoral research fellow in the Department of Geography and Tourism Studies at Brock University. She received her PhD from the University of Toronto's Centre for Drama, Theatre, and Performance Studies and the collaborative programs in Sexual Diversity Studies and Women and Gender Studies. Her primary research focuses on the intersections of queer geographies, pop culture, and performance. Zisman Newman was founder and chair of Toronto's Queer Theory Working Group at the Jackman Humanities Institute and co-founder of Equity in Theatre, a national organization that worked to improve equity in the professional Canadian performance industry.